D1528093

THE FATHERS OF THE CHURCH

A NEW TRANSLATION

VOLUME 126

THE FATHERS
OF THE CHURCH

A NEW TRANSLATION

EDITORIAL BOARD

FULGENTIUS OF RUSPE AND THE SCYTHIAN MONKS

CORRESPONDENCE ON CHRISTOLOGY AND GRACE

Translated by
ROB ROY MCGREGOR AND
DONALD FAIRBAIRN

Introduction and Notes by
DONALD FAIRBAIRN

THE CATHOLIC UNIVERSITY OF AMERICA PRESS
Washington, D.C.

Copyright © 2013
THE CATHOLIC UNIVERSITY OF AMERICA PRESS
All rights reserved
Printed in the United States of America

The paper used in this publication meets the minimum requirements of
the American National Standards for Information Science—Permanence
of Paper for Printed Library Materials, ANSI z39.48-1984.
∞

LIBRARY OF CONGRESS CATALOGING-IN-PUBLICATION DATA
Fulgentius, Saint, Bishop of Ruspa, 468–533.
[Selections. English. 2013]
Correspondence on Christology and grace / Fulgentius of Ruspe and the
Scythian monks; translated by Rob Roy McGregor and Donald Fairbairn ;
introduction and notes by Donald Fairbairn.
p. cm. — (The fathers of the church ; v. 126)
Includes bibliographical references (p.) and indexes.
ISBN 978-0-8132-0126-9 (cloth : alk. paper)
1. Fulgentius, Saint, Bishop of Ruspa, 468–533.—Correspondence.
2. Jesus Christ—Person and officesw—Early works to 1800.
3. Free will and determinism—Early works to 1800.
4. Grace (Theology)—Early works to 1800.
I. McGregor, Rob Roy, 1929– II. Fairbairn, Donald   III. Title.
BR65.F854E5 2013
232—dc23
2012038316

Rob Roy McGregor
dedicates this book to his wife, Kathryn,
and their son, Rob Roy III.

Donald Fairbairn
dedicates this book to his children,
Trey and Ella, who greeted him many times
as he came home from the office
by asking, "How's Fulgie?"

CONTENTS

PREFACE

This is the second volume in the Fathers of the Church series dedicated to the North African bishop and theologian St. Fulgentius of Ruspe (ca. 467–ca. 532). The first, translated by Robert Eno and published in 1997, is broad in scope, containing the *Life of the Blessed Bishop Fulgentius* and a number of the bishop's theological and moral treatises. This current volume is meant as a complement to that earlier one, and its focus is considerably narrower. It contains correspondence between Fulgentius (writing on behalf of a group of North African bishops) and a group of Latin-speaking monks from Scythia (near the mouth of the Danube River in modern-day Romania) between AD 519 and 523.

The correspondence between Fulgentius and the Scythian monks is significant—and striking—because it stands at the intersection of two great theological discussions: the primarily eastern Christological controversies between the Fourth Ecumenical Council (at Chalcedon in 451) and the Fifth (at Constantinople in 553) and the largely western discussions about grace (the so-called "Semi-Pelagian" controversy) that stretched from the closing years of St. Augustine's life (the discussion began in 427, and Augustine died in 430) to the Second Synod of Orange in 529. Contemporary western scholars normally treat these controversies over Christ and grace separately, but there were noteworthy points of contact between the discussions. In the 420s, John Cassian was the ardent opponent of both Nestorius on Christology and Pelagius on grace, even though he has subsequently been branded (probably unjustly) as the father of Semi-Pelagianism. The correspondence between Fulgentius and the Scythian monks from a century later is another significant instance of direct connection between the controversies over Christ and those over grace.

These connections suggest that we today may do well to treat Christology and grace more as two sides of the same coin than as separate theological issues. Both sets of issues deal fundamentally with the relation between God and humanity: Christological questions ask how divine and human are related in the person of the Savior, and grace-related questions ask how the divine and the human are linked in the conversion, Christian life, and final salvation of each Christian. We offer Fulgentius's correspondence with the Scythian monks to the English-reading world in the hope not only that it will aid our understanding of sixth-century Byzantine/Roman theology, but also that it will encourage and contribute to our own thinking about the relation between two of the Christian faith's most central doctrines.

These translations represent a collaborative effort between Dr. Rob Roy McGregor (a retired classicist, Romance languages specialist, and translator of Calvin's French sermons) and me. The stimulus that ultimately led to this volume began in the early 2000s when Dr. McGregor asked me whether there was something in my field written in French that he could translate for a general audience. Because I had long wanted to explore more fully the relation between grace and Christology in the Semi-Pelagian Controversy, I asked whether he would instead be willing to translate some of Fulgentius's writings from Latin. Dr. McGregor kindly agreed and did the initial translation of two of Fulgentius's writings included in this volume. Other tasks prevented me from being able to take up Dr. McGregor's work, and the project languished for several years. Eventually I was able to give attention to Fulgentius, and as Dr. McGregor translated the third document by Fulgentius, I revised his translations, added my own translations of the documents by the Scythian monks, compiled the notes, and wrote the introduction. I would like to acknowledge my debt to Dr. McGregor for his initial offer, his patience with me when it must have seemed to him that I was doing everything except writing on Fulgentius, and his diligent work on Fulgentius's writings themselves. Without him these translations would likely have never made the transition from being a nice idea in my mind to becoming an actual volume that could be useful to others.

I would also like to acknowledge my gratitude to Dr. Carole Monica Burnett, staff editor of the Fathers of the Church series, for her enthusiastic correspondence as I was working on this project and her superb work in checking and improving the translation.

Donald Fairbairn
Charlotte, North Carolina
March 2013

ABBREVIATIONS

ACO   *Acta conciliorum oecumenicorum.* Berlin.

ACW   Ancient Christian Writers. New York and Mahwah, NJ: Newman Press.

CCL   Corpus Christianorum Series Latina. Turnhout: Brepols.

CPG   *Clavis Patrum Graecorum.* Turnhout: Brepols.

CPL   *Clavis Patrum Latinorum.* 3d ed. Turnhout: Brepols.

CSEL   Corpus Scriptorum Ecclesiasticorum Latinorum. Vienna: Austrian Academy of Sciences.

FOTC   The Fathers of the Church. Washington, DC: The Catholic University of America Press.

LXX   Septuagint.

NPNF   A Select Library of the Nicene and Post-Nicene Fathers of the Christian Church, 1888. Reprints, 1956 (Grand Rapids: Eerdmans) and 1994 (Peabody, MA: Hendrickson).

PG   Patrologiae Cursus Completus: Series Graeca. Ed. J.-P. Migne. Paris.

PL   Patrologiae Cursus Completus: Series Latina. Ed. J.-P. Migne. Paris.

SC   Sources chrétiennes. Paris.

SELECT BIBLIOGRAPHY

Texts and Translations

For each work, the first citation is to the best available edition of the text. The parenthetical citation (if present) indicates the best available English translation.

Augustine. *De correptione et gratia.* PL 44:915–46. (NPNF, first series, 5.471–91).
———. *De dono perseuerantiae.* PL 45:993–1034. (FOTC 86.271–337).
———. *De gratia et libero arbitrio.* PL 44:881–912. (NPNF, first series, 5.443–65).
———. *De praedestinatione sanctorum.* PL 44:959–92. (FOTC 86.218–70).
———. *Ep. 194 ad Sixtum.* CSEL 57.176–214. (FOTC 30.301–32).
Cassian, John. *Conlationes.* SC 42, 54, 64. (ACW 57).
———. *De incarnatione Domini contra Nestorium libri 7.* CSEL 17.233–391. (NPNF, second series, 11.549–621).
Epistula Scytharum monachorum ad episcopos. CCL 91A.551–62, and CCL 85A.157–72. (*Journal of Ecclesiastical History* 35 [1984]: 247–55; re-translated in this volume).
Faustus of Riez. *De gratia.* CSEL 21.3–96.
Ferrandus (?). *Vita sancti Fulgentii.* In Lapeyre, G. G., ed. *Vie de Saint Fulgence de Ruspe de Ferrand, Diacre de Carthage.* Paris: Lathielleux, 1929. (FOTC 95.3–56).
Fulgentius of Ruspe. *De veritate praedestinationis et gratiae Dei.* CCL 91A.458–548. (Translated in this volume).
———. *Ep. 15.* CCL 91A.447–57. (Translated in this volume).
———. *Ep. 17.* CCL 91A.563–615. (Translated in this volume).
Maxentius, John. *Capitula Maxentii Ioannis edita contra Nestorianos et Pelagianos ad satisfactionem fratrum.* CCL 85A.29–30. (Translated in this volume).
———. *Libellus fidei.* CCL 85A.5–25. (Translated in this volume).
Prosper of Aquitaine. *De gratia Dei et libero arbitrio liber contra collatorem.* PL 51.213–76. (ACW 32.70–138).
Tanner, Norman P., ed. *The Decrees of the Ecumenical Councils.* Washington: Georgetown University Press, 1990.

Studies

Cappuyns, D. M. "L'origine des «Capitula» d'Orange 529." In *Recherches de théologie ancienne et médiévale* 6 (1934): 121–42.

Casiday, Augustine, and Frederick W. Norris, eds. *The Cambridge History of Christianity. Vol. 2: Constantine to c. 600.* Cambridge: University Press, 2007.

Davidson, Ivor J. *A Public Faith: From Constantine to the Medieval World, A.D. 312–600.* The Baker History of the Church, Vol. 2. Ed. Tim Dowley. Grand Rapids: Baker, 2005.

Davis, Leo Donald. *The First Seven Ecumenical Councils (325–787): Their History and Theology.* Collegeville, MN: Liturgical Press, 1983.

Dewart, Joanne McWilliam. "The Christology of the Pelagian Controversy." *Studia Patristica* 17 (1982): 1221–44.

Djuth, Marianne. "Faustus of Riez: *Initium Bonae Voluntatis.*" *Augustinian Studies* 21 (1990): 35–53.

———. "Fulgentius of Ruspe: The 'Initium Bonae Voluntatis.'" *Augustinian Studies* 20 (1989): 39–60.

Fairbairn, Donald. *Grace and Christology in the Early Church.* Oxford Early Christian Studies. Oxford: University Press, 2003.

Frend, W. H. C. *The Rise of the Monophysite Movement: Chapters in the History of the Church in the Fifth and Sixth Centuries.* Cambridge: University Press, 1972.

Gray, Patrick. *The Defense of Chalcedon in the East (451–553).* Studies in the History of Christian Thought 20. Ed. Heiko A. Oberman. Leiden: Brill, 1979.

Grillmeier, Aloys. *Christ in Christian Tradition. Volume One: From the Apostolic Age to Chalcedon (451).* Trans. by John Bowden. Rev. ed. London: Mowbray, 1975.

Grillmeier, Aloys, and Theresia Hainthaler. *Christ in Christian Tradition. Volume Two: From the Council of Chalcedon (451) to Gregory the Great (590–604). Part Two: The Church of Constantinople in the Sixth Century.* Trans. by John Cawte and Pauline Allen. London: Mowbray, 1995.

Gumerlock, Francis X. *Fulgentius of Ruspe on the Saving Will of God: The Development of a Sixth-Century African Bishop's Interpretation of 1 Timothy 2:4 During the Semi-Pelagian Controversy.* Lewiston, NY: The Edwin Mellen Press, 2009.

Lapeyre, G. G. *Saint Fulgence de Ruspe: un évêque catholique africain sous la domination vandale.* Paris: P. Lathielleux, 1929.

Maxwell, David R. "Christology and Grace in the Sixth-Century Latin West: The Theopaschite Controversy." Ph.D. diss., University of Notre Dame, 2003.

———. "Crucified in the Flesh: Christological Confession or Evasive Qualification?" *Pro Ecclesia* 13 (2004): 70–81.

McGuckin, John A. "The 'Theopaschite Confession' (Text and Histori-

cal Context): A Study in the Cyrilline Re-interpretation of Chalce-
don." *Journal of Ecclesiastical History* 35 (1984): 239–55.
————. *St. Cyril of Alexandria: The Christological Controversy.* Supplements
to *Vigiliae Christianae* 23. Leiden: E. J. Brill, 1994.
Meyendorff, John. *Christ in Eastern Christian Thought.* Rev. ed. Crestwood,
NY: St. Vladimir's Seminary Press, 1975.
Nisters, Bernhard. *Die Christologie des Hl. Fulgentius von Ruspe.* Münster-
ische Beiträge zur Theologie 16. Ed. F. Diechamp and R. Stapper.
Münster: Aschendorffsche Verlagsbuchhandlung, 1930.
O'Keefe, John J. "'Impassible Suffering?' Divine Passion and Fifth-Century
Christology." *Theological Studies* 58 (1997): 38–60.
Plagnieux, Jean. "Le grief de complicité entre erreurs nestorienne et
pélagienne: d'Augustin à Cassian par Prosper d'Aquitaine?" *Revue des
études augustiniennes* 2 (1956): 391–402.
Smith, Thomas A. *De Gratia: Faustus of Riez's Treatise on Grace and Its Place
in the History of Theology.* Notre Dame, IN: University of Notre Dame
Press, 1990.
Weaver, Rebecca Harden. *Divine Grace and Human Agency: A Study of the
Semi-Pelagian Controversy.* North American Patristic Society Patristic
Monograph Series 15. Macon, GA: Mercer University Press, 1996.

INTRODUCTION

INTRODUCTION

The background to Fulgentius's correspondence with the Scythian monks from AD 519 to 523 is a rope with many strands, both political and theological. I will present three of the major strands composing this rope: the Vandal rule of North Africa from 439 to 535, the Christological disputes in the Eastern Roman Empire from the Council of Chalcedon (451) until the time of this correspondence, and the Western theological discussion known as the Semi-Pelagian Controversy from its beginning in 427 until the time of this correspondence.

Vandal Rule of North Africa and the
Resurgence of Catholicism[1]

In the 370s, the nomadic Huns began to move westward out of Asia into the Balkans and the northern flanks of the Alps, in what is today East-Central Europe. The Huns attacked and displaced the previously sedentary Germanic tribes—Goths and Vandals—who had been living on the northern fringes of the Roman/Byzantine Empire. The Gothic and Vandal tribes, forced into an unfamiliar nomadic lifestyle, in turn began to threaten the Empire, especially its western regions. Most famously, in August of 410, the city of Rome itself came under the

---

1. The history of the Roman Empire's interaction with the northern European tribes has been told and re-told many times. An excellent short discussion comes in Chapter 11 of Ivor J. Davidson, *A Public Faith: From Constantine to the Medieval World, A.D. 312–600*, The Baker History of the Church, Vol. 2, ed. Tim Dowley (Grand Rapids, MI: Baker, 2005). See the bibliography to this chapter of Davidson's work (p. 426) for more detailed studies.

control of Alaric and the Goths. Later, in 429, Vandal invaders in Spain under the command of Geiseric crossed the Strait of Gibraltar into Latin North Africa (Morocco, Algeria, and Tunisia today), and by 439, they had captured most of the region, including Carthage, the major city (located in what is today Tunisia). Geiseric and his successors went on to rule North Africa for nearly a century.

Long before they attained supremacy over the Western Roman Empire, the Goths and Vandals had been converted from paganism to Christianity.[2] Their version of the faith, however, was "Arian" in that it rejected Nicene Christianity's affirmation that the Son was fully equal to and of the same substance as the Father. Accordingly, the Vandal rulers of North Africa— Geiseric (died 477), his son Huneric (died 484), and Huneric's successors Gunthamund (died 496) and then Thrasamund (died 523)—placed pressure on Catholic Christian leaders and churches to conform to their ways of speaking about the Trinity. In spite of these efforts by the Vandal rulers, non-Catholic or Arian Christianity was largely in decline from about 460 onwards. By the time of Thrasamund in the early sixth century, the rulers rarely resorted to violence against Catholics, although they still often used exile as a tool of political control. Fulgentius of Ruspe was born into this charged political and theological atmosphere.

We know the details of Fulgentius's life from a biography written not long after his death, *The Life of the Blessed Fulgentius,* perhaps by Ferrandus, a deacon in Carthage.[3] A young adult when Thrasamund came to power in 496, Fulgentius became part of a growing movement in the late fifth and early sixth centuries to regain Catholic intellectual supremacy in North Africa. In 502 or 507,[4] Fulgentius was ordained as the Catholic bishop of Ruspe (on the coast of the Mediterranean Sea in what is to-

2. The historical origins of the Christian movement among the Gothic and Vandal tribes are unclear, but much of the early work of christianization is attributed to the fourth-century missionary Ulfilas, who translated the Bible into Gothic.

3. See *The Life of the Blessed Bishop Fulgentius,* in Robert Eno, trans., *Fulgentius: Selected Works,* FOTC 95, 3–56. See also Eno's brief introduction to Fulgentius's life (pp. xv–xviii) and his select bibliography (pp. xi–xiii).

4. The date one gives for Fulgentius's ordination as a bishop depends on

day Tunisia) in violation of Thrasamund's prohibition against ordaining any new Catholic bishops. Thrasamund exiled him (along with sixty other bishops) to the island of Sardinia off the west coast of Italy. Because of his theological acumen, Fulgentius rose to a position of prominence among the exiled bishops, and Thrasamund recalled the now-famous bishop about the year 516, so that the Arian king could debate the Catholic theologian on Trinitarian dogma. When Thrasamund was unable to best Fulgentius in intellectual combat, he sent him packing for Sardinia again, and this second exile lasted from about 519 until the king's death in 523. Thrasamund's successor Hilderic (died 530) was pro-Byzantine,[5] and after Fulgentius returned from his second exile in 523, he saw the complete restoration of Catholic Christianity in North Africa. He died in 527 or 532, shortly before the Byzantines recaptured North Africa from the Vandals in 535. Thus the tense interaction between North African Catholics and their Arian Vandal rulers forms the backdrop for Fulgentius's correspondence with the Scythian monks, since that correspondence began during his second exile (519–23) and continued after his triumphant return to Ruspe upon Thrasamund's death.

Christological Disputes in the East
after Chalcedon

Meanwhile, in the East differing attitudes toward the Christological formulation adopted at the Council of Chalcedon (451) were proving to be even more divisive than differing Vandal and

---

the date one adopts for his death. We know from *The Life of the Blessed Fulgentius* 28–29 (see FOTC 95, 54–55) that he died on January 1 of some year, at age 65, after having been bishop of Ruspe for twenty-five years, that he was buried the next day, and that his successor as bishop (Felicianus) was ordained on a Sunday, exactly one year after Fulgentius was buried. Since January 2 fell on a Sunday in 528 and 533, Fulgentius died in either 527 or 532. J. Fraipont, Introduction to *Sancti Fulgentii Episcopi Ruspensis Opera*, CCL 91, pp. v–vi, argues for 527 as the year of Fulgentius's death, but Eno, Introduction to FOTC 95, pp. xv–xvi, prefers the year 532. Fulgentius's episcopate thus began in either 502 or 507.

5. Although Hilderic's father, Huneric, was an Arian, his mother, Eudocia, the daughter of the Byzantine emperor Valentinian, was a Catholic.

Roman views of the Trinity in the West. The issues surrounding
the Christological controversy were extremely complex and are
interpreted in various ways today, but I suggest that undergird-
ing the controversy as a whole was the issue of whether God the
Son himself personally entered human history to accomplish
mankind's salvation. In other words, was Christ really God the
Son who had become fully human while remaining the Second
Person of the Trinity, or was he a man who was somehow indwelt by God the Son? To state it yet another way, was Christ
really God, who after the Incarnation was also human, or was
he a man who was divine in the sense of being indwelt by God?
This issue is tied to the question of whether human salvation
is wrought fundamentally through the downward movement of
God himself to our condition, or primarily through the upward
elevation of mankind to God. If human salvation requires God
himself to step into human life personally, then a Christology
in which Christ, as a person, is God the Son incarnate becomes
essential. Conversely, if human salvation is a process of elevating
ourselves to the sphere of God, then a Christ who is essentially
a man like us but who is aided and indwelt by God will be the
best possible leader in helping us to rise up to God. Theodore
of Mopsuestia (died 428) and Nestorius (died ca. 451) argued
in effect that salvation was a process of elevating ourselves to
God and that Christ was a divinely inspired man who was our
leader in that process. In stark contrast, Cyril of Alexandria (ca.
375–444) argued that Christ was God the Son himself who took
humanity upon himself in order to come down personally to
the sphere of humanity and save us.[6]

In spite of the apparent clarity of these competing visions of
salvation and of Christ, the issues of the Christological controversy were clouded considerably by terminological problems. In
particular, the word *physis* (today rendered in English as "nature") was the source of much confusion and conflict. Many

6. For my treatment of the Christology of Theodore, Nestorius, and Cyril, see
Chapters 1–4 of Donald Fairbairn, *Grace and Christology in the Early Church* (Oxford: University Press, 2003). For an outstanding concise statement of this way of
viewing the controversy, see John J. O'Keefe, "Impassible Suffering? Divine Passion and Fifth-Century Christology," *Theological Studies* 58 (1997): 39–60.

Greek speakers used *physis* in the sense of "personal nature," and thus saw it in the same category as the words *hypostasis* and *prosopon* (both of which were regarded in the fifth century as being terms denoting the individual subsistence of Christ, or what we call "person" in English). Other Greek speakers used *physis* more as a synonym for the Greek word *ousia* (which referred to the innermost aspect of a being and is rendered "essence" in English). Theodore and Nestorius both used the word *physis* in the sense of "personal nature," and thus Nestorius's phrase "in two *physeis*" actually meant that Christ was two persons (the assumed man and God the Son who indwelt him). Cyril likewise normally used the word *physis* in the sense of "personal nature," which meant that his infamous slogan "one incarnate *physis* of God the Logos" actually referred to the one person of Christ, not to a single nature as we use the word "nature" today.[7] Notice here that to our ears, "two *physeis*" seems to be correct, and "one *physis*" seems to be problematic. The reason for this is that we are using the word *physis* to mean "inner reality" or "nature." But in the fifth century, three of the most central players in the controversy were all using the word *physis* differently from the way we do, which means that Nestorius's "two *physeis*" (= two personal natures, or two persons) was the problematic expression, whereas Cyril's "one incarnate *physis*" (= one person) was the more acceptable. The different ways of using the word *physis* made it difficult both for Christians at the time and for us today to understand what a given Christological thinker actually meant.

In 451, the Council of Chalcedon affirmed that Christ is acknowledged in two *physeis* and that the properties of both *physeis* come together into a single *hypostasis* and a single *prosopon*.[8] Through these statements, Chalcedon is acknowledging

7. For an excellent discussion of the patristic use of the Greek words *ousia, physis, hypostasis,* and *prosopon,* see John A. McGuckin, *St. Cyril of Alexandria: The Christological Controversy,* Supplements to *Vigiliae Christianae* 23 (Leiden: E. J. Brill, 1994), 138–45.

8. For the Greek text and English translation of the Chalcedonian Definition, see (*inter alia*) Tanner, ed., *Decrees of the Ecumenical Councils, Vol. 1: Nicaea I to Lateran V* (Washington, DC: Georgetown University Press, 1990), 86.

that the words *hypostasis* and *prosopon* refer to the one "person" of Christ (which was in accord with early fifth-century usage of those words), but it is stating that *physis* shall refer to the two inner realities within Christ (two "natures" in English). Thus Chalcedon was forging a relatively new use of the word *physis*, different from the way Cyril had normally used it. As a result, this confession of two *physeis* in Christ was the lightning rod that ignited the passions of Cyril's most adamant defenders in Egypt and Syria. Many people read Chalcedon as if it were using *physis* to mean "personal nature" and were convinced that the affirmation of two *physeis* within the one Christ implied that the Logos and the man Jesus were two distinct persons. As a result, they believed Chalcedon was rejecting Cyril and adopting a Nestorian view that Christ is a divinely inspired trailblazer who can lead us up to God. Furthermore, on the political front many in the East and West also resented the rising preeminence of Constantinople as a patriarchal see, and political jousting over the supremacy of one see or another (Antioch, Alexandria, Rome, or Constantinople) added to the firestorm that Chalcedon sparked.[9]

A generation after Chalcedon, the dispute had reached such a pitch that the Byzantine Emperor Zeno, in a drastic effort to bring unity to his empire, sought to bypass the beleaguered council altogether. In 482, he published the *Henotikon*,[10] a statement of faith rooted in the work of the first three Ecumenical Councils (Nicaea I [325], Constantinople I [381], and Ephe-

9. The standard treatment of the political aspects of the post-Chalcedonian Christological debates is W. H. C. Frend, *The Rise of the Monophysite Movement: Chapters in the History of the Church in the Fifth and Sixth Centuries* (Cambridge: University Press, 1972). See also Chapter 6 of Leo Donald Davis, *The First Seven Ecumenical Councils (325–787): Their History and Theology* (Collegeville, MN: Liturgical Press, 1983). For a detailed discussion of the theological issues, see Parts 1–3 of Aloys Grillmeier and Theresia Hainthaler, *Christ in Christian Tradition, Volume Two: From the Council of Chalcedon (451) to Gregory the Great (590–604), Part Two: The Church of Constantinople in the Sixth Century*, translated by John Cawte and Pauline Allen (London: Mowbray, 1995). A recent, relatively brief but very clear, treatment comes in Frederick W. Norris, "Greek Christianities," in *The Cambridge History of Christianity*, Vol. 2 (Cambridge: University Press, 2007), 87–109.

10. Greek text in PG 86:2620–25; English translation in (*inter alia*) Frend, *The Rise of the Monophysite Movement*, 360–62.

sus [431]), without direct reference—positive or negative—to Chalcedon itself. Emperor Zeno and Patriarch Acacius of Constantinople sought to use the *Henotikon* as the basis for imperial unity, but this tactic largely backfired: Rome promptly broke fellowship with Acacius because he did not directly *affirm* the authority of Chalcedon (thus producing the so-called "Acacian Schism"),[11] but many in the East rejected the *Henotikon* because it did not directly *repudiate* Chalcedon![12] Several decades of political-theological conflict ensued, with the debates focusing as much on whether a given see, bishop, or emperor had the right to craft or revise theological formulations as on what theological language about Christ actually was or was not correct. For much of this period, Anastasius (who became Byzantine Emperor upon Zeno's death in 491) led the effort to impose Zeno's *Henotikon,* rather than Chalcedon, as the standard for imperial unity.

In the second decade of the sixth century, another factor was publicly injected into the debate. A liturgical prayer called the *Trisagion* ("Thrice-holy"), which had been used at Chalcedon's opening session, read, "Holy God, Holy Mighty, Holy Immortal, have mercy on us." In 511, however, the new patriarch of Antioch, Peter the Fuller, added the words "who was crucified for us," so that the prayer now read, "Holy God, Holy Mighty, Holy Immortal, who was crucified for us, have mercy on us." Thus the attention turned from the Incarnation to the question of who died on the cross, God the Word or some sort of assumed man. The addition of "who was crucified for us" to the prayer made

11. This schism lasted until 518, and, as we shall see later in this introduction, the healing of that schism was a significant part of the background to the correspondence between the Scythian monks and Fulgentius.

12. John A. McGuckin, "The 'Theopaschite Confession' (Text and Historical Context): A Study in the Cyrilline Re-interpretation of Chalcedon," *Journal of Ecclesiastical History* 35 (1984): 241, points out that in the East, the *Henotikon* fractured the *imperium* into three parties: those who accepted the text as a conciliatory move with a fresh start (a return to Cyril and Ephesus rather than Chalcedon), those who accepted the text because it was basically Monophysite and who hoped the dyophysites would be won over to it, and those hard-line Monophysites who anathematized the *Henotikon* because it did not explicitly anathematize Chalcedon.

clear what was evidently implied previously—that the person who was crucified was one of the three Trinitarian Persons.

This addition to the *Trisagion* created a firestorm of protest and polarized the Eastern Empire dramatically, but the general effect was to begin a backlash against those who wanted to circumvent Chalcedon. This backlash is interpreted in various ways, but in my opinion it was the result of misunderstanding on the part of those who thought the *Trisagion* was addressed to the whole Trinity. In Antioch, where the understanding was that the prayer was addressed specifically to Christ, the addition was unobjectionable. In Constantinople, however, where the understanding was that the prayer was addressed to the Trinity as a whole, the longer statement "Holy God, Holy Mighty, Holy Immortal, who was crucified for us, have mercy on us," appeared to imply that the entire Trinity suffered on the cross. Many people, recoiling against the idea that the divine nature of the Trinity as a whole died on the cross (which was surely not what the defenders of the addition to the *Trisagion* meant), rejected this addition to the prayer. As part of this backlash, many in the East came to regard the Chalcedonian Definition more favorably as well.

The increasingly favorable view of Chalcedon gained momentum through two other events of the same decade. First, in 514 Vitalian (a Goth with a strong commitment to Chalcedon and family connections to one of the Scythian monks) led a successful military revolt in Thrace (northeastern Greece and southern Bulgaria today) that forced Emperor Anastasius to give him more power. Second, in July of 518 Anastasius died and was replaced as Byzantine Emperor by the pro-Chalcedonian Justin. In that very year, Justin had the phrase "who was crucified for us" removed from the *Trisagion* in the Constantinopolitan liturgy. As a result, Pope Hormisdas of Rome, sensing correctly that the mood in the capital was now more favorable to Chalcedon, sought to solidify the authority of Chalcedon (and, not coincidentally, the authority of the papal office itself) by publishing a document anathematizing the two prior emperors, Zeno and Anastasius, who had opposed the great council (or at least who had not defended it).[13]

13. *Libellus Hormisdae* (Latin text in CSEL 35.2, 520–22).

INTRODUCTION 11

This document was accepted in Constantinople, perhaps because Patriarch John of Constantinople was not strong enough to resist Pope Hormisdas. The acceptance of Hormisdas's work in Constantinople formally brought the Acacian Schism to an end, as Rome and Constantinople were reunited, at least in principle.

This shift in mood in Constantinople meant that the *Henotikon* could no longer be the doctrinal standard of the empire, but not nearly everyone was willing to return to Chalcedon as the standard, since many still feared that it did not adequately guard against Nestorianism. If Chalcedon was to be accepted, people would have to be convinced that its two-*physeis* language was not meant in the Nestorian sense that in Christ there were two distinct persons, the man and the Word who indwelt him. The Scythian monks took upon themselves the task of clarifying Chalcedon as they entered the Byzantine political-theological scene late in 518 or early in 519. The very fact that the Scythian monks attempted this task shows that they believed the issue was whether Christ, as a person, was God the Son or an indwelt man, that they affirmed the first of these, and that they believed Chalcedon also affirmed the first of these.

Discussions about Grace in the West

A third element of the historical-theological background to Fulgentius's correspondence with the Scythian monks was the Western discussion over grace, commonly called the Semi-Pelagian Controversy.[14] This dispute grew out of the earlier Pelagian Controversy, which had more-or-less come to a close in the year 418, when a synod in Carthage, a synod in Ravenna (the Western imperial court), and Pope Zosimus all condemned certain assertions attributed to Pelagius.[15] Later in the same year, Au-

---

14. The standard treatment of this controversy is Rebecca Harden Weaver, *Divine Grace and Human Agency: A Study of the Semi-Pelagian Controversy,* North American Patristic Society Patristic Monograph Series 15 (Macon, GA: Mercer University Press, 1996).

15. Principal among these were the assertions that Adam would have been mortal even if he had not sinned, that infants did not derive original sin from Adam, that the baptism of infants was not necessary, and that grace consisted merely of providing external instruction. For the Latin text of the decrees of

gustine wrote a letter to a priest named Sixtus,[16] in which he
insisted very strongly that God's grace in saving a person, and
thus also his election of a person to salvation, were absolutely
free and did not depend in any way at all on human merit. In
427, a monk by the name of Florus from the monastery of Hadrumetum (in modern Tunisia) found this letter and showed
it to his abbot Valentinus. Thus began a relatively friendly discussion between the monks and Augustine about whether one's
salvation depended on one's actions or whether God's election
of some to salvation was unrelated to any merits of their own.
In response to the monks' questions, Augustine wrote *On Grace
and Free Choice*[17] (in which he warns against any attempt to deni-
grate the gratuity of God's grace by tying God's gift of grace to
human merit) and *On Rebuke and Grace*[18] (in which he warns
against relying on grace so completely that one takes no responsibility for one's own actions, and thus he argues that it is appropriate and necessary to use rebuke to correct the faults of
the monks). These writings seem to have satisfied the monks of
Hadrumetum, because history knows of no further complaints
from them related to grace and election.

At this time, however, southern Gaul (modern France) was
a major center of monastic life and also somewhat of a hotbed
of disrespect for episcopal authority. As news of what Augustine
was teaching in North Africa (or perhaps merely *rumors* of what
he was teaching, since the barbarian invasions in the early fifth
century made intellectual traffic across the Mediterranean less
frequent than it had previously been) reached Gaul, the monks
began to grumble that if election to salvation were not based
in any way at all on human merit, then the monastic task itself
would be valueless, since that task involved intense personal ef-

the Council of Carthage, see CCL 149, 69–73. For an English translation, see
J. Patout Burns, ed., *Theological Anthropology*, Sources of Early Christian Thought
(Philadelphia: Fortress, 1981), 57–60.

16. Augustine, *Ep. 194 ad Sixtum* (Latin text in CSEL 57, 176–214; English
translation in FOTC 30, 301–32).

17. Augustine, *De gratia et libero arbitrio* (Latin text in PL 44:881–912; English
translation in NPNF, first series, 5, 443–65).

18. Augustine, *De correptione et gratia* (Latin text in PL 44:915–46; English
translation in NPNF, first series, 5, 471–91).

INTRODUCTION

fort to attain spiritual maturity. In 427 or 428, Augustine's *On Rebuke and Grace* reached Gaul and intensified the debate. Prosper of Aquitaine and a certain Hilary both wrote to Augustine,[19] asking for his help in refuting the monks who, as it seemed to them, simply refused to accept election/predestination as a logical corollary of grace. Augustine responded in 429 with the last two treatises of his life, *On the Predestination of the Saints*[20] (in which he argues that God's choosing a person for salvation is not based on any antecedent merits by which that person could have earned such election) and *On the Gift of Perseverance*[21] (in which he asserts that human action is the outworking of grace, by which God brings to salvation those whom he has chosen). Furthermore, Prosper followed Augustine's lead by writing *Against Cassian the Lecturer,*[22] a work in which he criticizes Cassian for arguing (in Conference 13 of his mammoth work *The Conferences*) that some people do not need grace to bring them to God, but that they can make the first move toward God on their own. Prosper appealed to Rome to get an official condemnation of Cassian, but he was unsuccessful, and the discussion died down for a couple of generations.

The controversy resumed about the year 475, when Faustus of Riez (also in southern Gaul) wrote his treatise *On Grace.*[23] In this work, he argues for what he calls a centrist position, which rejects the extreme of relying exclusively on God and that of relying solely on one's own effort. In the process, Faustus argues against an Augustinian understanding of election/predestination without actually associating such a view with Augustine

---

19. Prosper of Aquitaine, *Epistula ad Augustinum* (Latin text in CSEL 57, 454–68; English translation in FOTC 32, 119–29); Hilary, *Epistula ad Augustinum* (Latin text in CSEL 57, 468–81; English translation in FOTC 32, 129–39).

20. Augustine, *De praedestinatione sanctorum* (Latin text in PL 44:959–92; English translation in FOTC 86, 218–70).

21. Augustine, *De dono perseuerantiae* (Latin text in PL 45:993–1034; English translation in FOTC 86, 271–337).

22. Prosper of Aquitaine, *De gratia Dei et libero arbitrio liber contra Collatorem* (Latin text in PL 51:213–76; English translation in ACW 32, 70–138).

23. Faustus of Riez, *De gratia* (Latin text in CSEL 21, 3–96). For a detailed discussion of this work see Thomas A. Smith, *De Gratia: Faustus of Riez's Treatise on Grace and Its Place in the History of Theology,* Christianity and Judaism in Antiquity 4, ed. Charles Kannengiesser (Notre Dame, IN: University Press, 1990).

himself. Significantly, virtually the only thing he writes about Christology in the entire work is that just as it is a mistake to argue that Christ is solely human or solely divine, so it is also a mistake to assert that salvation is solely through human action or solely by grace. The two natures of Christ, then, become Faustus's justification for a dual understanding of human salvation as a product of both divine and human action.[24] Faustus's work did not elicit conspicuous disapproval from the monks of Gaul, but it produced a strong reaction when it came to the attention of both the Scythian monks and Fulgentius some forty-five years later.

As I mentioned in the preface, twentieth-century scholars have typically regarded the disputes about grace as a separate controversy from the disputes about Christ.[25] As David Maxwell points out succinctly, "A striking feature of the secondary literature on the Scythian controversy is that Christology and grace are never treated together in the same work. This characteristic of the secondary literature stands in stark contrast to the primary texts themselves which frequently discuss both doctrines together."[26] If one grants that the Semi-Pelagian Controversy was to a great degree a discussion about whether one should emphasize divine action or human action in one's discussion of human salvation, then the question of that controversy was basically this: Is God the primary actor in saving mankind, or do we somehow save ourselves with God's help? One should notice that this question is very similar to the question of the Christological controversy as I have described it above. In both controversies, the complex issues can be reduced (without an

24. Faustus, *De gratia* 1.1 (CSEL 21, 8).

25. For example, two of the most widely used multi-volume historical theology surveys, Adolf Harnack's *History of Dogma* and Justo González's *A History of Christian Thought,* both treat the Christological Controversy and the controversies over grace in separate *volumes.*

26. David R. Maxwell, "Christology and Grace in the Sixth-Century Latin West: The Theopaschite Controversy" (Ph.D. diss., University of Notre Dame, 2003), 6. Maxwell continues with a cogent discussion of the origin and progression of the assumption that the two controversies were separate, citing scholars from Loofs (writing in 1887) through Smith (writing in 1990). See Maxwell, "Christology and Grace in the Sixth-Century Latin West," 8–21.

egregious degree of oversimplification) to the same alternatives: Either we do not deserve salvation and cannot achieve it ourselves, so God must come down himself to save us; or we are able to rise up to God, and therefore what we need is simply a guide and an enabler, a man indwelt by God the Son in a way similar to the way we can be indwelt by God the Spirit. One may reasonably argue that the ideas of the two controversies have much in common.

Furthermore, as I have also mentioned in the preface, the two controversies did not merely have similar ideas; they also had direct historical connections between them. Both Cassian in the fifth century and the Scythian monks in the sixth explicitly connected the two, but scholars often discount the connections that Cassian and the Scythian monks make. For example, Charles Brand argues that Cassian's equation of Nestorius with Pelagius is a defensive mechanism; Cassian has to protect himself from the suspicion that *he* is a Pelagian, and he does so by equating Nestorius (falsely, in Brand's opinion) with the vilified Pelagius.[27] Similarly, John McGuckin and Thomas Smith both argue that the Scythian monks' linking of grace with Christology is merely a political move—an attempt to enhance their reputation in the anti-Pelagian West—not an actual reflection of their thought.[28] In contrast to such explanations, I suggest that it is more natural and more respectful of both Cassian and the Scythian monks to take them at their word.[29] They connected

27. Charles Brand, "Le *De incarnatione Domini* de Jean Cassien: Contribution à l'étude de la christologie en Occident à la veille du concile d'Éphèse" (Ph.D. diss., Université de Strasbourg, 1954), 155.

28. John A. McGuckin, "The 'Theopaschite Confession' (Text and Historical Context): A Study in the Cyrilline Re-interpretation of Chalcedon," *Journal of Ecclesiastical History* 35 (1984): 245; Smith, *De Gratia*, 3.

29. In Chapter 5 of *Grace and Christology in the Early Church*, I argue that Cassian views salvation not as mankind's rising up to God (as scholars often assume), but rather as a downward movement of God to make us his adopted children, and that the monastic task that dominates Cassian's writings is one of fostering an already-present union with God, not advancing toward such union. In Chapter 6, I argue further that Cassian's Christology (although terminologically deficient by later standards) does clearly stress that Christ is God the Son who has come down to earth to live as a man for our salvation. If my interpretation is correct, Cassian's thought not only shows legitimate connections between Nestorianism

grace and Christology because they saw these as two sides of the same coin, and Fulgentius agreed with them.

THE THEOPASCHITE CONTROVERSY,
THE SCYTHIAN MONKS, AND FULGENTIUS

This general historical-theological background—which we have considered in terms of three interwoven strands—should be enough to show that the two great theological controversies of the fifth and sixth centuries were indeed connected, and in fact one of their primary points of intersection was the correspondence between Fulgentius and the Scythian monks. With this in mind, I turn now to the particular discussion within those larger controversies to which the correspondence belongs: the early sixth-century Theopaschite Controversy. This dispute technically began with the addition of the phrase "who was crucified for us" to the *Trisagion* in 511, an event whose implications I have discussed above. At this point I will pick up the narrative with the arrival of the Scythian monks themselves.[30]

The monks, led by John Maxentius, were from Scythia, which was (as I mentioned in the preface) near the mouth of the Danube River in modern-day Romania. This was a region in which both Greek and Latin were spoken,[31] but they themselves spoke Latin more readily than Greek. In late 518 or very early 519, they traveled from their hometown of Tomi to Constantinople to appeal to the emperor to settle a dispute they had with their

_____

and Pelagianism, but also argues convincingly against both of them. See Donald Fairbairn, *Grace and Christology in the Early Church,* Oxford Early Christian Studies (Oxford: University Press, 2003). Augustine Casiday, *Tradition and Theology in St John Cassian,* Oxford Early Christian Studies (Oxford: University Press, 2007), 226–27, 256, generally agrees with me. Furthermore, Maxwell, "Christology and Grace in the Sixth-Century Latin West," 62–63, arrives independently at an appraisal of Cassian almost identical to mine.

30. For more of the details, see Frend, *The Rise of the Monophysite Movement,* 244–47; Maxwell, "Christology and Grace in the Sixth-Century Latin West," 77–93. See also Maxwell, "'Crucified in the Flesh': Christological Confession or Evasive Qualification?" *Pro Ecclesia* 13 (2004): 70–75.

31. A century earlier, Cassian—unparalleled at the time for his fluency in both languages—probably came from the same region, although some scholars place his birth in southern Gaul.

bishop Paternus.[32] While they were there, they clashed in March 519 with Dioscorus (a papal legate who was in Constantinople overseeing the healing of the Acacian schism) and a Constantinopolitan deacon named Victor about the acceptability of the monks' confession that "one of the Trinity was crucified in the flesh," a phrase with obvious parallels to the addition to the *Trisagion*, "Holy God ... who was crucified for us." The monks' phrase—called the "theopaschite confession"—appears in John Maxentius's *Twelve Chapters*,[33] which may be the earliest writing by the monks and which is included in this volume. As Dioscorus reported this dispute to Pope Hormisdas, he dropped the crucial qualifier "in the flesh" from the monks' confession that "one of the Trinity has suffered in the flesh," thus giving the mistaken impression that the monks failed to distinguish the Son's suffering in his human nature from suffering in his divine nature as the Logos.

In the late spring or early summer of 519, John Maxentius wrote a *Declaration of Faith*[34] against the Deacon Victor, and the monks presented this *Declaration* to Dioscorus and Patriarch John of Constantinople. Dioscorus rejected their work, perhaps not because he disagreed with it but because he felt the Chalcedonian Definition itself was sufficient and did not need the explanatory notes that the monks put forward. Emperor Justin also rejected the monks' case, but the monks, rather than returning to Tomi, departed for Rome to make their case to Pope Hormisdas, while John Maxentius himself stayed behind in Constantinople. They arrived in Rome in August.

Meanwhile, the emperor's nephew Justinian (who would himself become emperor in 527) wrote to Pope Hormisdas warning him that the monks were troublemakers. But something (per-

32. Technically, they should have appealed to the patriarch of Constantinople, but because the Acacian schism had not yet been healed, Constantinople was out of fellowship with Rome, and thus with Latin-speaking Tomi. So they appealed to Emperor Justin rather than to Patriarch John.

33. *Capitula Maxentii Ioannis edita contra Nestorianos et Pelagianos ad satisfactionem fratrum* (Latin text in CCL 85A, 29–30).

34. *Libellus fidei* (Latin text in CCL 85A, 5–25). The *Declaration* is not included in this volume, but the expanded version of it sent to Fulgentius and the other exiled bishops is included.

haps a recognition of the significance of the monks' theology)
changed his mind, and he almost immediately wrote a second
letter and sent it by special courier to arrive in Rome before the
first one. His second letter encouraged Hormisdas to send the
monks back to Constantinople, and from the summer of 519 onwards, Justinian was a strong ally of the monks and their Christology. Hormisdas initially received both the monks and their
Declaration warmly, but he refused to send them back and instead
asked Emperor Justin to send Victor to Rome so that Hormisdas
could adjudicate the case between Victor and the monks. Hormisdas kept them in Rome for fourteen months, changed his
tone, and began to refer to the theopaschite confession as a nov-
elty (although he never called it heretical), and ultimately refused to affirm them. In the fall of 520, the monks left Rome under some duress. (Hormisdas claimed that they were disturbing
the peace, but they claimed to have been forced out of Rome by
pro-Chalcedonian rabble-rousers.) During their stay in Rome in
519, the monks sent a letter (essentially an expanded version of
the *Declaration*) to Fulgentius and the other North African bishops exiled on Sardinia,[35] and Fulgentius responded on behalf of
the exiled bishops,[36] affirming the monks' beliefs on both Christology and grace. Both the monks' letter and Fulgentius's very
long response are included in this volume.

Meanwhile, back in Constantinople, John Maxentius apparently continued the debate in the absence of his monastic brothers. In the spring or early summer of 520, a North African bishop named Possessor, who was in Constantinople, wrote to Pope
Hormisdas indicating that he, the general Vitalian, and Justinian
wanted to know what the pope thought about Faustus's *De gratia.*
Evidently, then, in Constantinople the Scythian monks (or at least
John Maxentius after the others left for Rome) had been arguing
that Faustus's thought on grace was opposed to that of Augus-

35. *Epistula Scytharum monachorum ad episcopos.* This letter is numbered as *Ep.*
16 in the collection of Fulgentius's letters, and the Latin critical text is in CCL
91A, 551–62. (It is also printed with the other writings of the Scythian monks in
CCL 85A, 157–72.)

36. *Epistula* 17 in the collection of Fulgentius's letters (Latin critical text in
CCL 91A, 563–615).

tine. Hormisdas recognized this as the same controversy the rest
of the monks had brought to him in Rome, and he responded to
Possessor[37] by accusing the monks of contentiousness while arguing that Faustus was not as high an authority as Paul, the Fathers,
the councils, or Augustine. John Maxentius later pointed out that
in Hormisdas's response, he did not deal with the Christological
question with which the monks had started. At some point between 520 and 523, the monks may have written another letter
to Fulgentius asking specific questions about grace, because, after the death of the Vandal North African Emperor Thrasamund
in 523 (and the consequent end of the North African monks'
exile), Fulgentius wrote a second letter to the Scythian monks[38]
addressing questions he says the monks asked him. At about the
same time, Fulgentius wrote his long treatise *The Truth about Predestination and Grace*.[39] Both of these documents are included in
this volume.

The Scythian monks were unsuccessful in swaying opinion
either in Constantinople or in Rome. Their failure, however,
does not necessarily imply that the church in either city substantially disagreed with their Christology or their understanding
of grace. As we have seen, Hormisdas originally received them
warmly, Justinian was their tireless defender, and of course, they
won the approval of Fulgentius and the other North African
bishops.[40] A generation later, their Christology was vindicated

37. *Epistula* 70 (Latin text in CCL 85A, 115–21).

38. *Epistula* 15 in the collection of Fulgentius's letters (Latin critical text in
CCL 91A, 447–57).

39. *De veritate praedestinationis et gratiae* (Latin critical text in CCL 91A, 458–
548).

40. In fact, writing in 1930, Nisters demonstrated that the monks' arguments
precipitated a shift in Fulgentius's Christological language. Prior to his correspondence with them, Fulgentius often referred to Christ's humanity as *homo* ("man")
and seemed to regard the one person of Christ as a combination of divine and
human. During and after the time of his correspondence with the monks, however, Fulgentius shifted toward a much stronger insistence that the person of
Christ is the Logos, and he also began much more consistently to use *humanitas*
("humanity") rather than *homo* to refer to the human nature of Christ. See Bernhard Nisters, *Die Christologie des Hl. Fulgentius von Ruspe,* Münsterische Beiträge
zur Theologie 16, ed. F. Diechamp and R. Stapper (Münster: Aschendorffsche
Verlagsbuchhandlung, 1930), 91–92.

at the Fifth Ecumenical Council (Constantinople II) in 553, as
that council affirmed that the Christ who suffered on the cross
was indeed one of the Persons of the Trinity.[41] Furthermore, the
monks' theology of grace had a fairly direct impact on the subsequent course of the Semi-Pelagian Controversy. John Maxentius composed a florilegium of anti-Pelagian statements by Augustine[42] and had these sent to Rome. Later, Pope Felix IV used
capitula 3–10 of Maxentius's florilegium to reply to some questions posed by Caesarius of Arles about grace, and Caesarius in-
corporated these *capitula* as Canons 1–8 of the Second Synod of
Orange in 529 (which brought the Semi-Pelagian Controversy
to a close).[43] In light of the later success of the monks' ideas,
it may be that their initial failure came about not because the
Church fundamentally disagreed with their views, but rather
because neither Constantinople nor Rome was willing to jeop-
ardize the fragile peace that the healing of the Acacian Schism
had brought about.

Be that as it may, the course of the Theopaschite Controversy
and the writings of both the monks and Fulgentius indicate a
very strong connection between Christology and grace. They
argue that both in the Incarnation itself and in the salvation
of individual believers, God is fundamentally the one who acts
to bring humanity to himself, and human action (both Christ's
and ours) is carried out under the divine, not independently.
As Maxwell helpfully concludes, the relation between Christology and grace is primarily characterized by two points: "First,
human actions originate in God both in the case of Christ and

41. See the *capitula* of the Second Council of Constantinople, in Tanner,
ed., *Decrees of the Ecumenical Councils, Vol. 1*, 114–22. Notice that *capitula* 2, 3,
5, 6, and especially 10 distinctly resemble the affirmations that the monks and
Fulgentius make in the writings included in this volume.

42. These were not the same as the *capitula* against both Nestorius and Pelagius, translated in the appendix to this volume. Instead, they are found in CCL
85A, 251–73.

43. Compare Maxentius's *capitula* 3–10 (Latin text in CCL 85A, 252–59)
with the Synod's *capitula* 1–8 (Latin text in SC 353, 154–61; English translation
in J. Patout Burns, trans. and ed., *Theological Anthropology* [Philadelphia: Fortress Press, 1981], 112–15). See also D. M. Cappuyns's discussion in "L'origine
des «Capitula» d'Orange 529," in *Recherches de théologie ancienne et médiévale* 6
(1934): 121–42.

in the case of Christians. Except in the case of sin, humanity never acts independently from God. Second, God's role as subject does not evacuate humanity from Christology or soteriology, but humanity finds its fulfillment precisely because God acts through human experiences, human actions, and even human decisions."[44] The brief writings by the Scythian monks included in this volume and the much longer ones by Fulgentius in response stand not only as examples of the intimate connection between grace and Christology in patristic thought, but also as a reminder to us today of the priority of the divine in every aspect of human salvation.

MANUSCRIPT TRADITION AND EDITIONS OF THESE DOCUMENTS

The manuscripts of the correspondence between the Scythian monks and Fulgentius translated in this volume are extant in two codices. The first (N) dates from the eighth or ninth century and is housed in Rome,[45] and the second (*Port.*) dates from the twelfth century and is housed in Grenoble.[46] In both of these codices, the order of the writings is as follows: *Ep.* 15 (the *second* of Fulgentius's letters to the monks), then *The Truth about Predestination and Grace* (the *last* of these four writings to be composed), then *Ep.* 16 (the monks' letter to the North African bishops—thus the *earliest* of the documents in this correspondence), and finally *Ep.* 17 (Fulgentius's *first* letter to the monks). The manuscript of the monks' letter was published in 1556 by Gravius[47] and also appeared in editions in 1573 by Plantinus[48] and in 1587 by Henricpetrus.[49] The three writings

44. Maxwell, "Christology and Grace in the Sixth-Century Latin West," 242.

45. Rome, Bibl. Naz. 1006 (Cheltenham 12260), saec. VIII–IX (ex abbatia S. Crucis, sed fortasse Nonantulae confectus), fol. 1ᵛ–125.

46. Grenoble, Bibl. Munic. 226 (134), saec. XII (e Cartusia Portarum), fol. 95–179.

47. Editio Bartholomei Grauii, Louanii, 1556 (iuxta codicem quem Iohannes Hesselius in abbatia Parcensi repperit).

48. Editio Christophori Plantini, Antuerpiae, 1573, pp. 363–437 (text taken from Gravius's edition).

49. Editio Sebastiani Henricpetri, Basiliae, 1587.

by Fulgentius were published in 1612 by Sirmond[50] and in 1649
by Chiffleti.[51] A complete text of the monks' letter and Fulgentius's responses was published in 1684 by Quesnel and Mangeant.[52] When J. Fraipont published the critical texts of these
writings in 1968 in Corpus Christianorum Series Latina,[53] he
compared the various editions with the two manuscripts themselves, and made relatively few corrections to the edition of
1684.[54] We have used Fraipont's text with only a few alterations
in preparing these translations.

The two writings by the Scythian monks translated in the appendix to this volume are extant in a ninth-century codex (*L*)
housed at the Bodleian Library in Oxford.[55] The texts were published by Schwartz in 1914 in *Acta conciliorum oecumenicorum*[56]
and were re-edited by Glorie in Corpus Christianorum Series
Latina in 1978.[57] We have used Glorie's text without alteration.

50. Editio Iacobi Sirmondi, S.J., Parisiis, 1612. This edition is missing most
of Book Three of *The Truth about Predestination and Grace*.

51. Editio Petri Francisci Chiffletii, S.J., Diuione, 1649. This edition includes
only Book Three of *The Truth about Predestination and Grace*.

52. Editio Paschasii Quesnel et Lucae Mangeant, *Sancti Fulgentii Ruspensis
Episcopi Opera, quae sunt publici iuris, omnia*, Parisiis, 1684.

53. CCL 91A, 445–615.

54. The editor of the critical text of the monks' writings (published in
1978), Fr. Glorie, repeated Fraipont's text of the monks' letter to the North
African bishops, without the critical apparatus but with a full set of notes indicating similarities between that letter and Maxentius's *Libellus fidei*. See CCL
85A, 157–72.

55. Oxford, Bodleian Library, Laud.misc.580. S. IX², fols. 9–12.

56. *ACO* 4.2, 10–11.

57. CCL 85A, 29–36.

*CORRESPONDENCE ON
CHRISTOLOGY AND GRACE*

LETTER FROM THE SCYTHIAN MONKS
TO THE BISHOPS

OUR SERVANT Peter the Deacon, along with John, Leontius, another John, and the rest of the brothers who were sent to Rome in the cause of the faith, writes to the most holy lords who should be named with all veneration: Datianus, Fortunatus, Januarius, Albanus, Horontius, Boethos, Fulgentius, and the other bishops and those who are distinguished in the confession of Christ.[1]

1. (I.) We believe it will be useful, highly necessary, and particularly profitable for the holy churches of God if we present to you, holy brothers, what we and all the holy churches of the East defend concerning the Incarnation and the divine economy, in the face of the heretics who never stop troubling the ancient faith of the Church with their depraved and wicked arguments. In doing so, we pray that we may win your agreement, blessed brothers, for we believe that we differ in no way from your holy and glorious confession, especially since we do not doubt that the Holy Church of God is made alive by one and the same Spirit everywhere. If all the Orientals learn that you, holy brothers, agree with them (or rather with the Catholics) in all the dogmas, they will all be filled with no small joy, but rather an abundant happiness.

---

1. As explained in the introduction, the monks wrote this letter during their stay in Rome in 519, to the North African bishops whom Thrasamund had exiled to Sardinia. The standard title of the letter is *Epistula Scytharum monachorum ad episcopos*, and the letter is preserved as *Ep.* 16 in the collection of Fulgentius's letters. The Latin critical text may be found in CCL 91A, 551–62 (also printed in CCL 85A, 157–72). John McGuckin has translated this letter in *Journal of Ecclesiastical History* 35 (1984): 239–55, and we have made use of his translation in composing the new one here.

2. As a result, we humbly beseech and petition you, blessed brothers, to conduct a careful examination of the matters set out below, and once you have discussed them (as is fitting for most true and fearless preachers of Christ), to disclose to us your judgment in writing. If by God's help you confirm that our exposition that we are placing before you is in harmony with the Catholic faith and the apostolic traditions (as we do not doubt you will), then we will easily be strengthened by the authority of such strong and tested bishops and will be able to shut the mouths of those who speak evil. Then, most holy lords who are most worthy before God, we will be able to persevere in the faith of the Holy Fathers and to return thanks to God, who has glorified you by granting you to confess his holiness. And now we beseech you to examine closely the following matters.

3. (II.) Therefore, in accordance with the tradition of the Holy Fathers, we confess our Lord Jesus Christ in two united and unconfused natures (that is, the natures of divinity and humanity), in one person or subsistence. We do not accept those who preach one incarnate nature of God the Word and who turn away from the faith of the venerable Chalcedonian council. Nor do we admit those who deceitfully profess two natures yet have difficulty in confessing the one incarnate nature of God the Word because they think that this is contrary to the profession of the two natures.[2] Contrary to their opinion, the phrase "one incarnate nature of God the Word" signifies nothing other than two natures ineffably united, as the blessed Cyril (bishop of the city of Alexandria)[3] wrote in his second letter to Succensus (bishop of Diocaesarea). Cyril wrote thus: "If we were to speak of one nature of God the Word and then to stop without saying the word 'incarnate,' we would essentially be abandoning the economy. In that case, one could appropriately reply to us deceivers, 'Where is his perfection in humanity?' Or 'how does

2. The point of these seemingly convoluted sentences is that both "one nature" and "two nature" confessions can be orthodox, depending on what one means by "nature."

3. Bishop of Alexandria in the early fifth century. An ardent student of Athanasius's writings, Cyril dominated the Christological controversy.

our substance subsist?' For indeed, when one uses the word 'incarnate,' one thereby implies both the perfection of humanity and the manifestation of our essence. As a result, people should stop supporting themselves with such fragile reeds and abandoning the economy or denying the Incarnation."[4]

4. (III.) We believe that the blessed Virgin Mary is *Theotokos,* or "Bearer of God," not simply on account of the dignity of the man who was born from her—some people are even fearless enough to preach impiously that this man was God by grace and not by nature! Instead, we believe that Mary is *Theotokos* properly and in truth, because she truly and properly gave birth to God the Word incarnate and made man, the Word who was united essentially or naturally to flesh.

5. Therefore, we also confess that the union of natures that came about was in every respect an essential or natural one, but we do not mean this in the same sense as those who contend that God the Word was at work in Christ in the same way as he was at work in a prophet. The blessed Gregory of Nazianzus[5] has refuted these people when he writes to Cledonius.[6] He says: "If anyone says God the Word was at work by grace, as in a prophet, and does not confess that the union came about essentially,[7] let him

4. Cyril of Alexandria, *Second Letter to Succensus* (= *Ep.* 46), par. 4. Greek text and English translation in *Cyril of Alexandria: Select Letters,* trans. Lionel Wickham, Oxford Early Christian Texts (Oxford: Clarendon Press, 1983), 88–91. Latin version by Dionysius Exiguus (with some minor differences from the text translated here) in *ACO,* 1.5, 301.

5. Fourth-century bishop of Sasima, but native and resident of Nazianzus, both in Asia Minor. He was chosen as bishop of Constantinople in 380 and briefly headed the Council of Constantinople (Second Ecumenical Council) in 381, before being asked to resign. His "Theological Orations" on the Trinity, preached in Constantinople in 380, have gained him the title "Gregory the Theologian."

6. Cledonius was a presbyter at Nazianzus in Asia Minor (modern-day Turkey) who was acting as Gregory's deputy while the bishop himself was at a spa in Xanxaris recovering from the trauma of trying to lead the Council of Constantinople. Gregory wrote this letter to Cledonius in 382 to counter the Apollinarian insistence that God the Son assumed human flesh, but not a human mind, at the Incarnation.

7. When the monks quote Gregory as saying that "the union came about es-

be devoid of the greater operation, or rather full of the worse."[8] Nor do we maintain this in the same sense as those who attempt to construe the union of the natures in terms of an illustration or of favor or good will (either personal or subsistent),[9] or in terms of authority or power or an equality of honor. The blessed Cyril, whom we mentioned a little above, anathematizes these when he writes against Nestorius:[10] "If anyone divides the substances[11] in the one Christ after the union and relates them merely with an association in terms of honor, dignity, or power, instead of saying that they have come together into a natural union, let that person be anathema."[12] God the Word united a human nature to himself and was made man—not in an empty, nominal way, not in a small part of himself, but by the very nature in which he is divine just as the Father is, equal to the Father in all ways except that the one is Father and the other is Son.

---

sentially," they are actually strengthening the language Gregory used. The word he used in Greek for "the union came about" (*synaptomai*) was used in the fourth century not only for the union of natures in Christ, but also for an individual Christian's connection to God. Fifth-century christology would later deem this word insufficient to describe the christological union, and here in the early sixth century the monks' alteration of Gregory's language by using the Latin *unitio* rather than *societas* reflects the later developments.

8. Gregory of Nazianzus, *First Letter to Cledonius* (= *Ep.* 101), par. 22. Greek text in SC 208, 46. English translation from Greek in *St. Gregory of Nazianzus: On God and Christ,* trans. Lionel Wickham et al., Popular Patristics Series (Crestwood, NY: St. Vladimir's Seminary Press, 2002), 157.

9. Cf. John Maxentius's third anathema in the appendix to this work.

10. Bishop of Constantinople in the early fifth century. Nestorius was deposed at the Council of Ephesus in 431 and spent the last two decades of his life in exile in Upper Egypt.

11. The Greek word *hypostasis,* which Cyril uses here, had originally been a synonym for the Latin *substantia,* but by Cyril's time it had become a synonym for the Latin *persona.* Accordingly, the Latin version of Cyril's letter should have written *personae* ("persons") or *subsistentiae* ("subsistences") here, rather than *substantiae* ("substances"). Despite the imprecision in the Latin version, however, the next sentence makes clear that the monks are speaking of Christ as a single person, God the Son.

12. Cyril's third anathema from his *Third Letter to Nestorius* (= *Ep.* 17), written on November 30, 430. Greek text and English translation in *Cyril of Alexandria: Select Letters,* 28–29. Latin version by Dionysius Exiguus (almost identical to the text translated here) in *ACO* 1.5, 243.

6. In addition, the Holy Fathers preach that Christ Our Lord is compound[13] as a result of the union of divinity and humanity. When Paul of Samosata[14] was unwilling to confess this, he was condemned by the Synod of Antioch as a result of the arguments of Malchion, a priest of the same Antiochene church, a man most learned in all matters, who was subsequently elected by all the bishops who had convened against the aforementioned Paul.[15] This Malchion took up the central debate of this council and refuted the heretic by saying, among other things:

A compound may truly be made from entities that were previously uncombined, as in the case of Christ Jesus, who was made as a unity from God the Word and a human body of the seed of David. He was by no means in any kind of division afterwards, but subsisted in unity. But it seems to me that you are unwilling to profess a compound on these terms, so you argue that the Son of God is in him not substantially but merely by participation in the Wisdom.[16] For you have said that the Wisdom might suffer loss and therefore cannot be compounded with anything else. So you do not think that the divine Wisdom could remain undiminished just as he was before he emptied himself out.[17] So in this emptying out, which the Wisdom underwent by virtue of mercy, he existed undiminished and immutable. You even say that the Wisdom dwelt in him[18] just as we dwell in houses, as one in another, yet we are not part of the houses, nor is the house part of us.[19]

13. The Latin word *compositus* naturally lends itself to a translation as "composite" in English. The translation "composite," however, might imply that two entities have been combined to make the person of Christ. Instead, what the monks intend here is that a single person, God the Word, was formerly simple (that is, only God) but is now complex or compound since he has added humanity to who he already was as God. Therefore, throughout this book we use "compound" to render the adjective *compositus* and the noun *compositio*.

14. Third-century bishop of Antioch. He was condemned at two or three synods in Antioch in 268 for teaching that the man Jesus became Son of God when the Holy Spirit descended on him.

15. Malchion was a third-century presbyter in Antioch who led the interrogation against Paul of Samosata and may have written the synodal letter that condemned him, a letter from which the monks quote in this passage.

16. In this passage the word "Wisdom" is referring to the Logos, the Second Person of the Trinity. We indicate this by adding the article "the" in front of "Wisdom" and by using the masculine pronoun "he."

17. Cf. Phil 2.6.   18. That is, in the man Jesus.

19. The acts of the Synod of Antioch survive only in fragments, which Henri de Riedmatten has collected in *Les actes du procès de Paul de Samosate*, Paradosis 6

The blessed Athanasius, who refuted the vanity of the heretics, also spoke in a similar way in the treatise entitled "That the Christ is One."[20] After he had demonstrated that their speculations on the deity of the Son of God were excessive, he continued in this way:

And in a similar way they investigate the Incarnation. They say, "How is God made flesh? How does he receive a body? How is the uncontainable one joined to a tiny little body? How is the uncreated one united to the created? The uncircumscribed one to the circumscribed? And how can that great, immense, and indivisible one be divided into parts? For if that greatness is confined to a small space, then either that which is great has been made little, or only a part (not the whole divinity) has been united to the flesh." And this is impious to believe. Because of this, those who say "How?" or "In what manner?" have fallen headlong. In this faithless manner of thinking, have these people not posited an indwelling instead of an Incarnation, human action instead of unity and compounding, and two subsistences and two persons instead of the one substance of our Lord Jesus Christ?[21] Have they not impiously and improperly propounded a dogma of a quaternity in place of the holy and ineffable Trinity?[22]

7. Again the blessed Gregory[23] says in his sermon *On the Son:* "To state the matter in a single idea, just as you ascribe the higher things to the divinity and thus to that nature that is shown to be superior to the passions and to the body, so you indeed attribute the lower things to the compound[24] who for your sake emptied himself out and was incarnate."[25] Thus, from this we believe most

(Fribourg: Editions St-Paul, 1952). On pp. 148–50 Riedmatten discusses the fragment translated here.

20. Athanasius was the leader of the Nicene party during the height of the Arian controversy in the fourth century. This work is one whose attribution to Athanasius is questionable. It may have been written by an unknown follower of Apollinarius in the latter part of the fourth century. (See *CPG* 2, no. 3737.)

21. Notice again the confusion between "subsistence" or "person" on one hand and "substance" on the other. To be consistent, one would need to write "instead of the one subsistence of our Lord Jesus Christ."

22. Ps (?)-Athanasius, *That the Christ is One*. Greek text in PG 28:124C.

23. Gregory of Nazianzus.

24. That is, to God the Son considered in his post-incarnate state, in which he possesses humanity as well as the deity he has always possessed.

25. Gregory of Nazianzus, *Third Theological Oration* (= *Or.* 29), par. 18. Greek text in A. J. Mason, ed., *The Five Theological Orations of Gregory of Nazianzus,* Cam-

rightly that even after he assumed flesh, the full and perfect God the Word suffered no increase or diminution. On the contrary, by his union he brought ineffable glory to the nature he assumed.

8. (IV.) But on this matter of the Trinity, even after the mystery of the Incarnation, the Trinity remains intact because the same God the Word, even with his own flesh, is one of the Trinity. And this is not because his flesh is of the substance of the Trinity, but because it is the flesh of God the Word who is one of the Trinity. For he, and no other person,[26] was the one "who ascended into heaven, he who had descended from heaven, the Son of man who is in heaven."[27] And for this reason we profess that God the Word suffered in the flesh, was crucified in the flesh, and was buried in the flesh, in accordance with the blessed Cyril when he says: "If anyone does not confess that God the Word suffered in the flesh, was crucified in the flesh, tasted death in the flesh, and was made the firstborn from the dead, even though as God he is Life and the Life-giver, let that person be anathema."[28]

9. Similarly, we say that the man was Christ the Word in accordance with the saying of the blessed John: "that which was from the beginning, that which we have heard, that which we have seen with our eyes, that which we have looked upon and touched with our hands, concerning the Word of Life."[29] For the Word could not be touched by human hands according to

bridge Patristic Texts (Cambridge: University Press, 1899), 101–2. English translation from Greek in *St. Gregory of Nazianzus: On God and Christ*, 86.

26. The word "person" does not occur here, but the Latin adjective *alius* is masculine, indicating that the monks are speaking of the Son as a person, not of his divinity as a nature. Among both Greek and Latin writers in the fourth through sixth centuries, it was common to write of Christ as "one" and "another" with the pronouns for "one" and "another" in neuter forms, but not as "one" and "another" with the pronouns in masculine form. The best way to render this in English is to write that Christ is one thing and another thing (or "one nature and another nature"), but he is not one person and another person.

27. Jn 3.13.

28. Cyril's twelfth anathema from his *Third Letter to Nestorius* (= *Ep.* 17). Greek text and English translation in *Cyril of Alexandria: Select Letters*, 32–33. Latin version by Dionysius Exiguus (virtually identical to the text translated here) in *ACO* 1.5, 244.

29. 1 Jn 1.1.

the nature of his deity unless he became man. But as for this child whom the blessed Virgin bore, whom she wrapped in cloths, whom she placed in a manger, whom she had circumcised on the eighth day, whom the just man Simeon clasped to his bosom, who (the evangelists indicate) was subject to his parents, and who (those evangelists bear witness) advanced in age and wisdom,[30] it is beyond doubt that this one was by nature God, the one through whom all things—visible and invisible—were made, the Only-Begotten one and the Firstborn "in whom all things hold together,"[31] according to the Apostle Paul. And the prophet Isaiah also bears witness of this fact in a clear voice when he says: "A child has been born to us, a son has been given to us, whose power is in his shoulder, and he will be called 'Messenger of great counsel,' 'Wonderful,' 'Counselor,' 'Mighty God,' 'Lord,' 'Father of the coming age,' 'Prince of peace.'"[32]

10. Consequently, we believe that there can be no agreement with those who assert that the mighty God was united to that child but do not believe that that child was himself the mighty God. This is especially clear since the psalmist testifies that the "throne into the age of ages" belongs to no one else, but wholly to the one who was born of the Holy Spirit and the Virgin Mary and was baptized in the Jordan by John so that he might sanctify the waters. For the psalmist says: "Your throne, O God, lasts into the age of ages; the scepter of your reign is a scepter of justice. You have loved righteousness and hated iniquity, and therefore your God has anointed you with the oil of gladness above all your fellows."[33] How, then, could God be anointed, whose throne lasted into the age of ages, unless he became man?

11. (V.) Therefore, according to this saying of the prophet, God was made Christ, but Christ was not made God. The latter is

30. See Lk 2, especially 2.52.   31. Col 1.16–17.
32. Is 9.6.

33. Ps 44.7–8 (45.6–7 modern). Throughout this book, citations of the Psalms list the chapter and verse in the Vulgate first, followed by the chapter and verse in modern translations. If the monks' or Fulgentius's text is closer to the Vulgate translation following the Septuagint than to the Vulgate translation following the Hebrew, this fact is indicated by the notation "following LXX."

what the heretics say when they dare to assert that Christ is God
by advancement, not by nature. God was anointed because he
himself was made man. There is not one person who is God and
another person who is man, but the same one is God and the
same one is man. The same one who is the natural son of the
Virgin is the natural Son of God.[34] For this reason we believe and
confess that there were two births of God the Word; that is, one
before the ages from the Father according to his divinity, and the
other in the last days, from the holy Virgin according to the flesh.
We execrate those who deny the birth of God the Word according to the flesh, for they even draw back from confessing that the
wondrous deeds and the sufferings are of one and the same Son
of God—something the entire Church of God confesses.

12. Moreover, we also accept the four councils that are in
keeping with the sense of our exposition: that is, the council of
the 318,[35] the council of the 150 who condemned the impious
Pneumatomachians,[36] the first council at Ephesus where the most
blessed bishops Celestine of Rome and Cyril of Alexandria presided,[37] and the holy and venerable council held at Chalcedon.[38]

34. In these two sentences, the words translated "person" and "one" do not
actually occur, but we have added them to convey the force of the masculine
adjectives *alter* and *idem*. See note 26, above.

35. The First Ecumenical Council, held at Nicaea in 325. It condemned
Arius and affirmed the full equality of the Son to the Father. It also produced
a creed that was eventually expanded to form what we call the Nicene Creed.

36. The Second Ecumenical Council, held at Constantinople in 381. It rejected Pneumatomachianism (the denial of the full deity of the Holy Spirit) by
affirming the full equality of the Spirit to the Father and the Son. It also produced—or at least ratified—the creed we now call the Nicene Creed.

37. The Third Ecumenical Council, held at Ephesus in 431. The Roman
pope Celestine was not actually present but sent legates to the council. Cyril was
the presiding bishop. There were two rival councils held at Ephesus in 431 and
another one in 449. The one headed by Cyril in 431 was ultimately called the
correct and ecumenical council, while the other one in 431 (headed by John of
Antioch with the help of Nestorius) was rejected. The council at Ephesus in 449
was also subsequently rejected by the Church. (Pope Leo of Rome referred to it
as a "robber synod.") When the monks here refer to the "first council at Ephesus," they are considering the one in 449 to be the second, although they reject
it. They are disregarding the rival council of 431.

38. The Fourth Ecumenical Council, held at Chalcedon in 451. This is the

13. In addition we embrace the letters of the blessed Leo.[39] We anathematize all who hold opinions contrary to the doctrines of the Church, including all the writings of Theodore of Mopsuestia and his disciple Nestorius and all those who hold opinions similar to those of the same Nestorius.[40] We anathematize all the writings that oppose the twelve chapters of the blessed Cyril, which he published against the said Nestorius;[41] and we add to this condemnation Eutyches and Dioscorus with their companions and all those whom the apostolic see has justly and rightly condemned.[42]

14. (VI.) Now that we have discussed these matters, it follows that we should declare to you, blessed brothers, what we should believe about the grace of Christ by which he has plucked us from

---

council that produced the Chalcedonian Definition. For further information about these councils, see the introduction to this volume.

39. Roman pope at the time of the Council of Chalcedon. When the monks refer to the letters of Leo, they mean most notably Leo's *Ep.* 28, more commonly called the *Tome* (Latin text in *ACO* 2.2.1, 24–33; English translation in NPNF, 2d series, vol. 12, 38–43). Many people, both ancient and modern, have considered Leo's *Tome* to be inconsistent with Cyril's anathemas, but the monks show here that they believe them to be consistent. In *Grace and Christology in the Early Church,* 218–20, I argue that Leo, like Cyril and (in my opinion) Chalcedon, affirms that the personal subject of Christ is God the Word.

40. Theodore, bishop of Mopsuestia in what is today southern Turkey, died in the year 428, just as the Christological Controversy was brewing. Before becoming bishop of Mopsuestia, he had been Nestorius's teacher in Antioch, and Nestorius later became the bishop of Constantinople in 428. Nestorius's proclamation of his teacher's theology in the imperial capital was the immediate catalyst for the controversy. As mentioned above, Nestorius was condemned at Ephesus in 431 and exiled to Upper Egypt four years later. Theodore was condemned posthumously at the Fifth Ecumenical Council in 553.

41. The monks quote the third and twelfth of these anathemas in paragraphs 5 and 8 above. One may find the Greek text and English translation of all twelve anathemas in *Cyril of Alexandria: Select Letters,* 28–33.

42. Eutyches was a monk in Constantinople in the mid-fifth century, and Dioscorus was the bishop of Alexandria after Cyril's death in 444. Both of them adhered to extreme versions of Cyril's theology and refused to speak of two natures in Christ at all. Both were condemned at Chalcedon. Significantly, the Oriental Orthodox Churches (that is, the so-called "monophysites") also condemned Eutyches, although they regard Dioscorus as a saint.

the power of Satan, according to what has been handed down to us. For even on this matter your approval is most necessary to us.

15. Thus we believe that the Creator of all made Adam good, free from any assaults of the flesh and endowed with great freedom so that by his own capacity he might either do good, or (if he should so desire) admit evil. Death and immortality were to some degree placed within the freedom of his choice. For he was capable of both, so that if he kept the commandment, he would become immortal and have no experience of death; but if he disdained the commandment, then death would follow at once. He was then seduced by the cleverness of the serpent and voluntarily became a violator of the divine law. So according to what had been foretold to him, he was condemned by the just decree of God to the punishment of death. He was completely (that is, according to body and according to soul) changed for the worse, lost his personal freedom, and was sold into slavery to sin.

16. Because of this, no man has been born without being bound by this chain of sin, except the one who was born in a new mode of begetting so that he might destroy this chain of sin: "the mediator between God and men, the man Christ Jesus."[43] What else could have been—or can be—born from a slave except a slave? And Adam fathered sons not while he was free, but only after he was made a slave of sin. Therefore, just as every man is from him, so every man is a slave of sin through him. As the Apostle says: "Because of one man all men have come under condemnation,"[44] and again, "through one man sin entered into this world, and death through sin, and so death passed to all men, for in him all have sinned."[45] Therefore, those who say that only death, not sin, has passed into the human race are ut-

---

43. 1 Tm 2.5.   44. Rom 5.18.

45. Rom 5.12. In this passage, the phrase here translated "for in him all have sinned" is ambiguous in Greek. It could refer either to death, to Adam, or to the entrance of sin and death into the world in general. The Latin version of this passage resolves the ambiguity by indicating that all have sinned in Adam, and therefore that somehow sin—not just death—is transmitted from one generation to the next.

terly mistaken, since the Apostle bears witness that both sin and, through it, death are brought into the world.

17. Therefore, no one at all is delivered from this condemnation and death except by the grace of the Redeemer. Although he was the Lord and indeed God, he was made a slave "by taking the form of a slave,"[46] so that he might free us from perpetual servitude and the devil's power and might lead us back to true freedom. As a result, he said this to the Jews: "Then you will be truly free if the Son sets you free."[47] They thought they were truly free, but in fact by their most vain intention they were slaves to human cares. In order that false freedom might become true freedom (that is, that human freedom might become Christian freedom), that very freedom needed a liberator, through whose grace it might be able to turn away from human cares so as to contemplate and long for the things that pertain to life eternal.

18. Indeed, without this grace human freedom can contemplate and long for human things, but it cannot contemplate or desire or long for divine things. The primary and principal foundation of these divine things—and to a great degree the basis and fount of all good things—is to believe in the crucified Lord of glory.[48] Such belief undoubtedly does not spring from the freedom of the natural choice, because it is not flesh and blood that reveals this, but the heavenly Father reveals this to whom he wills[49] by drawing him to true freedom, not by violent compulsion but by inpouring sweetness through the Holy Spirit so that we may soon say with faith, "Jesus is Lord." No one can say this through the freedom of the natural will, but only through the Holy Spirit.[50]

19. Therefore, those who say, "It is my responsibility to will to believe and God's responsibility to help by grace," prattle on in vain. For the Apostle testifies that the very act of believing (which means giving assent to the truth) is given to us by God, when he

46. Phil 2.7.   47. Jn 8.36.
48. Cf. 1 Cor 2.8.   49. Cf. Mt 16.17.
50. Cf. 1 Cor 12.3.

says, "For it has been given to you by Christ, not only that you may believe in him, but even that you may suffer for his sake."[51]

20. (VII.) Our opponents say that if God causes unwilling people to will to believe, but (in our opinion) there is no one who can naturally believe in the Son of God or will anything good that pertains to eternal life, then why does God not cause all people to will to believe, since there is no favoritism with God,[52] especially when it is written of him that "he wills all men to be saved and to come to the knowledge of the truth"?[53] They argue that according to our opinion, either God wills and is unable, or the divine Scripture is lying. Since it is impious to think either, it remains to say (in our opponents' opinion) that God does not rouse up human will to believe, but instead he waits for it to come from man so that there may be a fitting reward for those who will to believe and a just condemnation for those who refuse to do so.

21. If these matters are really the way such heretics say they are, then those heretics have comprehended the unsearchable and incomprehensible judgments of God.[54] If, as they themselves wish to say, God condemns those who are unwilling to believe but saves those who are so willing, then there is nothing at all that needs any further investigation. But if they are right, the Scripture that bears witness to the incomprehensible judgments of God is greatly mistaken. On the other hand, as a way of believing in and demonstrating the incomprehensible judgments of God, we say that from one lump of perdition some are saved by God's goodness and grace, while others are abandoned to a just and hidden judgment.

22. Otherwise, let those who think that this is contrary to divine justice and goodness tell us, if they can, why it was that the one "who wills all men to be saved and to come to the knowledge of the truth"[55] did so many great works in Chorazin and

51. Phil 1.29.
52. Cf. Rom 2.11, Eph 6.9, Col 3.25, Jas 2.1.
53. 1 Tm 2.4.   54. Cf. Rom 11.33.
55. 1 Tm 2.4.

Bethsaida but did not will to do any in Tyre and Sidon, even though (as he himself testifies) if he had done any such works there, "would they not have been penitent in sackcloth and ashes?"[56] Or why did he prohibit the Apostle from preaching the word of salvation in Asia and Bithynia?[57]

23. If they admit that these things cannot be understood, then let them return to their senses, realize that they are but men, and stop speculating about why God should save some by a free gift yet abandon others to a just and hidden judgment, since God has the power "to make from the same lump one vessel for honor and another for dishonor."[58] Let them cry out together with us, or rather with the Apostle: "O the depth of the riches of both the wisdom and knowledge of God! How unsearchable are his judgments, and his ways past finding out! For who has known the mind of the Lord? Or who has become his counselor? Or who has first given to him and it will be repaid to him? For from him and through him and in him are all things; to him be the glory into the ages of ages. Amen."[59] Therefore, it is obvious that anyone who says, "grace does not come to me unless I first will it," is not simply opposing us but is completely opposing the Apostle. Saying this amounts to nothing else than saying that one must first give to God in order to receive back from him.

24. (VIII.) But as for us, we follow that very apostle, and we affirm that the source of all good thoughts, the harmony among those thoughts, and even the good will itself, are from God and through God and in God. He is the one who inwardly forgives and corrects the wills of men, wills that had been evil and entangled in earthly deeds. He does this by the inpouring and working of the Holy Spirit, as it is written, "The will is prepared by the Lord."[60]

25. The blessed Basil, bishop of Caesarea,[61] concurs with this in his *Prayer at the Sacred Altar,* which almost the whole East

---

56. Mt 11.21.
57. Cf. Acts 16.6–7.
58. Rom 9.21.
59. Rom 11.33–36.
60. Prv 8.35, following LXX.
61. This is the fourth-century father Basil the Great, who was one of the ma-

uses. Among other things, he says, "Lord, grant strength and protection. Make those who are evil to be good, we pray. Preserve those who are good in goodness. For you are able to do all things, and there is no one who may contradict you. When you will, you save, and no one resists your will."[62] See how succinctly and definitively the distinguished teacher previously brought an end to this [future] controversy. Through this prayer he teaches that those who are evil are made good not from themselves, but by God, and they persevere in that goodness not by their own strength but by the assistance of divine grace.

26. The blessed Innocent, bishop of the apostolic see, spoke similarly in his letter to the Council of Milevis:[63] "We must ascribe all the efforts, works, and merits of the saints to the praise and glory of God, for no one can please him in any other way than the way he himself has given."[64] That African council repeats and explains the Pope's idea[65] more clearly and more carefully in its letter to Pope Zosimus.[66] The council says,

---

jor influences on early Greek monasticism, the possible composer of one of the major liturgies of the Eastern Churches, and a key leader in the latter phases of the Arian Controversy leading to the Second Ecumenical Council in Constantinople in 381. Basil was a good friend of Gregory of Nazianzus, whom the monks have cited previously in this letter.

62. This prayer is not present in the current versions of the Liturgy of Saint Basil and is not extant in its complete form. See McGuckin's extended note on the passage in *Journal of Ecclesiastical History* 35 (1984): 253–54n.

63. Innocent I, the pope from 402 to 417, condemned Pelagius's thought in January 417. The Scythian monks argue that the passages they quote in this paragraph are from correspondence between Innocent and the North African Council of Milevis (held in 416 as part of the deliberations of the Pelagian Controversy) and between that council and the subsequent pope, Zosimus (pope from 417 to 418). We possess this correspondence only as an addendum to *Ep.* 21 by Pope Celestine I (pope from 422 to 432), who took part in the later Semi-Pelagian Controversy and the Nestorian Controversy. It is not clear whether the quotations in this paragraph were originally written in the 410s, as the monks allege here, or in the 430s. If the latter, it is also not clear whether they were written by Celestine himself or by Prosper of Aquitaine.

64. Addendum to Celestine, *Ep.* 21 (Latin text in PL 50, col. 533A).

65. That is, the Council of Milevis was explaining Pope Innocent's idea to Pope Zosimus.

66. In the summer of 417, Zosimus presided over a Roman synod that reversed Innocent's condemnation of Pelagius. But then in the following year, he

In the letters that you arranged to have sent to all the provinces, you made the assertion that we must ascribe all good things to their author, from whom they originate.[67] Thus, we have by the inspiration of God brought all these matters before the consciences of our brothers and fellow-bishops. We therefore accept this formulation so that you may cut down all those who extol freedom of choice over and against God's assistance as if you were sweeping through them with the drawn sword of truth. What might you do with this free choice other than making us conscious of our complete unworthiness? If, by God's inspiration, you have recognized this fact faithfully and wisely and have expressed it trustingly and truthfully, it is surely because "the will is prepared by the Lord."[68] God himself touches the hearts of his children so that the virtuous may accomplish something through their Father's inspirations, "for as many as are led by the Spirit of God, these are sons of God."[69] God touches our hearts in this way so that we may not think that our choice is absent in any particular good action of the human will, and even more, so that we may not doubt that his grace precedes that will. For God works in the hearts of men, and in free choice itself, in such a way that holy thoughts, pious counsels, and every motion of the good will may all be from God. Through him we are able to do any sort of good thing, but "apart from him we can do nothing."[70]

27. The most blessed Celestine addresses these ideas in a concurring way in his letter given to the Gauls. He says,

When the prelates of the holy people, in their [divinely] mandated office, are engaged in seeking God's mercy, they do so on behalf of the

---

reviewed the entire proceedings of the Pelagian Controversy and condemned Pelagius, thus bringing that dispute more-or-less to a close.

67. This sentence makes it seem as if the Council of Milevis believes it is reminding Pope Innocent of what he wrote, not informing Pope Zosimus of what his predecessor wrote. Either the members of the Council are not aware that Innocent has died, or this confusion is an indication that these words do not originally derive from the 410s.

68. Prv 8.35, following LXX.

69. Rom 8.14. The Latin word translated "led" in this biblical quotation is the same word (the verb *agere*) that is translated "accomplish" earlier in the sentence. Furthermore, notice the parallel between "Spirit" in the biblical quotation and "inspirations" earlier in the sentence. The double word-play is that those in whom God does his work by his Spirit are able to do their own works by God's "in-Spiriting."

70. Addendum to Celestine, *Ep.* 21 (Latin text in PL 50:533B–C). Final Scripture quotation is from Jn 15.5.

human race. The whole Church joins with them, asking and beseeching earnestly that God may give faith to the faithless, set idolaters free from the errors of their faithlessness, lift the veil from the hearts of the Jews so that the light of truth may appear to them, cause the heretics to recover their senses in their understanding of the Catholic faith, give the schismatics a restored spirit of love, bestow the remedies of penitence to the lapsed, and finally, open the halls of heavenly mercy to the catechumens who have been led to the sacraments of regeneration.

The effect of these prayers shows that one does not ask the Lord for these things either carelessly or in vain, since he deigns to draw many people out of every kind of error. He plucks people from the power of darkness and transfers them to the kingdom of his beloved Son,[71] and he makes vessels of mercy out of vessels of wrath.[72] One can sense that this is the work of God to such a degree that when one gives thanks and praise for the illumination or correction of people such as these, one must ascribe such praise to the God who has brought the changes about.[73]

A little bit later, Celestine also writes:

Since we have accepted these ecclesiastical laws and these documents that have come from divine authority, we are strengthened by God's help to such a degree that we confess him to be the author of every good desire and work, every achievement and virtue by which one reaches out to God from the beginning of faith. We may not doubt that God's grace precedes all human merits and that only through God may we begin to choose anything good, or to accomplish it. As God gives this gift of his assistance, there is no question of his taking away free choice. Rather, he sets it free so that having been in darkness, it becomes light; having been wicked, it becomes upright; and having been foolish, it becomes prudent.[74]

The same teacher also concludes this very letter like this: "We believe that these writings have taught us according to the aforementioned canons of the apostolic see and that these are quite sufficient for the confession of God's grace (from whose

71. Cf. Col 1.13.

72. Cf. Rom 9.21.

73. Addendum to Celestine, *Ep.* 21 (Latin text in PL 50:535B–536A). Notice that our source for this quotation is the same collection of quotations added to Celestine's *Ep.* 21. The monks' attributions of the quotations in the previous paragraph to Innocent and the Council of Milevis in the 410s and of this quotation to Celestine in the 430s are not corroborated by the independent information we possess today about these quotations, but the monks' attributions may nevertheless be correct.

74. Addendum to Celestine, *Ep.* 21 (Latin text in PL 50:536B).

work and honor absolutely nothing should be detracted). Anything that may appear contrary to the previously detailed beliefs, we do not regard as appropriately Catholic."[75]

Most holy brothers, we have not considered it necessary to set these things before you as if you were ignorant men, but we have judged it useful to include these matters in our humble treatise in order to refute the madness of those who take refuge in dogmas that are new and have never before been heard in the churches.

28. Since we have been instructed in the teachings of all the holy fathers, we anathematize Pelagius and Celestius, together with Julian of Eclanum and all those who think like them.[76] We particularly anathematize the books of Faustus, bishop of the Gauls, who came from the monastery of Lérins.[77] There is no doubt that he wrote these books in opposition to the idea of predestination, and in the text he opposes not only the tradition of all these holy fathers, but even that of the Apostle himself. He links the assistance of grace to the presence of human effort and completely invalidates the whole grace of Christ by impiously professing that the ancient saints were not saved by the same grace that saves us, as the most blessed Apostle Peter teaches,[78] but that they were saved by their own natural capacity.

Peter, a deacon by God's mercy, has signed.
John, a monk by God's mercy, has signed.
Leontius, a monk by God's mercy, has signed.
John, a lector by God's mercy, has signed.

75. Addendum to Celestine, *Ep.* 21 (Latin text in PL 50:537A–B).

76. Pelagius was a British monk who came to Rome in the late fourth century or at the turn of the fifth, fled to North Africa after the sack of Rome in 410, and then left North Africa for Palestine around 412. His alleged teaching that Adam's sin was not transmitted to his posterity and that grace was primarily (or exclusively) external was the focus of the Pelagian Controversy from 412 to 418. Caelestius and Julian of Eclanum were two of Pelagius's followers. Caelestius was the one whose teaching first attracted Augustine's attention in North Africa in 412, and Julian was Augustine's primary target in the 420s.

77. Faustus was bishop of Riez in southern Gaul in the latter part of the fifth century. The book the monks cite here is his work *On Grace*, written around 475. The Latin critical text of this work (called *De gratia* in Latin) may be found in CSEL 21, 3–96.

78. Cf. Acts 15.11.

FULGENTIUS'S FIRST LETTER TO
THE SCYTHIAN MONKS

DATIANUS, FORTUNATUS, Boethos, Victor, Scholasticus, Horontius, Vindicianus, Victor, Januarius, Victorianus, Fontius, Quodvultdeus, Fulgentius, Felix, and Januarius[1] send greetings in the Lord to the beloved and highly esteemed saints and brothers in the faith and grace of Christ: Peter the deacon, John, Leontius, another John, and to the other brothers whom you mentioned in your letter[2] and who were sent to Rome together with you in the cause of the faith.[3]

1. (I.) Our blessed brother, Deacon John, directed by your fellowship, presented to us the letter that you sent. After examining it, we simultaneously and eagerly acknowledged both your faith and your salvation. Or more precisely, your salvation became obvious to us through your acknowledgment of the faith. For in this life the only true salvation of men is correct faith in God, "faith that works through love,"[4] through which faith apostolic authority testifies that we have been saved by divine grace, saying, "By grace you have been saved through faith, and this is not from yourselves. It is a gift of God, not from works, lest any-

---

1. This list of senders includes eight names not listed among the addressees in the monks' letter to the bishops: two Victors, Scholasticus, Vindicianus, Victorianus, Quodvultdeus, Felix, and a second Januarius. This list does not include Albanus, who is listed among the addressees of the monks' letter.

2. This list of addressees corresponds exactly to the list of the senders of the monks' letter to the bishops. Fulgentius's second letter (*Ep.* 15) has a slightly different list of addressees.

3. As explained in the introduction, Fulgentius wrote this letter on behalf of the North African bishops exiled to Sardinia. He wrote it to the Scythian monks in 519, while they were in Rome. The Latin critical text may be found in CCL 91A, 563–615.

4. Gal 5.6.

one be exalted."[5] And since love must adhere continually to the correct faith (which enables that love to practice good works effectively, and thus to "cover a multitude of sins"),[6] therefore the teacher of the Gentiles in faith and truth then adds, "For we are his workmanship, created in Christ Jesus for good works, which God has prepared so that we may walk in them."[7] He added this lest he dare, out of the presumptuousness of human pride, to claim anything for himself after that faith (through which we have been freely saved) has been approved, and so that instead he might assign even the grace of good works to the benefits of divine goodness. We rejoice that you, under God's guidance, are walking in such good works and accomplishing them. To be sure, are "not slothful in concern," but instead you are "fervent in the Spirit,"[8] who is the Lord you serve with a very laudable devotion. Therefore, love deriving from a pure heart, a good conscience, and an unfeigned faith spurs you (for the sake of the fellowship of the faith) to examine more carefully the secret reasons for our exile, secrets that need to be made known. Thus, because the word of God, which is living and powerful,[9] is not bound,[10] we will also demonstrate (by means of a public reply written back to you, beloved brothers) those same truths that we also receive and hold by the holy authority of the canonical books, and also by the things the Fathers taught and instituted. These are truths about the Incarnation and economy of our Lord Jesus Christ, and about grace (which is granted freely to the unworthy in such a way that it brings about in us both the beginning and the completion of a good will). We trust in the Lord (from whom faith is also imparted to us so that we may believe with our hearts, leading to righteousness, and from whom a word is given so that we may confess with our mouths, leading to salvation),[11] that he will guide both our understanding and our pen equally, so that we may give an appropriate response to your question. He will so guide us that in our response we may state those things that the reality of our

---

5. Eph 2.8–9.
6. Cf. Jas 5.20, 1 Pt 4.8.
7. Eph 2.10.
8. Rom 12.11.
9. Cf. Heb 4.12.
10. Cf. 2 Tm 2.9.
11. Cf. Rom 10.10.

redemption implies about the Incarnation of the Lord, and that we may say those things about the grace of God that the celestial majesty itself has freely imparted to us.

2. (II.) You say, therefore, that "in accordance with the tradition of the Holy Fathers," you confess "our Lord Jesus Christ in two united and unconfused natures (that is, the natures of divinity and humanity), in one person or subsistence."[12] As a consequence of this, you also assert that you believe that "the blessed Mary is, properly and in truth, the Bearer of God; because, in other words, she truly and properly gave birth to God the Word incarnate and made man, and united essentially or naturally to flesh."[13] Let it suffice for us to identify these points from the tenor of your letter. The other things that your profession about the Incarnation of the Lord includes depend on these points.

3. Therefore, if anyone refuses or hesitates to believe and preach either that there are two natures or that there is one person in our Lord Jesus Christ, or if anyone refuses to confess that the same one, that is, the Word Incarnate, truly born of the Virgin Mary for our salvation, is God and man, the Catholic faith recognizes and shows such a one to be as much a stranger as he is an ingrate who opposes the mystery of human redemption. For this is that "great mystery of godliness" recommended to all the faithful by the mouth of the Apostle, "the mystery that was made manifest in the flesh, was justified in the spirit, appeared to angels, was proclaimed among the nations, was believed on in this world, and was taken up in glory."[14] This is, of course, the Word who was in the beginning and was with God and was God,[15] that is, the Only-begotten Son of God and the power and wisdom of God,[16] through whom and in whom

12. Scythian Monks' Letter to the Bishops (= *Ep*. 16), par. 3 (Latin text in CCL 91A, 552, and CCL 85A, 158; English translation in this volume, p. 26).

13. Scythian Monks' Letter to the Bishops (= *Ep*. 16), par. 4 (Latin text in CCL 91A, 552, and CCL 85A, 159; English translation in this volume, p. 27).

14. 1 Tm 3.16.   15. Cf. Jn 1.1–2.

16. Cf. 1 Cor 1.24.

all things were made and without whom nothing was made.[17] This same is the Only-begotten God, "although he existed in the form of God...."[18] (That is, he was equal in all things to the one who begat him, he possessed a unity of natural essence with him, and he was in that nature which he, being eternal, has from the Father—that which the Father naturally is. The same one was true God, most high and immutable; and he was not a different God from the Father, but instead, although the personal distinction remained, he was naturally one God with the Father. And of course, he was neither less than nor subsequent to the Father, nor of a different power, nor of another essence.) This same one, "although he existed in the form of God, nevertheless he did not regard being equal with God as something to be forcibly kept, but he emptied himself by taking the form of a slave."[19] The same one "was made in the likeness of men"; the same one was "found to be in the human condition."[20] In him there could be no thought of forcibly keeping, because the begotten fullness of natural equality remains in him, since he is from the Father's substance by an ineffable and eternal birth. Therefore, "he emptied himself by taking the form of a slave." Thus indeed, God willed to be man naturally, and so the Lord of all things took on a servile nature without loss of his own sovereignty. Correspondingly, having emptied himself, he compassionately accepted the form of a slave. The holy Apostle of the New Covenant, after being made a fit minister by God, just as he himself bears witness,[21] also himself testifies about this form, lest anyone of us who hears about the emptied Son of God should by evil thought imagine that the form in the Only-begotten God has lost or diminished its equality with the Father's form, and lest such a person, by following the crooked, circuitous ways of the serpent's deception, should not hold to the path of right faith. To prevent this from happening, Paul clarified that emptying by removing the unclear elements, when he added subsequently: "by taking the form of a slave." Therefore, the Only-begotten God's emptying was his taking

17. Cf. Jn 1.3.   18. Phil 2.6.
19. Phil 2.7.   20. Ibid.
21. Cf. 2 Cor 3.6.

the form of a slave, since there was no loss or diminishment of his divinity. The divine nature, to be sure, cannot be diminished or increased in any way, because it is immutable and remains always what it is. For if that true and most high God, who "for our sakes became poor although he was rich, so that we might become rich through his poverty,"[22] had been emptied in the sense of losing his fullness (even saying this is wicked!) or had undergone some change when he accepted the form of a slave, then blessed John the evangelist would not have said about the incarnate Word: "And we have seen his glory, the glory as of the Only-begotten from the Father, full of grace and truth."[23] So the Word who was made flesh began to be human flesh in human reality, but in divine reality he did not cease to be the Word. For this reason, the wonderful kindness of God the Redeemer effectually accomplished the mystery of taking up and redeeming man, because the divine majesty could never admit of any change or diminishment.

4. Therefore, the Word of God, the very same God the Word, when he took human flesh from the flesh of his mother, did indeed receive the form of a slave in such a way that he deigned to become what he in fact became. But he did this while remaining in the form of God, that is, eternal and immutable God through that unity of person in which he received the form of a slave. Indeed, when "he was made in the likeness of men, he was found to be in the human condition."[24] Although in all ways he had immutable deity from the nature of the Father, nevertheless he who was not created deigned to be created, and he who was not created but begotten from the Father willed to be born from a woman. In this manner "the Word was made flesh"[25] so that there might be "one mediator between God and men, the man Christ Jesus,"[26] "who is God over all things and is blessed into the ages."[27] He is the one true Son of God and Son of man, one and the same from the Father without beginning, always having been the begotten God, but indeed also truly God according to

22. 2 Cor 8.9. 23. Jn 1.14.
24. Phil 2.7. 25. Jn 1.14.
26. 1 Tm 2.5. 27. Rom 9.5.

the flesh, conceived and born in time from his mother. It was not that the Only-begotten God received an unconceived flesh, but rather, God himself was conceived in that flesh in the profoundest humility. Indeed, according to the flesh God himself was created in and from the Virgin, and in fact he who had created his own mother was created from and in that flesh.

5. (III.) If, however, God the Word had become flesh in the Virgin in such a way that he had not come from her, it is certain that God himself would not have possessed the substance of flesh from the flesh of his mother but would simply have passed through the Virgin. In such a case, he could not have accomplished the mystery of becoming the mediator for our salvation, because in that case Christ the Son of God would not have unconfusedly united true, full humanity and divine substance in himself. Therefore, the medical remedy (as it were) that divine goodness employed was that the Only-begotten God, who is in the bosom of the Father,[28] should become man, not only in a woman but also from that woman. Without doubt we are commanded by the prophets of God to believe and confess this. Indeed, the prophet did not keep silent about the fact that God was made man, but he said: "Mother Zion will say, a man, truly a man, was born in her, and the Most High himself has established her."[29] Isaiah, also filled with the Holy Spirit, foretold the mystery of the coming Incarnation of the Son of God thus: "Behold, a virgin will conceive in her womb and will bear a son, and his name will be called Emmanuel, which is translated 'God with us.'"[30] Therefore, because the one whom the Virgin conceived in her womb and bore is called "God with us," we recognize that indeed God has been conceived in the Virgin's womb and has been born. The Gospel also says of Mary: "She was found to be with child by the Holy Spirit."[31] Joseph, too, Mary's husband (with whom she did not have sexual relations and experience corruption of the flesh, but who was the witness

28. Cf. Jn 1.18.
29. Ps 86.5, following LXX (87.5 modern).
30. Is 7.14; cf. Mt 1.23.
31. Mt 1.18.

to and guardian of her sacred virginity and purest fruitfulness) is thus advised by an angel's oracle: "Joseph, son of David, do not be afraid to take Mary as your wife, for what has been born in her is of the Holy Spirit."[32] It is also shown by heaven-sent words that he [the one born in her] was made from her, for the Apostle says: "But when the fullness of time came, God sent his own Son, made from a woman, made under the law."[33] Likewise, as he was writing to the Romans, he established this excellent beginning of his letter in order to show that he set a true and stable foundation of faith: "Paul, a slave of Jesus Christ, called to be an apostle, set apart for the Gospel of God, which he had promised through his prophets in the holy Scriptures concerning his Son, who was made from the seed of David according to the flesh."[34] Also when writing to Timothy, his beloved son in the faith, he chiefly urges him with anxious affection to remember this faith, saying, "Remember that Christ Jesus (who was from the seed of David) arose from the dead according to my Gospel."[35] Also the angel Gabriel is found to have used this consolation when speaking to the blessed Virgin herself, namely, the future bearer of her Creator, indeed of the Creator of all things: "The Holy Spirit will come upon you, and the power of the Most High will overshadow you; therefore that holy thing that will be born from you will be called the Son of God."[36]

6. To this belongs the mystery of our salvation, because our father Abraham ordered the steward of his household to place his hand under his loins and swear by the God of heaven.[37] One should not suppose that he did this apart from the prophetic spirit, that is to say, at the time when the chosen vessel hinted that all things happened as figures.[38] Therefore, holy Abraham, the father of the nations, did not do this because he believed that there was already some natural union with the God of heaven in his flesh. Instead, he did this so that he might show that the God of heaven was going to be born as a man from that

---

32. Mt 1.20.
34. Rom 1.1–3.
36. Lk 1.35.
38. Cf. 1 Cor 10.11.

33. Gal 4.4.
35. 2 Tm 2.8.
37. Cf. Gn 24.2.

flesh which would bring the Truth from among the descendants of Abraham himself. Therefore, that Truth is the one Christ the Son of God in the natures of divinity and flesh. In him the one-ness of person does not confuse the human and divine natures, and the unconfused oneness of the natures does not make them exist as two persons. Consequently, the truth of our recon-ciliation and salvation remains because God the Only-begotten became true man for us, and the man who was conceived and born was none other than the Only-begotten God.

7. Therefore, the blessed Mary both conceived and bore God the Word inasmuch as he was made flesh. God the Word did not insert the flesh in which he was conceived into her womb. Nor did God himself, who was to be conceived, take on the ma-terial of conceived or formed flesh apart from her. Instead, he assumed that flesh from her as he was being born. He received the nature of human flesh from and in the Virgin herself, and the eternal God was temporally conceived and born according to that nature. To be sure, the virginal conception was the very act of accepting flesh, because apart from temporal flesh that spiritual nature of the Word of God that was begotten without beginning from God the Father could not have been conceived in the womb of that saint who was herself both mother and spiritual virgin. Likewise, apart from union with the Word of God, flesh could in no way be engendered in the inmost vir-ginal womb that had not been inseminated by intercourse with a man. Therefore, when God who was to be conceived in her ar-rived, at that very time, the nature of the Virgin who conceived offered this flesh from itself. Thus one must not imagine that there was any interval of time between the origin of the con-ceived flesh and the arrival of the Majesty who was to be con-ceived. Indeed, there was one conception of divinity and flesh in the womb of the Virgin Mary, and there is one Christ the Son of God, conceived in both natures so that thereafter he might begin to erase the stain of the corrupted offspring, which was seen to exist in each person who was born.

8. (IV.) For because all men are born of intercourse between male and female, then because of their very conception they

have the beginning of original sin spread upon them by that contact. For that sin—which the first man incurred when he was led astray by the devil's malice even though he was good by nature—passed into his descendants along with its punishment, that is, death—a fact that holy David truly declared, saying, "Behold, I was conceived in iniquities, and in sins my mother bore me."[39] Thus, as the merciful and just Lord sought to destroy the vestiges of human iniquity, it was absolutely necessary that the immaculate one deign to unite an immaculate human nature to himself in the very act of conception, an act which ordinarily the devil was accustomed to rule as his own portion and dominion by inflicting the stain of original sin. Therefore, the Only-begotten God accepted the conception and birth of his human nature, a nature that he willed to assume truly and completely. May it never be that any Catholic would believe or say that the Only-begotten God, who was to redeem us by his own blood in that flesh by which God himself was made man, might reject the beginnings of human conception, when in fact God was going to suffer the extremes of human mortality in that same flesh, while remaining immortal himself. For just as the true and living God did not lose his unchangeable and indestructible natural condition as he died in the flesh, so also the same God who was naturally infinite and eternal did not lack his natural infiniteness when he was conceived in circumscribed flesh; and when he was born in the flesh temporally, he did not lose his natural eternality in which he was the eternal God from the Father and in the Father. For by that life he wanted his death to be the death he assumed in the flesh, and that eternality had its [temporal] conception in his mother.

9. Therefore, God the Word, that is, the Only-begotten Son of God, who is in all things (just as he himself bears witness) "the Alpha and the Omega, the Beginning and the End,"[40] thus did not initially refuse to be conceived in flesh according to human nature, just as God, by dying in the same flesh, later paid the debt of human nature. For human nature would have been

---

39. Ps 50.7 (51.5 modern).
40. Rv 1.8.

in no way sufficient and satisfactory for removing the sin of the world, unless it had passed into the oneness of God the Word, not by a confusion of the natures, but only by a unity of person. To be sure, when the Word became flesh by a wondrous union, he created his nature that he received from us. Nonetheless, in that divine and profoundly wondrous union, the divinity of the Word was not changed into flesh, and the true humanity of the Word absolutely preserved the natural reality of our race. Therefore, a virgin (and one must constantly call to mind the fact that she was a virgin) both conceived and gave birth to God the Word himself, according to the flesh that was made in her. The one she bore was the Only-begotten God, the very power and wisdom of God,[41] the radiance of eternal light and the flawless mirror of God's majesty, the image of his goodness, the splendor of glory, and the figure of his substance. The one she bore was the one whom the unchangeable and eternal divinity of the Father begat as the eternal and unchangeable one, without any beginning of his nature. The virginal womb first conceived and gave birth to this same one: God and man complete and entire in human nature.

10. (V.) When, however, we say, "The Lord Christ is God and man," we point not to a duality of persons, but to the fact that a very true union of both natures has taken place without any mingling. To be sure, the same God who is man is the same man who is God; for human nature was wondrously united to God the Word in such a way that the true God himself would become true man, and indeed in such a way that the true humanity of the incarnate Word would possess no other person than the incarnate Word. For it was a human substance, not a person, that was added to God. Therefore, God with his own flesh is one Christ—the Son of God and the Son of man, the same one at the same time both Word and flesh. Indeed, the same Word is flesh, for the same God is man.

11. (VI.) But God the Word did not receive flesh in some way without becoming flesh, since the evangelist says: "The Word

41. Cf. 1 Cor 1.24.

was made flesh."[42] And the most high and most great God did not assume the nature of flesh in the way [he dwelt] in one of the patriarchs or prophets. In that case, God would certainly have been in that man, but God himself would not have been a man. May it never happen that the Christian conscience holds to such an understanding or that anyone among the faithful permits himself to be defiled by such great ungodliness. For when "the Word was made flesh," divinity thus deigned to unite humanity miraculously to itself in such a way that for the life of the world, that humanity of his would come into being as divine humanity in one and the same God and man, Christ, while preserving the reality of both natures. For God, "not withholding his mercies in his anger,"[43] was made man for this purpose: that whatever he had created whole in man, God might make it completely whole again once he had taken it into himself.

12. As a result, he possessed this marvelous quality of being both God and man because he was truly conceived and born according to the flesh. Consequently, the Virgin ineffably conceived and bore the God of heaven, and the Virgin Mother remained inviolate—after all, an angel has truthfully proclaimed that she was full of grace and blessed among women.[44] By the power and work of prevenient grace, the Holy Spirit came over her and the power of the Most High overshadowed her.[45] As she was about to conceive the one who was God and the Son of God, she neither desired nor engaged in intercourse, but instead, while maintaining her virginity in both mind and body, she received from him what she was about to conceive and give birth to, by a gift of uncorrupted fertility and fertile purity. Thus did the holy Virgin conceive God the Word as he, the Creator of angels and men, was himself made according to the flesh; and in the same way she gave birth to the Redeemer of men. For the holy Virgin Mary did not conceive God without his assuming flesh, or conceive flesh without its union with God, because the

42. Jn 1.14.
43. Ps 76.10, following LXX (77.9 modern).
44. Cf. Lk 1.28, 42.
45. Cf. Lk 1.35.

one whom the Virgin conceived belonged jointly to the God of the Virgin and to the flesh of the Virgin.

13. This is the grace by which it came about that God (who came to take away sins because there is no sin in him) was conceived from sinful flesh and born as man in the likeness of sinful flesh. To be sure, the flesh of Mary had been conceived in iniquity in accordance with human practice, and so her flesh (that gave birth to the Son of God in the likeness of sinful flesh) was indeed sinful. For the Apostle bears witness that "God sent his own Son in the likeness of sinful flesh."[46] That is to say, he sent the one who, "although he existed in the form of God, nevertheless did not regard being equal with God as something to be forcibly kept, but emptied himself by taking the form of a slave. He was made in the likeness of men."[47] For that reason, the Son of God (the same one who was made in the likeness of men) was sent in the likeness of sinful flesh so that he might become like men in the true flesh that he himself had created and so that God (created in the flesh without sin) might remove our dissimilarity to himself. He understood this dissimilarity in our flesh to be a result not of his work but of our sin. Therefore, as the Son of God appeared, he was sent in the likeness of sinful flesh, because human mortality was present in his true human flesh, but not human iniquity. When it is said that truly the likeness of sinful flesh is in the Son of God, or rather that the Son of God is in the likeness of sinful flesh, one must believe that the Only-begotten God did not take the defilement of sin from the mortal flesh of the Virgin, but that he received the full reality of its nature so that the Source of truth might arise from the earth, the Source whom the blessed David announces in a prophetic word, saying: "Truth has sprung out of the earth."[48] Consequently, Mary (whom God accepted) truly conceived and bore God the Word incarnate.

14. (VII.) But she gained the privilege of conceiving and bearing God-made-man not because of human merits, but because of the condescension of the Most High God who was be-

46. Rom 8.3.   47. Phil 2.6–7.
48. Ps 84.12 (85.11 modern).

ing conceived and born from her. For if God the Word had not been born as a true and full human being by uniting human nature (taken from the Virgin) to himself in an exceptional way, he could never have been the source of spiritual birth from God for us who had been born carnally. But in order that the divine birth might be given to those who had been carnally born, the divine majesty was first conceived and born in the true flesh of the Only-begotten Son. For salvation was far from sinners, and our iniquities separated us greatly from God. Because we were held bound by the fetters of death from the very moment of our fleshly birth, and because we could be set free from this death only by the blessing of spiritual birth, God was born of man so that men might be born of God. For this reason, therefore, Christ the Son of God, that is, the true God and eternal life, was born and died in true flesh so that we might be reborn spiritually in the one name of the Trinity through the sacrament of baptism. The Apostle teaches this, saying: "We who have been baptized in Christ Jesus have been baptized in his death."[49]

15. Therefore, the first birth of Christ, the Son of God, was from God, and the second was from man. But our first birth is from man, and our second is from God. And since God received true flesh from the womb as he was about to be born, he thus granted the Spirit of adoption to us who have been reborn through baptism. That which he was not by nature through his first birth, he was made by grace through his second birth. This happened so that what we were not by nature through our first birth, we might become by grace through our second birth. But God conferred grace on us as he was born from man; and we received grace freely, so that we might become participants in the divine nature, as a gift from the God who was born in flesh. Therefore, because the Son of God became the Son of man, "as many as received him" (just as the blessed John the evangelist testifies) "to them he gave the power to become sons of God, to those who believe in his name, who have been born not from blood,[50] nor from the will of the flesh, nor from the will of

49. Rom 6.3.
50. The Latin word used here, like the Greek word it translates, is actually

man, but from God."[51] Indeed, after the eternal birth that the co-eternal Son possesses from the Father, if that Only-begotten Son (who is in the bosom of the Father) had not undergone a second birth for the sake of justifying man, then since man had been conceived in iniquity, he would not be free from the entanglements of his first birth. But according to the blessed John's word, "for this purpose the Son of God has appeared, that he may destroy the works of the devil."[52] Thus, since his first birth (by which he is true God and eternal life from the nature of the Father) had no beginning [in time], the same God took on the beginning of a second birth in time from the Virgin.

16. (VIII.) Therefore, because the status of his life remains unchangeable, that living Speech of God is, after his first birth, naturally one life with the Father from whom he was born, for "just as the Father has life in himself, so also he has granted the Son to have life in himself."[53] The very same Son of God was born by grace in the nature of flesh to die for those who were dead, so that we, after the death that we have after our first birth from the flesh, might be reborn to life in the grace of the Spirit. But the true and living God, indeed, God who is the Truth and Eternal Life, would not be able to taste death unless he himself became true man; and the same man who tasted death would not be strong enough to conquer death unless he was the true God and Eternal Life. For which man will destroy death by death except that man who is a man in such a way that he is also God? Or who will rescue his own soul from the hand of hell? Thus, according to the flesh that he received from us, the Only-begotten living and true God was conceived and born, and likewise, after he was dead, he arose. Since the purpose of his coming was "to seek and to save that which had perished,"[54] he "was handed over for our offenses and arose for our justification."[55] But the

---

plural: "not from bloods." The idea is that this spiritual birth of the Christian is not like fleshly birth, which (in ancient understanding) involves the mingling of the parents' blood.

51. Jn 1.12–13.　　　　　　　52. 1 Jn 3.8.
53. Jn 5.26.　　　　　　　　　54. Lk 19.10.
55. Rom 4.25.

death of God's Son (which he undertook only in the flesh) destroyed both of our deaths, namely, that of the soul and that of the flesh, and the resurrection of his flesh bestowed on us the grace of both spiritual and bodily resurrection. This happened so that, after we had first been justified by faith in the death and resurrection of God's Son, we might be raised from the death of unbelief, by which we were held in bondage while we were by nature sons of wrath (just as others also).[56] Furthermore, this happened so that after the first resurrection (that is, of the soul, which was granted to us by faith, even in accordance with this flesh in which we now live), we might rise again, never to die again. The true God and Eternal Life deigned to take on himself the destruction of our death for no other purpose than to give us (those who believe in his resurrection) his life, which will remain for ever. Therefore, the Lord of glory also endured the abuse of the cross in order to give his glory to his faithful ones, just as he himself bore witness, saying, "And I have given them the glory that you have given me."[57] Therefore, the Word-made-flesh is one complete Christ. With respect to the term "flesh," however, this one must be accepted as a complete man, that is, a rational soul and flesh. For just as Christ, God's Son, received our true, but sinless, flesh, so he also received his own true, but sinless, soul. He put on our flesh with its condition of human mortality, and in the same way he truly accepted our soul with its weaknesses, yet without the stain of human iniquity. Christ did this so that, as his divinity bore our weaknesses by his power in his soul, he might preserve righteousness without sin, and so that through righteousness he might remove the punishment of mortality from his flesh itself, by the gift of resurrection. Therefore "Christ, rising from the dead, dies no more, and death will not dominate him any more."[58]

17. (IX) In keeping with the usage of words in Scripture, it is certainly customary to indicate both the flesh and the soul with the single word "flesh," as it is written: "I will pour out a mea-

56. Cf. Eph 2.3. 57. Jn 17.22.
58. Rom 6.9.

sure of my Spirit upon all flesh,"[59] and, "All flesh shall see God's
salvation,"[60] and, "As you have given him power over all flesh,"[61]
and, "Unless those days had been shortened, no flesh would be
saved."[62] In keeping with this custom, just as the whole man is
indicated in some passages of the Holy Scriptures with the word
"flesh," so also in other places the [same] whole man is designated by the word "soul" alone. For the patriarch Abraham left
his land, his relatives, and the house of his father at the command and with the help of the God who called him (for he was
in no way able to fulfill what God commanded without the help
of the one who had commanded). As he departed, he took with
him the men whom he possessed, and the narrative states that he
took with him the souls he had acquired in Haran. Likewise, as
Jacob was going down to Egypt, Holy Scripture reminds us that
seventy-five souls were in his caravan.[63] The blessed Apostle Peter
also says that eight souls were saved through water at the time of
the flood.[64] Also, in the Acts of the Apostles, when the Jews were
suddenly and wonderfully conscience-stricken by the preaching
of that same blessed Peter and were converted from being faithless to being full of faith by the right hand of the Most High, it
is written that "about three thousand souls were added on that
day."[65] We understand from these testimonies that when either
"flesh" or "soul" is used alone, full and complete human nature is
meant. Therefore, the Word made flesh is one complete Christ;
one from both and in both (that is, human and divine natures).
In him the glorious union of both natures remains absolute, so
that whoever diminishes Christ's humanity to stress his divinity or
detracts from the divinity to stress his humanity denies Christ by
a sacrilegious infidelity and blasphemous preaching. And John
the Apostle, filled with truth, testifies "that every spirit that denies
Jesus is not from God, and this one is an antichrist."[66]

18. (X.) What Christian could be unaware of or doubt the fact
that before he became flesh, God the Word was not Christ, but

---

59. Jl 2.28; cf. Acts 2.17.   60. Lk 3.6.
61. Jn 17.2.   62. Mt 24.22.
63. Cf. Gn 46.27.   64. Cf. 1 Pt 3.20.
65. Acts 2.41.   66. 1 Jn 4.3.

was only God? But at that time the same God the Word (who was always in the form of God) began to be Christ when he, God, emptied himself and took the form of a slave without diminishing the fullness of his nature. Therefore, God became Christ so that Christ might be perfect God and man, for the Word deigned to become flesh so that the flesh might be able to be designated by the name "Word," that is, God. For the flesh of Christ was not Christ before it was assumed by the Word; neither did flesh itself, that is, some man himself, take upon himself the form of the living God. Instead, God, who was in the form of God, took the form of a slave. God, equal to the Father, was "made in the likeness of men and was found to be in the human condition."[67] He who was rich became poor on our account so that we might become rich through his poverty.[68] Therefore, the Word-made-flesh is one Christ; but that Word without flesh was the eternal God. Not only was the flesh of Christ apart from the Word not ever Christ, but that flesh had not even been conceived as a person. Therefore, the Word-made-flesh was eternal before he became flesh, but the flesh of the Word took its personal beginning in God the Word himself. But because the Word-made-flesh is one Christ, the Son of God and of man, the Word is not one person and the flesh another person.[69] Instead, one and the same person is without beginning since he is eternal God begotten of the Father, and this same person has a temporal beginning according to the flesh. This same God was made man from a virgin, and he is one Only-begotten Son of God from eternity in his divinity and with a beginning in his flesh. From eternity (that is, in his divinity), he is surely the Creator of things visible and invisible; and from the beginning (in his flesh), he is the one saving his people from their sins. From eternity in his divinity, the same one is co-eternal with the Father (from whom he came forth ever living); and from his beginning in his flesh, he came after his mother (from whom he was born in time so as to die in time). For the Apostle testifies that "at the right time Christ died for the ungodly."[70]

---

67. Phil 2.7.   68. Cf. 2 Cor 8.9.

69. In this passage, as elsewhere, we add the word "person" to convey the force of the masculine Latin pronouns.

70. Rom 5.6.

18 *bis*. Therefore, it was not the Trinity (that is, not the Father and the Son and the Holy Spirit together), nor the Father alone or the Holy Spirit alone—(that is, not the one who begat the Son or the one who proceeded from the Father) [who was born for us]. Rather, it was the Son alone (that is, the one whom the Father begat as the co-eternal and coequal Son for himself in the unity of their nature—one person of the Trinity, Christ the unique Son of God). This happened so that the one who was conceived and born from the womb of his Virgin Mother according to the flesh in order to save us would be the same one who was the true and most high God from the bosom of God the Father. It was not the Trinity, but the Only-begotten from the Father, Christ the Son of God, who was a child in the flesh and grew in the flesh. The Father (who is perfect and infinite) recognizes him to be his equal in perfection and infiniteness through the unity of divinity. It was not the Trinity, but the one who was "the way, the truth, and the life,"[71] Christ the Son of God, who mercifully lived through the course of time in the flesh through the human states from infancy to mature young manhood. Since he was eternal in the unity of the Father's nature, he wondrously created the ages, and since he was unchangeable, he made the uncertainties of temporal circumstances certain. It was not the Trinity, but Christ, the splendor of the Father's glory, who suffered in the flesh for us and who was the sole person born from his Father God and was himself the impassible God. Therefore, we sincerely believe what must not be doubted: that Christ the Son of God himself tasted death in the flesh for our sakes while still preserving the immortality of his divinity. As we hear in the truthful preaching of the holy Apostle John, he is the true Son of God the Father and true God and eternal life.[72] It was not the Trinity, but the Word-made-flesh, Christ the Son of God, who deigned to be crucified and die in that flesh and who arose. Since he remains the Life, he raised his very own flesh from the tomb. It was not the Trinity, but Christ (who is God over all things),[73] who ascended in the flesh into heaven in the sight of his disciples, and who is com-

71. Jn 14.6.
73. Cf. Rom 9.5.

72. Cf. 1 Jn 5.20.

ing back from heaven in the flesh. He did not desert heaven when he took flesh on earth, and in his divinity he did not desert his own followers on earth when he ascended into heaven in the flesh. For he promised this when he said: "Lo, I am with you always, even to the end of the age."[74] Therefore, he who is in the form of God is God, according to the prophecy of the blessed Jeremiah: "He is lofty and has no end; he is highly exalted and infinite."[75] Shortly thereafter the same prophet says of him: "He is our God, and no other will be compared to him; he has laid hold of the complete path of instruction and has given it to Jacob his son and to Israel his beloved."[76] In the form of a slave (in which he was made a little less than the angels),[77] he was (as the same prophet says) "afterwards seen on earth and interacted with men."[78] Unbelieving men saw the same mortal and changeable man, but those who now truly believe in him with a clean heart are going to see him as God, immortal and unchangeable by nature. For true faith now cleanses the hearts of men, so that the glory of the future resurrection will make those hearts able to see God.

19. (XI.) But what is true faith except believing unhesitatingly that one and the same Christ is true God and true man, and proclaiming that he, one and the same, was begotten of God the Father according to the divinity and was born of the Virgin Mary according to the flesh? Apostolic authority certainly testifies that Christ is one and the same person, who is "from the fathers according to the flesh," who is "God over all things and is blessed into the ages."[79] One and the same was "crucified because of weakness," but "is alive because of God's power";[80] one and the same also does mighty works among men and endures sufferings on behalf of men, because when Christ the Son of God was doing miracles according to his divinity, his suffering humanity was present in the same God. And when the same Christ, the Son of God, was suffering according to the flesh, his

74. Mt 28.20.
76. Bar 3.36–37.
78. Bar 3.38.
80. 2 Cor 13.4.

75. Bar 3.25.
77. Cf. Heb 2.9.
79. Rom 9.5.

impassible divinity was present in the same man. Therefore, this is why the properties of the natures do not divide the person of Christ the Only-begotten Son of God, and the unity of the person cannot mingle or remove the characteristics of each nature, because the one who says that he himself is the Truth by nature has preserved both in his one self by maintaining the reality of the natures. Therefore, we do not separate the impassible divinity of Christ from his humanity in his sufferings, nor do we think that his humanity should in any way be separated from his divinity in his miracles. Consequently, we do not separate or mix Christ in the miracles and the sufferings, since blessed Peter, by revelation from the Father, confessed him as the Son of the living God,[81] and since Christ himself had previously said that he was really the Son of man.[82] Therefore, true faith does not separate or divide the true Christ in his sufferings and miracles, because the unity of his person does not allow any division within him, and the reality of both natures continues unconfused. For the God Christ "was handed over for our offenses," because he is true man; and the same man Christ "arose for our justification,"[83] because he is true God. If the same true God were not true man, he could not be betrayed and die; and if the same true man were not true God, he would not be able to release and raise himself from the pains of hell. But because there is not one person who is God and another who is man, but the same one is Christ, God and man, it is in fact the same God Christ who underwent death in his flesh, and the same man Christ who destroyed death in his divinity. To be sure, the same Christ, Son of God, who could not die in his divinity, died in his flesh, since the immortal God took on the mortality of that flesh. And the same Christ, Son of God, died in the flesh and was raised because, even while he was dead in the flesh, he did not lose the immortality of his divinity.

20. Subsequently, the fact is that even after his resurrection, just as he demonstrated by his genuine wounds and by actually eating fish and honey that his flesh was solid and real, so also,

81. Cf. Mt 16.16.   82. Cf. Mt 8.20, *inter alia.*
83. Rom 4.25.

when he entered through closed doors, he showed that the true power of eternal divinity was present in him. He showed both of these facts so that people might recognize that the weakness of the dying Christ according to one nature and the majesty of the other nature both belonged to the same person who was resurrected. Because of this, when Thomas is commanded to experience the reality of the wound by placing his hand in the side of the dead and resurrected Christ, he acknowledges the real power of divinity in the wounds of the one who suffered and rose again. And when he is commanded to touch with his fingers the places of the nails, he declares with a confession of faith that Christ is his Lord and God, saying: "My Lord and my God!"[84] For he realized that the one who arose from the dead in his own flesh by the power of his own divine nature was none other than the one who, being from the nature of God the Father, is the true God and eternal life.

21. As he informed us of the truth of this faith, the Founder and Redeemer of the human race, the Creator of and Sharer in our nature, showed by his real wounds that his flesh was real and showed by the power of his resurrection that he was truly divine. He did this to demonstrate that we must believe and preach that he is one and the same God and man. After this, when he said to his apostles: "Go, teach all peoples, baptizing them in the name of the Father and the Son and the Holy Spirit,"[85] he simultaneously proclaimed that the divine and human natures reside in him, the one Son. Therefore, the Teacher and Bestower of eternal salvation gave this form of holy baptism lest anyone separate the natures of the same Son of God (a teaching that will be obtained by a deadly error). If such a person believed either that the human nature of the Son of God was alien to the work of human redemption in the sacrament of baptism or that two persons were present in the Christ whom we confess, that one would no longer be a true worshiper of the Trinity, but he would be a pernicious champion of a quaternity, and he would be worshiping sons—not the Son—along with the Father and

84. Jn 20.28.
85. Mt 28.19.

the Holy Spirit. For no one would think even remotely that faith in Christ as one person is to be rejected, since the same person is the only Son in the Trinity with the Father and the Holy Spirit. This one person is Christ Jesus, who created the world and shed his blood for us. Therefore, everyone who is washed in the name of the Father and the Son and the Holy Spirit in the sacrament of holy regeneration is not truly baptized unless his baptism is in fact in Christ's death and in his name. From this fact, one may clearly see that we have been buried with him in death through baptism, and in Christ's name alone (with the Father and the Holy Spirit) is it certain that we have been baptized. This is what the Roman Church (which is the summit of the world, enlightened—as if by brightly shining rays—by the words of two great lights, namely Peter and Paul, and embellished with their bodies), along with the whole of Christendom, holds and teaches. And she also believes this without hesitation, leading to justification, and she confesses this without doubting, leading to salvation. For these are the words that blessed Peter preached about the Son of God to the Jews: "Be penitent and be baptized, every one of you, in the name of Jesus Christ for the remission of sins."[86] Furthermore, so that we might believe very confidently that we have been baptized into the death of Christ, blessed Paul placed (as if in a most excellent mirror to be seen by all) this mystery of our salvation in that letter which he wrote to the Romans, saying: "We who have been baptized in Christ have been baptized in his death; for we have been buried with him through baptism into death."[87]

22. Therefore, whoever confesses (in accordance with the rule that the Lord established by his own mouth and authority) that he has been baptized in the one name of the Father and the Son and the Holy Spirit, and nevertheless tries to claim that there are two persons in Christ, should do one of two things: Either let him deny that he has been baptized in the death of Christ (an obvious blasphemy), so that it will be clear that he is an enemy of the apostolic preaching, or let him acknowledge

86. Acts 2.38.
87. Rom 6.3–4.

that he is a worshiper of a quaternity, not of the Trinity. If he truly fears the abyss of both blasphemies, let him hold the correct opinion of the Catholic faith with his whole heart, and let him not doubt that he has been baptized in the death of Christ when he was baptized in his name. He should acknowledge one natural name of the Father and the Son and the Holy Spirit, and he should recognize that he has been baptized in the name and death of the one who hanged on the cross, from whose side flowed the mystery of the spring and the cup. If one acknowledges this, let him also confess the one who was crucified for us, the one who is the power of God and the wisdom of God, the one whom Paul both trusts in and preaches, saying: "But we preach Christ crucified, to the Jews a stumbling block and to the Gentiles foolishness, but to those who have been called, both Jews and Greeks, Christ, the power of God and the wisdom of God."[88] This is the great mystery of godliness, whereby the Only-begotten true God surely deigned to become true man, to be born in time although he is eternal, to suffer although he is impassible, to be crucified although he is uncircumscribable, to die although he is immortal, and to be included among the finite although he is infinite (not only in the manger when he was born but also in the tomb when he died). All of these things truly happened to God the Son in accordance with the reality of his flesh, because, as the divine and human natures remained in him without confusion or separation, there was one person of the Son of God, Jesus Christ, in the reality of both natures.

23. (XII.) Divine kindness has thus conferred free grace upon the human race. Through this grace, all iniquity (not only the iniquity contracted by human generation but also the iniquity added by the sins of our own wills) may be blotted out. Moreover, the capacity for holy knowledge that had been lost long ago in the first man may indeed be regained through the second man. This capacity was held in bondage, and the bondage was accustomed to reigning while sin had dominion in our bodies, until the Man-God died and was raised in the flesh for the sake of men. Where the sin of delinquent man abounded,

88. 1 Cor 1.23–24.

the grace of the Redeemer abounded even more,[89] to the point that man's choice (which was free only to do evil when it was under the domination of sin) received anew the condition of true and saving freedom granted by the gift of prevenient grace. As we are sustained by the help of grace itself, we will explain (to the extent we can in a brief letter) this grace of God—not the grace by which we are born as human beings, but the grace by whose work we have been released from the bonds of original and actual sin through faith. We will do this so that on this question our response will not be absent from your investigation, or rather, from your profession.

24. Therefore, whoever does not wish to bear the name of the Christian religion fruitlessly or even condemnably, let him believe very firmly that our God (that is, the holy Trinity, which is the one, most high, and true God), because of his free goodness made the first man good, in his image, and he placed in the man the ability to know him and to love him. Furthermore, God created for the first man not only the gift of a good will, but rather, a whole and healthy freedom of choice that the man might use to possess and watch over righteousness. God did this so that if man did not use his implanted capacity for freedom and initiative to abandon the grace of God that was sustaining him, God's goodness would grant man eternal life as a reward. If, however, man disregarded divine justice and separated himself from grace, justice would be visited upon that sinner. Accordingly, the good and just Creator set up a condition that was just on both sides for that man whom he placed in a living body and endowed with the gift of intelligence and righteousness. If that man maintained obedience (which is the first virtue), he would transition from the state of an ensouled body (in which he had been created) to a spiritual and immortal status without the death of the body (because that body had no iniquity of soul). And if he had kept the commandments, he would also have received as a divine gift not only perfect and indestructible bodily immortality, but also such grace in his soul as he needed to live in a holy and upright manner. As a result, if he had not

89. Cf. Rom 5.20.

sinned while he was able to sin, he would afterwards have become completely unable to sin any longer.

25. Therefore, the "first man" created was "of the earth, earthy."[90] He did indeed receive the grace by which he would become unable to sin if he were unwilling to sin. He had not yet received the grace by which he would be neither willing nor able to sin at all. As a consequence, the good and just Lord would certainly have deemed it necessary to bestow that grace afterwards as a reward, if previously the slave had voluntarily preserved this initial grace in his actions. Therefore, if he had neglected to obey a good and just command, the sinner would have undergone the death of the soul that he himself had perniciously inflicted upon himself by doing wrong, and he would have even been punished with difficulties in the present life through the death of the body. (Someone who had been unwilling to preserve righteousness in his heart would not have been allowed to hold onto his condemned fleshly life of sin forever.) And if he had obstinately transgressed the saving commands and had been willingly liable to spiritual death, he would have been subsequently bound fast by the necessity of bodily death as a punishment. For unless the soul had preceded by dying through sin, the body would never have followed by dying in punishment. The apostolic authority teaches this when it says: "The body is indeed dead because of sin."[91] Therefore, after sin had been committed by a voluntary lie, the sinner deserved to hear in these words the sentence of the God who punishes: "You are earth, and to earth you will go."[92] Consequently, if man did not become dust by sinning, he would not be returning to dust as flesh.

26. (XIII.) Therefore, that man was created without any necessity to sin, and in his very act of sinning he lost the health of his soul by doing wrong; and he immediately lost the capacity to think about those things that pertain to God. For he forgot to eat his [spiritual] bread and was stripped of his garment of faith

90. 1 Cor 15.47.   91. Rom 8.10.
92. Gn 3.19.

and injured by the wounds of carnal desires. He lay oppressed by the dominion of sin to such an extent that he could possess no beginning of a good will unless he received it as God freely gave it. He was indeed a slave of sin; he was free from righteousness. For this reason he became alienated from righteousness because he was willingly dedicated to the dominion of iniquity. Therefore, having been sold under sin, he bound in himself all the descendants who would be born through sexual intercourse with the bonds of mortal servitude, which is what blessed Paul clearly taught with these words: "Through one man sin entered into the world, and death through sin, and so death passed to all men, because in him all have sinned."[93] All of us throughout the entire world have borne this sin in the one whom the Father formed first. In that man, all who could not sin of their own accord sinned before being born. Hence it came about that the condemned mass was now increasing the number of sons of wrath, and that mass simultaneously infused both iniquity and death into the posterity of that man. The result was that everyone who would be born from the seed of that sinner through the law of sin (a law that certainly persists in the mortal body throughout life) received the blemish of the parental sin in the very beginning of conception. Therefore, everyone was going to lead a brief, unhappily distressful life subject to sin and death under the heavy yoke that "lies on the sons of Adam from the day they leave their mother's womb until the day they are buried in the mother of us all."[94] For it is written: "Man who is born of woman has but a brief life and is full of wrath,"[95] and this wrath would also draw the one who was mortally born to the second death if it should find him departing from this life wretchedly, separated from the grace of God the Redeemer.

27. Therefore, so that the grace of the compassionate God might release us from the bond of original sin (by which we were held bound through the first man), there came forth the "one mediator between God and men, the man Christ Jesus."[96] For the transgression of the first man had made us sinful and

93. Rom 5.12.   94. Sir 40.1.
95. Jb 14.1.   96. 1 Tm 2.5.

mortal, but because God is immortal and righteous, he applied to our wounds the appropriate remedy: the Only-begotten God, who was born immortal and righteous of the Father, was also born as a man from man. In that human nature in which he became the mediator between God and men, he possessed righteousness from his Father and death from his mother. He contracted sin neither through his birth nor in his life, so that he might free us from all sin and so that we might receive from him righteousness, by which we might be released from the bond of eternal death so that through him we might be able to be righteous in this life and immortal after this life. Therefore, because he was born miraculously (that is, uniquely) in the likeness of sinful flesh, he is the only male opening the womb who may truly be called the one holy to the Lord. To be sure, it was not the lust of a husband during intercourse that opened the womb of his mother, but the omnipotence of the Son who was being born. He is the only one in whom the prince of the world found nothing as that prince came into the world. He alone is a man "unaided, set loose among the dead."[97] He alone "knew no sin," and as a result he was sufficient to become sin for us (that is, a sacrifice for sins), "so that we might be the righteousness of God in him."[98] He alone is "the bread that comes down from heaven and gives life to the world,"[99] and the bread that he gives is his flesh for the life of the world.[100] The flesh is indeed that of the righteous and immortal God, and when flesh that is born with the penalty of death and the pollution of sin receives his flesh, righteousness and life are granted to that flesh.

28. (XIV.) Therefore, if some people try to claim that death alone (and not sin as well) has passed from the first man to the human race, it is a wonder that they do not understand in what nets their opinions are entangled. First, they imply that God is unjust inasmuch as he causes children to die, even though (in the view of these people) the children are not infected with any contamination of original sin, and the children cannot, because

97. Ps 87.5–6, following LXX (88.4–5 modern).
98. 2 Cor 5.21.   99. Jn 6.33.
100. Cf. Jn 6.52 (6.51 modern).

of their young age, commit any sin by their own will. But the Apostle defines death as the wages of sin[101] and says again that the sting of death is sin,[102] by which death, with its sting, was indeed introduced into man. Thus sin is called the sting of death, not because sin entered the world through death, but because death entered through sin; just as we call a poisoned cup the cup of death, not because the cup is given by death, but because death is associated with that cup. Therefore, by what justice is a child subjected to the wages of sin if there is no pollution of sin in him? Or how do we know he has been pricked by death if he has not felt the sting? And since there is no iniquity with God (who made man in his image), what kind of justice is it if God's image [man], who can do nothing evil of himself, is not allowed to enter the kingdom of God unless he is redeemed by the blood of God's Son? In truth, whoever does not enter by that Son will be tormented by the endless pains of eternal fire. By what justice, then, does a just God impose punishment upon children who are born without sin, in whom he finds no cause for punishment? What kind of kindness on the part of the Creator God is it if he creates his own image [man] and condemns him in the absence of any iniquity, since "God who takes vengeance is not unrighteous"?[103] If these people do not want to live in fatal godlessness by insulting God himself, let them admit that the first man transmitted sin with death to all men.

29. (XV.) On the contrary, such people must see and avoid another impiety in this opinion of theirs. For when they say that children do not inherit original sin from Adam, they thus assert that those who (according to their own admission) possess human flesh do not actually possess sinful flesh. But since they do not deny that children possess human flesh when they deny that their flesh is sinful, they are consequently denying that human flesh is actually sinful flesh. Nevertheless, they concede to the Apostle who compels them to admit that "God sent his own Son in the likeness of sinful flesh."[104] For this reason, therefore, the blindness of a godless confession compels them to pretend (by

101. Cf. Rom 6.23.
102. 1 Cor 15.56.
103. Rom 3.5.
104. Rom 8.3.

a profane faithlessness) that the very flesh of Christ is not human, but of a different nature. The reason for this is that they deny that human flesh is sinful, but they do not deny that Christ came in the likeness of sinful flesh. Therefore, they say that the flesh in which children are born is human flesh, but nevertheless they try to deny that such human flesh is sinful flesh. But they agree with our confession that Christ came in the likeness of sinful flesh. Therefore, either they should not say that the flesh of Christ is human, or they should agree that all human flesh, in the likeness of which God sent his Son, is sinful flesh. When they have agreed to that, there will remain no difficulty in showing them that children possess the sin of the flesh. For if it is not false to speak of sinful flesh, then flesh itself has sin in itself. If it does not truly possess sin, it is wrongly called sinful flesh. But the disciple of the truth, Paul, is trustworthy when he calls the flesh about which we are speaking sinful flesh. Therefore, just as it is really flesh when it is called flesh, so indeed it really possesses sin in itself when it is called sinful flesh by the Apostle's own mouth.

30. But perhaps they will say that the Son of God was sent in the likeness of that sinful flesh such as men possess when they can already sin in accordance with their own will (whereupon their flesh is rightly called sinful flesh), rather than being sent in the kind of flesh that children have at birth, when they have no particular will to sin. But in this line of reasoning, they do not consider that if the flesh of children had been different in quality from the flesh of adults, God would have come only in the likeness of the flesh of children (who, they say, have no original sin). For the flesh of Christ would be more similar to children's flesh (with which it would have had a common reality in substance and quality) than to the flesh of adults (with whom only the nature of the flesh, not the stain, would have been shared with him). But perhaps they want Christ's flesh to have had only a likeness of nature with the flesh of adults, and also to have shared purity with the flesh of children. Therefore, let them confess that children—whom they assert to be surely born in human flesh, but they deny they are stained by con-

tact with original sin—are in the likeness of sinful flesh. They
must be shown that a great absurdity follows them in this assertion as well. For while they deny that children have original sin
when they are born, they do not deny that they possess human
flesh. They concede, however, that the Son of God received
sinless human flesh from the Virgin. It follows, therefore, that
they admit there is no difference between the flesh of the Only-
begotten of God who is born of the Virgin and the flesh of any
other child. The logical conclusion of this is that they would
say that all children (who they say are born without sin) do not
need the help of a Savior. By implying this, they run into the
trap of the Pelagian error[105] while unfaithfully contradicting the
Catholic faith. For if they assert that children are born without
sin, what remains for them to say except that there is nothing
in the children that needs to be cleansed by spiritual regeneration? And if they remove the blot of original sin from children
as they are born, what else are they doing but lying against divine truth, when they see that children receive the sacrament of
baptism for the remission of sins? Since this sacrament is given
to children and adults alike, we should acknowledge that everyone possesses the blot of original sin.

31. Therefore, whoever wishes to acquire true and eternal
salvation must cast off a heretically evil thought and must not
doubt that those whom he sees born with the penalty of sin
are also born with sin. Let such a person hear the blessed Job,
who says that "there is none clean from filth, not even an infant
whose life upon the earth lasts but one day."[106] Let him reflect
with humility upon the sorrows of the blessed David's devout
heart, as he says: "Behold, I was conceived in iniquities, and in
sins my mother bore me."[107] Let him also consider that the sacrament of circumcision was enjoined upon the revered Abraham,
a sacrament that comes with a terrible threat to the child. On

---

105. Pelagius was reputed to have argued that Adam's sin affected his posterity only in an external way, by giving human beings a bad example. In this
view, there was no transmission of sin from generation to generation.

106. Cf. Jb 14.4.

107. Ps 50.7 (51.5 modern).

that occasion, to be sure, the faithful and just God (who does not inflict wrath where he finds no guilt) speaks thus to our father Abraham: "The male child who has not been circumcised in the flesh of his foreskin on the eighth day, that soul shall be cut off from his people, for he has transgressed my covenant."[108] Therefore, whoever denies original sin in children born according to the flesh must explain in what way an eight-day-old infant could have transgressed God's covenant unless he transgressed in that way in which all have sinned.[109] For the Apostle asserts that before they are born, infants have done nothing good or evil.[110] So let us now consider that those born—not only within the first eight days after their birth (at which time infants were commanded to be circumcised), but also after the day of circumcision, during the whole time of their infancy—are unable to transgress God's covenant. As a result, the knowledge of that same covenant cannot be made known to them either.

32. Or is anyone trying to remove original sin in children from the blessed Paul's statement in which he says that death reigned "from Adam to Moses, even in those who did not sin in the likeness of Adam's transgression"?[111] If anyone does try to deny this, he is refuted by another statement of the same Apostle: "Through one man's offense, all men have come under condemnation,"[112] which he explains a little later by saying: "Through the disobedience of one man, many were made sinners";[113] and when he is speaking of the Jews and the Greeks, he adds more generally: "For all have sinned and come short of God's glory, being justified freely by his grace through the redemption that is in Christ Jesus."[114] For unless a person has accepted both ideas in keeping with the profession of Catholic belief—that is, unless he says that infants have done nothing wrong at least by their own works, and that he knows that all men in general have sinned in that first man—then do not such statements by the Apostle immediately put such a person in great difficulties?

---

108. Gn 17.14.
110. Cf. Rom 9.11.
112. Rom 5.18.
114. Rom 3.23–24.

109. That is, by original sin.
111. Rom 5.14.
113. Rom 5.19.

33. (XVI.) Neither natural capacity nor the letter of the holy law delivers anyone from this sin that fleshly birth introduces originally, but only the faith of Jesus Christ, the Son of God, who came "to seek and to save that which had perished."[115] He "died for the ungodly,"[116] giving "himself for us," as the Apostle says, "as an offering and a sacrifice to God, as a sweet-smelling savor."[117] In this mediator between God and men, the status of human nature has been restored and the work of fulfilling the law has been accomplished; for the weakness of nature has in no way been able to stand up to his power. Since "all our days have passed away, and we have passed away in [God's] wrath,"[118] this weakness is deprived of both illumination and power, it sins blindly apart from the law, and, as a result, it does not know it is sinning. For this reason it is said: "I would not have known covetousness, unless the law had said, 'You shall not covet.'"[119] In addition, not only has the hearing of the law removed no one from the power of darkness, but indeed that hearing has increased sinners' transgression. Without the grace of faith, to be sure, a known law condemns more harshly than an unknown law. To the degree that ignorance of sin is diminished, to that degree is the sinner's guilt increased. Therefore, the Apostle says: "For the law brings about wrath; for where there is no law there is no transgression."[120] The same Apostle also says that the law "was added because of transgression"[121] and that "Scripture has shut up all things under sin so that justification might be given to believers by the faith of Jesus Christ."[122] Therefore, concerning the ability of free choice alone (which, the haughtier it is by nature, the more subject it is to the dominion of sin and death unless it is preceded by the help of God's grace, by which a good will is restored and preserved in man), how does it guarantee for itself the beginning of a good will and work? For this will could neither keep God's command when it was healthy nor obtain a remedy of healing (however small) from the law

---

115. Lk 19.10.   116. Rom 5.6.
117. Eph 5.2.
118. Ps 89.9, following LXX (90.9 modern).
119. Rom 7.7.   120. Rom 4.15.
121. Gal 3.19.   122. Gal 3.22.

when it was wounded; but instead it increased sin because of its knowledge of the command. For "the law entered so that sin might abound,"[123] and no one can be set free from this sin except through the Lamb of God who takes away the sins of the world.[124] For what frees us from the body of this death is neither the free choice of man nor the holy, just, and good command of the law, but only the grace of God through Jesus Christ our Lord.[125] "For the law of the Spirit of life in Christ Jesus has freed us from the law of sin and death."[126]

34. (XVII.) The Spirit of life, however, has set us free not by finding faith in any man, but by giving it. For God (who justifies the ungodly) himself inspires faith in the unbeliever by the grace of his good will, and this faith works through love. From this the unbeliever gains the capacity to think correctly, as the Apostle testifies, saying that "we are not to think that anything comes from our own power, as if it were from us; but our sufficiency is from God."[127] For, in truth, according to the same Apostle, "God gives" to those whom he wills "penitence to know the truth so that they may regain their senses apart from the snare of the devil, who holds them captive to his will."[128] Therefore, when that first of the apostles (who is also worthily called blessed because of the word of truth) was speaking about the faith of the Gentiles, he said that God had cleansed their hearts by faith; and again he said that the same grace was divinely given to the Gentiles as also to the Jews, so that they might believe. The apostles and elders in the teaching of the Holy Spirit recognized this to be the free gift of grace, and they all with one accord agreed with blessed Peter's statement: "God, therefore, also gave the Gentiles penitence leading to life."[129] Certainly our Savior himself summons the human will by the authority of his own voice, saying, "Be penitent and believe the Gospel."[130] When he does so, it is clear that a man receives from God penitence leading to life so that he may begin to believe in God,

123. Rom 5.20.
125. Cf. Rom 7.24–25.
127. 2 Cor 3.5.
129. Acts 11.18.

124. Cf. Jn 1.29.
126. Rom 8.2.
128. 2 Tm 2.25–26.
130. Mk 1.15.

just as he cannot believe at all unless he receives penitence as a gift from the compassionate God. But what is man's penitence if not a change of his will? Therefore, God, who himself gives penitence to man, changes man's will.

35. Accordingly, if anyone says: "It is my role to will to believe, but it is the role of God's grace to help," let him change the order of the words. Or rather, let him not change the order but preserve it; let him neither put what is last in first place nor put what is in first place last. For he is wrong to place God's grace after his own will, since that will cannot be good if grace is absent. So do not let him say: "It is my role to will to believe, but it is the role of God's grace to help," but let him say: "It is the role of God's grace to help so that it is my role to will to believe." Then and only then does he truly and rightly put his willing into action, since prevenient grace has begun to help. For "faith that works by love"[131] makes the one to whom it is given humble, for "love is not puffed up."[132] So let no one doubt that he is given faith by the help and gift of grace, lest he (that is, a man who is not sound of mind but has already been judged with respect to his weakness) try to assign to himself the beginning of faith and even the penitence that God gives, leading to life. In assigning these things to himself, he would be deprived of the benefit of so great a remedy whose grace he, stubborn and ungrateful, fights against. One must be urged by the divine words to have humility of heart, since those words show that the good will itself (by which we begin to will to believe) is prepared and directed from the beginning by the Lord, as Solomon says: "The will is prepared by the Lord.[133] And in the Psalms, David sings: "The steps of a man will be guided by the Lord, and he will greatly desire his way."[134]

36. (XVIII.) If it is true (according to their way of thinking) that we have the capacity to will to believe before God's grace begins to help us, then it is wrong to call it grace, because it is not freely given to man, but it is the reward for a good will. For

131. Gal 5.6.
132. 1 Cor 13.4.
133. Prv 8.35, following LXX.
134. Ps 36.23 (37.23 modern).

(as they would have it) grace finds in us something that grace itself did not give. If that is indeed the case, we first give the will to God, and thus we receive grace not because of the mercy of the one who gives, but because of the fairness of the God who rewards. Nevertheless, "who has first given to him and it will be repaid to him?"[135] Surely no one, because "man can receive nothing unless it has been given to him from heaven."[136] For what does he have that he has not received? And if he has received it, why does he boast as if he has not received it?[137] But if God never creates a good will, but instead hopes to find one, then his mercy never actually goes before man. And where is it that David says: "My God, his mercy will come before me"?[138] And in the same way, may God's mercy go before us, or when it goes before, may it discover what kind of persons we are, as the teacher of the Gentiles shows us not just through the example of someone else, but by using himself as an example, when he says: "I was previously a blasphemer and a persecutor and an aggressor, but I obtained mercy because I acted in ignorance and unbelief."[139] Therefore, how was Paul (who was blind and unbelieving, who was unaware that he was a blasphemer and a persecutor and an aggressor) able to muster up from within himself any will to believe? As he considers this fact with a humble heart, he says in another place: "I am not worthy to be called an apostle, for I persecuted the church of God."[140] And immediately he ascribes his faith not to his own will, but to the grace of the merciful God, saying: "But by the grace of God, I am what I am."[141] And what was he already, if not faithful? But he obtained God's mercy in order to be faithful, just as he himself testifies when he says: "I give my judgment, just as I obtained mercy from the Lord to be faithful."[142] For even when he confessed that at first he had been a blasphemer, a persecutor, and an aggressor, he did not stop attributing his faith and love to grace, for he added immediately: "And the grace of God, which is in Christ Jesus, abounded exceedingly in faith and love."[143]

135. Rom 11.35.
136. Jn 3.27.
137. Cf. 1 Cor 4.7.
138. Ps 58.11 (59.10 modern).
139. 1 Tm 1.13.
140. 1 Cor 15.9.
141. 1 Cor 15.10.
142. 1 Cor 7.25.
143. 1 Tm 1.14.

37. Therefore, if the grace of God did not give Paul faith, one must not believe that it gave him love either. In that case, Paul lied (may it never be!), since he said that "God's love has been poured out in our hearts through the Holy Spirit who has been given to us."[144] But because Paul was not able to lie in Christ (who was speaking in him), let us confess most firmly that the Spirit himself has given us faith, since we cannot deny that through the Spirit, God's love has been poured out in our hearts. So since Paul was a blasphemer and a persecutor and an aggressor, the reason he was helped by the grace of God was not that he willed to believe. Instead, he received the gift of prevenient grace with the result that he was willing to believe. Grace did not find any beginning of faith in his will, but it found blasphemy, brutality, violence, and ignorance, all bound up in unbelief. Up to that point, his will was blind, and as a result not only was he unable to believe, but he was also unable to anticipate the very beginning of his faith. For if he had anticipated his ignorance, he would not have acted in ignorance. Therefore, in Paul's case, it is appropriate to attribute not only the beginning of faith but even the recognition of unbelief itself to the gift of prevenient mercy. For God's mercy conferred this knowledge on him so that as he was illumined and aided, he might recognize and shun his unbelief. In fact, the Lord is our illumination and our salvation; he illumines us so that we may acknowledge our sins, and he heals us so that we may live righteously, separated from our sins. For this reason, he himself, who confesses that he obtained mercy in order to be faithful, instructs us salvifically: "Therefore, it is not of the one who wills or of the one who runs, but of God, who shows mercy."[145] For in reality we are illumined by the gift of prevenient mercy so that we may will, and we are sustained by the help of subsequent mercy so that we may run. Therefore, in us there is no power of a living soul but only the pride of dead flesh, and the result is that each person attributes to himself the good will by which he begins to will to believe.

144. Rom 5.5.
145. Rom 9.16.

38. (XIX.) Indeed, since the time the first man willingly corrupted and subverted his nature, weakness grew so much that if the prior free choice of any given man were not continually healed and helped by the medicine of divine grace, his choice would surely be free, though not good; it would be free, though not upright; it would be free, though not whole; it would be free, though not righteous; and the more it is free from goodness, uprightness, wholeness, and righteousness, the more it is made captive by mortal servitude to evil perversity, weakness, and iniquity. For "the one who commits sin is a slave of sin,"[146] and "by whatever someone has been overcome, by that also he has been made a slave."[147] As sin reigns, a man does indeed have free choice, but this is freedom without God, not freedom under God. That is, he is free of righteousness, not free under grace, and therefore he is free in the worst and most servile way, because he has not been set free by the free gift of the merciful God. The Apostle clearly implies this when he says: "For when you were slaves of sin, you were free of righteousness."[148] Therefore, he who is free of righteousness cannot serve righteousness; for as long as he is a slave of sin, he is not found to be suitable for anything but serving sin. No one becomes free from such servitude to sin except one who is freed by the grace of the Liberator, Christ, so that when he is indeed freed from sin, he becomes a slave of God. Our Liberator himself, however, explains how one may become such by saying: "If the Son sets you free, you will be truly free."[149] Therefore, the chosen vessel explains to us the benefit of liberating grace by testifying not only that we are free, but also that we have been set free. He does this with these words: "But now, since you have been set free from sin and have become slaves of God, you have your fruit leading to sanctification, the outcome of which is truly eternal life."[150]

39. This true freedom, which is not born of human choice but is conferred by God's free mercy, takes its beginning from a good will and obtains its full effect through the fruit of sancti-

146. Jn 8.34.
148. Rom 6.20.
150. Rom 6.22.
147. 2 Pt 2.19.
149. Jn 8.36.

fication in eternal life. But just as it was the case in natural birth that the divine work of forming the person altogether preceded the will of the person being born, so is it the case in the spiritual birth (by which we begin to put off "the old man, which is being corrupted by deceitful desires,"[151] so that we may put on "the new man, which is created in the righteousness and holiness of truth")[152] that no one can acquire a good will by his own initiative unless his very mind (that is, our inner man) is renewed and remade from God. Therefore, the blessed Paul commands us not to be conformed to this age,[153] but to be remade in the newness of our mind.[154] And lest we think we ought to attribute the beginning of that remaking even partially to our ability, the Lord uses the prophet to show that he himself is the Former of light when he says: "I the Lord form the light and create darkness."[155] The blessed Apostle also confirms this in his preaching when he says: "God, who commanded the light to shine out of darkness, has shined in our hearts."[156] And in another place he says about the same light that God had already formed: "For once you were darkness, but now you are light in the Lord."[157] But since some have lapsed from their laudable formation as light into the censurable formlessness of darkness, he shows the affection of a godly mind by speaking thus: "My little children, for whom I am again in the pains of childbirth until Christ is formed in you."[158] But how is Christ to be formed in them unless he begins to dwell in them, that is, through faith? The blessed Paul thus confirms this by saying: "In the inner man, so that Christ will dwell in your hearts through faith."[159] Therefore, as long as we are being remade, we are being renewed, and in the way that we are being renewed, we are being made alive.

40. (XX.) Our life, however, takes its beginning from faith, "for the righteous one will live by faith."[160] Blessed Paul points out that this faith is not born from our will but is given to each

---

151. Eph 4.22.   152. Eph 4.24.
153. Reading *saeculo* rather than *saecula.*
154. Cf. Rom 12.1.   155. Is 45.7.
156. 2 Cor 4.6.   157. Eph 5.8.
158. Gal 4.19.   159. Eph 3.16–17.
160. Gal 3.11. Cf. Hab 2.4.

person by the Holy Spirit when he says: "For to one is given the word of wisdom through the Spirit, but to another the word of knowledge according to the same Spirit, and to another faith by the same Spirit."[161] Thus, we received the Holy Spirit not because we believed, but so that we might believe. In fact, let us recognize that the form that exists spiritually in our faith came first in the flesh of Christ. For Christ, the Son of God, was conceived and born of the Holy Spirit according to the flesh. The Virgin could not at any time conceive or give birth to that flesh if the Holy Spirit were not causing the emergence of that very flesh. In the same way, faith cannot be conceived or increased in the human heart unless the Holy Spirit infuses it and nurtures it. For we were reborn by the same Spirit, by whom Christ was born. Therefore, according to faith Christ is formed in the heart of each believer by the same Spirit by whom he was formed in the womb of the Virgin according to the flesh. Therefore, the prophet calls to the Lord on behalf of the faithful: "Because of our fear of you, O Lord, we have conceived in our womb and given birth; we have produced the Spirit of your salvation upon the earth."[162] Therefore, the angel announced that the Virgin Mary was full of grace not only before she conceived Christ, but even before she knew she was going to conceive him, since she had no prior knowledge of this or any prior will to conceive the Son of God. Her ignorance of what was coming shows that the Virgin's obedient will itself (through which the conception of the Lord and Savior took place) was the result of God's grace. In just the same way, before a man begins to will to believe, grace is given and poured into his heart so that Christ may begin to be formed in him through faith. And when Christ is formed in each person, he forms himself, for he himself initiates faith in the heart of each believer. Consequently, we are strongly advised in the letter written to the Hebrews to look "to Jesus, the author and perfecter of our faith."[163] There is no doubt that just as he is thus the author of our faith, inasmuch as he gives faith to those who do not possess it, in the same way he is the perfecter of that same faith, for he adds to it by increasing

161. 1 Cor 12.8–9. 162. Is 26.18.
163. Heb 12.2.

it in those who possess it, and he perfects it by a sacred work. For the blessed Apostle James says that the faith of our father Abraham "was perfected by works."[164]

41. Therefore, the author and perfecter of our faith is Jesus, for "he himself works in us both to will and to accomplish according to his good will."[165] But if he is the author of our faith only in the sense that he is waiting for our will so that faith may take its origin from us, it follows that he should also be called the perfecter of our faith only in the sense that he expects the faith that has risen from us to continue to perfection by our effort. In this way God is deprived of everything if both the beginning and the perfection of our faith are dependent on the power of human choice. Since it would be extremely impious to say that, let us (if we do not oppose the salvific words of the sacred Scriptures) believe without any hesitation that God both begins and accomplishes in us all the things that pertain to the beginning or the growth of a good will. He is himself the one who "works in us both to will and to accomplish according to his good will." Let us, therefore, cry out with humility of heart and with true faith along with the prophet: "I know, O Lord, that the way of a man is not found in himself and that it is not the role of a man to correct his way."[166] Therefore, the way of a man is not found within himself, but he receives it from God, and it is not the role of a man to correct the way that he does possess from himself. Therefore, he does not have his own will within himself, nor does he correct his will unless he receives the gift of spiritual grace along with uprightness of heart. Consequently, Solomon says: "But the Lord directs the hearts."[167] The blessed Apostle James also testifies that "every excellent gift and every perfect gift is from above, coming down from the Father of lights."[168] Through Ezekiel he promises the grace of a new heart to some of those lights, saying: "I will give you a new heart, and I will give you a new spirit, and the stony heart will be removed from your flesh, and I will give you a fleshly heart,

164. Jas 2.21.
166. Jer 10.23.
168. Jas 1.17.

165. Phil 2.13.
167. Prv 21.2.

and I will put my Spirit in you, and I will cause you to walk in my righteous ways and keep my statutes and do them."[169] Likewise, the blessed Paul, in an effort to restrain the audacity of human presumption, says: "For who makes you different? And what do you have that you did not receive? But if you received it, why do you boast as if you did not receive it?"[170] We must humbly and salvifically recognize with Paul and at the same time confess that we are what we are by God's grace,[171] if indeed we are anything. By this grace, human choice is not removed, but healed; it is not taken away, but corrected; it is not set aside, but illumined; it is not done away with, but supported and preserved. This happens so that where man had weakness in his capacity to choose, he may begin to have strength; where he was going astray, he may return to the path; where he was blind, he may receive light; and where he was wicked, serving impurity and iniquity, there—preceded and helped by grace—he may serve righteousness leading to sanctification.

42. (XXI.) And we marvel that there are some who say: "If God causes unwilling people to will to believe, but there is no one who can naturally believe in the Son of God or will anything good that pertains to eternal life, then why does he not cause all people to will, since 'God is not a respecter of persons'?"[172] From these words that have been inserted into your letter, it appears that those who ask that question give no consideration at all to what they are saying. If (as they would have it) God were to find any sort of beginning of a good will in any man whatsoever, then God would be a respecter of persons. But since he has not found a good will in anyone, but has granted it freely to whomever he chose, we know he is not a respecter of persons since the generosity of him who gives is free in the case of each person. They also say: "Why does he not cause all people to will?" Can it

---

169. Ezek 36.26–27.   170. 1 Cor 4.7.

171. Cf. 1 Cor 15.10.

172. Acts 10.34. The quotation by the monks' opponents in which this biblical text occurs is from the Scythian Monks' Letter to the Bishops (= *Ep*. 16), par. 20 (Latin text in CCL 91A, 559, and CCL 85A, 168; English translation in this volume, p. 37).

really be that he does not do this in anyone just because he does not do it in all? "Does the potter not have power over the clay to make of the same lump one vessel for honor and another for dishonor?"[173] By their line of reasoning, one is compelled either to fault justice in the case of vessels of wrath, which, because of their deserts, he has justly prepared for destruction; or to fault mercy in the case of vessels of mercy, which, without any deserts but solely by the gift of grace, he has prepared for glory. We have also instructed those people that, in accordance with the testimony of Scripture, the will itself has been prepared by the Lord.[174] If it is not given by God but is found in man, the statement of Scripture that it is prepared by the Lord is false. But all Scripture is divinely inspired, and all that it says is true because all the things it says come from universal truth, for "the words of the Lord are pure words."[175] Therefore, God himself, who prepares the will, also gives it. If God does not give it to man by his grace, man will never be able to will to believe in God, for grace does not find such a will in man, but instead produces it in him.

43. (XXII.) But when we say that no one can believe in God unless his heart is illumined by God's grace so that he may believe, we do not mean that the possibility of believing can in no way exist in human nature, but we point out that in order to be able to possess it, a man ought to hope and pray for it. In fact, if the possibility of believing had not been given naturally to man in his first condition when he began to believe in the Son of God, he would never have committed sin by faithlessness. And such capacity to believe was not innate in every nature whatsoever, for God did not make every nature rational. "God does not care for oxen, does he?"[176] Wickedness is not punished in them, nor is goodness crowned. But the divine words teach us that God does care for all men.

44. Consequently, faith (whose Creator deigns to provide such great care that one may say rightly that even the hairs of

173. Rom 9.21.   174. Cf. Prv 8.35, following LXX.
175. Ps 11.7, following LXX (12.6 modern).
176. 1 Cor 9.9.

our head are numbered) is compatible with human nature. As a result, when human nature realizes that it is so greatly loved by God, it loves God who loves it, and it clings to him by the faith of a pure heart. Faith is the way to blessedness for such a pure heart, and faithlessness occasions great distress for it. Therefore, faithlessness is justly punished, since it does not believe in the Son of God, for its sin is its unbelief, just as faith is power—not the kind of faith that is found in demons, but the kind God gives his saints, whom he justifies from impiety. Such is the "faith that works through love."[177] "The demons also believe, and tremble,"[178] but they do not love him from whom they withdraw because of pride. Since the first man, under diabolical persuasion, fell into this pride (through which he lost humility), he lost faith. Upon losing faith, he lost divine protection. For it is written: "He who does not believe in God is not protected by God."[179] As a result, "the earth and ashes begin to be proud because their heart extends into their lives."[180] So that men may return to the heart itself, the divine word does not cease to exclaim: "Return, you transgressors, to the heart."[181] Truly, "they are flesh, a wind that passes and does not return,"[182] and a lost sheep can never will to return, unless the good shepherd first searches for it and brings it back on his shoulders. This is why the good shepherd has come to seek and to save the lost sheep that cannot seek its shepherd before it is sought by him, but is preceded by the one who seeks it so that it may seek. But the shepherd would look for it in vain if the sheep being sought were unable to seek the shepherd. But the kindness of the shepherd who is seeking gives that ability to the sheep so that it may also have the will to seek the shepherd. It is being sought so that it may seek, and it is illumined so that it may believe. This is divinely accomplished in man, because God infuses faith into him so that by the gift of grace, man's nature may receive the power to believe (power that it had lost). God infuses this faith so that man's corrupt nature may (having been instructed through

---

177. Gal 5.6.   178. Jas 2.19.
179. Cf. Sir 10.15.   180. Sir 10.9–10.
181. Is 46.8.
182. Ps 77.39, following LXX (78.39 modern).

grace) begin to seek that which it was not able to seek. And God infuses this faith so that through the work of the physician (who is needed not by the healthy but by the sick),[183] his weakness may be cast out and his nature may be healed. This is the kind of health the person was praying for who kept saying: "I said, 'Lord, be merciful to me; heal my soul, for I have sinned against you.'"[184] If human nature were healthy, no one would be praying for the healing of the saints; and if human nature were incapable of being healed, everyone would be praying in vain for healing. Therefore, human nature can be healed, but it receives the gift of such healing by the same grace that it received at the beginning of creation. For if man could in no way be healed in his nature, the heavenly physician would not have come to heal him. But on the other hand, if he were able to heal himself, he would not need the heavenly physician. In fact, he is healed by faith. If a person could gain such faith from himself, God would not give it to him. But God gives it, for "to another faith is given by the same Spirit,"[185] just as the Apostle says: "God, therefore, has dealt to each one a measure of faith."[186]

45. (XXIII.) Therefore, man cannot believe naturally for the simple reason that it is divinely granted him to believe. On this matter in particular, we know that man was created in order to have faith, because from ancient times human nature has been renewed by faith. For in this way, every man has been damaged by the voluntary sin of the first man so that God, by his own good will, is able to heal man's will if he wishes. "For he created," as it is written, "so that all things might exist; and he made the nations of the earth healthy."[187] Truly, lest one think that the beginning of health comes from man in and of himself, the divine word soon adds: "And in them is no fatal poison."[188] Consequently, although the devil took faith from the first man, even so he did not take away the power of giving back to God what he had given, and the devil was not able to corrupt human nature to the extent that afterward it would be unable to receive

183. Cf. Mt 9.12.   184. Ps 40.5 (41.4 modern).
185. 1 Cor 12.9.   186. Rom 12.3.
187. Wis 1.14.   188. Ibid.

again, through God's generosity, what it had lost. Indeed, the Omnipotent One, who was able to form human nature, is also able, by healing infirm nature, to form it again and preserve it through grace. Just as nature itself had received saving faith in the first man from God, so now it receives saving faith as a gift of divine goodness, in those predestined individuals whom the same God creates in order to save them through faith from [the sin of] their [first] parents.

46. Therefore, man is able to believe naturally in God because God so grants. Indeed, not to believe in God is against man's nature; since man does not possess unbelief as a result of his creation by God, but he possesses it by his willing transgression of the command. And by this transgression, he can through his own effort be deprived of health and light, with the result that he is able to increase, but not remove, his own blindness and infirmity with respect to his choice. Nevertheless, only through the omnipotent Creator is it possible for one's ability to choose to be illuminated and healed. So for the glory of his name, God grants the unbeliever not only to be able to believe, but even to attain to the immortal and incorruptible condition of life through the grace of faith. And once he receives grace for grace, he is not at all able to sin, and he is joyfully able to see what he has believed. For this reason, that voice of faith resounds in the Psalms: "I believe I will see the goodness of the Lord in the land of the living."[189] Therefore, although God did not make human nature to be corrupted by guilt, he nonetheless is able to heal the corrupted nature by grace in accordance with his omnipotent kindness. So God heals and illumines man's choice so that a man may believe in God naturally. The result is that man can have faith, but he cannot have it unless it is a gift from God.

(XXIV.) It does not follow that all the things we can possess are things we can acquire of ourselves. Even our flesh is made by God in such a way that it is able to live naturally. This very

189. Ps 26.13, following LXX (27.13 modern).

ability, however, is not something the flesh possesses of itself, but life itself comes from the soul. Therefore, it is clear that life has to be managed by the soul so that it may begin to inhabit the flesh naturally. Our flesh can indeed live, but only if the soul, which is its life, is in it.

47. In this way, we are given no small example of God's grace in our soul and flesh. For just as the flesh does not have life from itself, but receives it from the soul, so man cannot have faith unless he receives it as a gift from God who gives it. And also, just as the fact that the flesh lives is the work of the soul alone, so also the fact that man believes is the work of grace alone. And just as the flesh can do nothing if the soul ceases to quicken it, so also man can will nothing rightly if the help of grace departs from him. Therefore, the life-giving power of the soul that is present sustains the flesh so that it may be able to live and function. Likewise, man is continually aided by the help of life-giving grace so that he may will or do the good. Moreover, it is important to note that our flesh is made alive by the soul, that it may receive the ability not only to function well but also to function badly. And since grace makes us alive, it supplies us with help not only to will well but also to work well. Therefore, let a man recognize that of himself, he is naturally able to believe; for he possesses both the nature that allows belief and the capacity to believe (which is not given by God to irrational animals). We must not think, however, that he is so capable of having faith that he could imagine the beginning of faith as resulting from his own will. Therefore, the man who wills has faith, but God, who gives faith, changes and directs the will of man. For "the Lord will give sweetness, and our land will give its fruit."[190]

48. (XXV.) Therefore, concerning those whose nature is healed by God's gift so that they may naturally believe in God, those who have been freely justified by faith and also receive the help of subsequent grace to do good works, the Apostle says the

190. Ps 84.13, following LXX (85.12 modern).

following: "For when the Gentiles, who do not have the law, naturally do the things pertaining to the law, they (although they do not have the law) are a law to themselves, and they show the work of the law written in their hearts."[191] To be sure, the ones who speak against grace strive to assign this passage of the Apostle only to unbelieving Gentiles. Thus, they argue that the passage means simply that even those who do not receive the grace of faith preserve by a certain natural law those things that pertain to honorable customs and the things that hold human society together. As a result, even [such unbelieving Gentiles] use the equity and severity of laws to restrain those who strive to break them. Those, however, who interpret the passage this way do not realize that their opinion is utterly undercut by the Apostle's prior statement when he says: "For it is not the hearers of the law who are righteous before God, but it is the doers of the law who will be justified."[192] But the same blessed Apostle demonstrates that no one can be justified without faith, when he says: "And knowing that a man will not be justified by the works of the law, but by the faith of Jesus Christ, we also believe in Christ Jesus with the result that we are justified by the faith of Jesus Christ and not by the works of the law. Consequently, no flesh will be justified by the works of the law."[193] And a little later, as he commends the grace of faith by which true righteousness is bestowed on each person, he says: "I do not nullify the grace of God; for if righteousness comes by the law, Christ has died in vain."[194] Likewise, he declared that our father Abraham was not justified by works of the law, but by faith, when he said: "Just as Abraham believed God, and it was credited to him as righteousness."[195] And in order to show that in the same way the Gentiles (whom the divine word promised to the seed of Abraham) were being justified by faith, Paul continued by adding: "Know, therefore, that those who are of faith are children of Abraham. And since God foresaw in Scripture that the Gentiles would be justified by faith, he declared to Abraham beforehand, 'In you all nations will be blessed.' Therefore, those who are of faith will be blessed

---

191. Rom 2.14–15.   192. Rom 2.13.
193. Gal 2.16.   194. Gal 2.21.
195. Gal 3.6. Cf. Gn 15.6, Jas 2.23.

with faithful Abraham."[196] And he confirms that this man, our father Abraham, was justified not by works but by faith, when he speaks thus in another passage: "For if Abraham has been justified by works, he has reason to boast, but not before God. For what does the Scripture say? 'Abraham believed God, and it was credited to him as righteousness.' But to one who works, a reward is granted not as a gift but as a debt. But indeed to one who does not work but believes in the One who justifies the unrighteous, his faith is credited as righteousness."[197]

49. Therefore, the Apostle says that when these Gentiles "naturally do the things pertaining to the law," "they show the work of the law written in their hearts."[198] Thus the Apostle testifies that he is speaking of those who are being justified, and he remembers that Abraham our father was justified not by works but by faith. Since the Apostle asserts all this, and since he himself testifies that "everything that is not of faith is sin"[199] and that "without faith it is impossible to please God,"[200] who would dare to accept the Gentiles as the referent in this passage if it were known that they are not justified by faith? Because if it is known that Abraham (to whose seed the Apostle recalls that the Gentiles have been promised) was justified by faith, then if anyone claims that the Gentiles can be justified not by faith, but by works, what can we say except that he is denying that they belong to Abraham's seed, to whom the nations were promised? For Abraham (as the Apostle says) "is the father of all the uncircumcised who believe, so that righteousness may be credited to them as well."[201] Therefore, inasmuch as "there is one God, who justifies the circumcision by faith and the uncircumcision through faith,"[202] the Apostle has made it clear that he is speaking of those who are being justified, for he is discussing the Gentiles who naturally do the things that pertain to the law and the Gentiles who have the work of the law in their hearts. Such an understanding is consistent

196. Gal 3.7–9. Cf. Gn 12.3.
197. Rom 4.2–5. Cf. Gn 15.6, Jas 2.23.
198. Rom 2.14.   199. Rom 14.23.
200. Heb 11.6.   201. Rom 4.11.
202. Rom 3.30.

with the truth because the Gentiles whom God justifies by the gift of faith are understood in the same passage, and inasmuch as he grants them the grace of faith, he writes in their hearts the work of his law when he grants justification. Their nature has been renewed through the grace of the New Testament even without the letter of the Old Testament, and this has happened so that they may have the work of the law written upon them in order that they may begin to belong to the people of God, not by the merit of preceding works, but by the free gift of justification. The divine teaching has graciously deigned to make this known to us by the prophetic word, as holy Jeremiah says: "'Behold, the days are coming,' says the Lord, 'when I will make a new covenant with the house of Israel and the house of Judah,'"[203] and a little later: "'For this is the covenant that I will make with the house of Israel after those days,' says the Lord. 'I will place my laws in their hearts and write them upon their inward parts, and I will be their God and they will be my people. And none of them will teach his neighbor and his brother, saying: "Know God"; for they will all know me, from the least of them to the greatest of them, for I will forgive their iniquities, and I will remember their sins no more.'"[204]

50. (XXVI.) This knowledge is the kind by which one knows God so as to receive divine forgiveness of sins as a gift resulting from propitiation, but such knowledge is far from the so-called knowledge of those who, "although they knew God, did not glorify him as God or give thanks, but became futile in their speculations. Thinking they were wise, they became fools and exchanged the glory of the incorruptible God for the likeness of the corruptible image of man."[205] For these did not know God because, without the grace of faith ("that works through love"),[206] they were rendered without excuse because of their very knowledge. But the others, who know God through understanding by faith, are rendered exempt from accusation. "For who will accuse God's elect?"[207] No one indeed, for "all things

203. Jer 31.31.
205. Rom 1.21–23.
207. Rom 8.33.

204. Jer 31.33–34.
206. Gal 5.6.

work together for good for those who love God."[208] For this reason, no one accuses them because God justifies and glorifies those who were foreknown, predestined, and called according to his purpose. He does this so as to exclude any boasting on the basis of deeds of the law, by which arrogant man has exalted himself, so that "he who boasts may boast in the Lord"[209] by the law of faith, "which works through love."[210]

51. But in the case of those who know God but do not glorify him as God, that knowledge is not profitable for salvation. Since this is so, then what about those who preserve something good in their character and works, but that good does not relate to the purpose of Christian faith and love? How can they be righteous before God? To be sure, certain good things associated with a fair human society can be found in such people; but because these things are not done through faith in and love for God, they cannot be profitable [for salvation]. As a matter of fact, it is possible for a person who does not love God to believe that God exists; but it is in no way possible for a person who does not believe in God to love God. For each individual can believe that something exists that he does not love, but no one can love what he does not believe exists. And the Apostle says that apart from love, faith and other good works cannot profit anyone; for he says: "If I have all faith, so that I could remove mountains; and if I distribute all my means for food for the poor, and if I give my body to be burned, but do not have love, it profits me nothing."[211] Therefore, if works with faith cannot profit one without love, how have works that have not been done in faith been profitable? This is why the blessed Apostle rightly prays for the Thessalonians that "may God fulfill by his power every act of your good will and the work of your faith."[212] Likewise he had previously stated this in the same place where he was speaking of the Gentiles naturally doing the law. There he says: "But glory and honor and peace to each one who does good, to the Jew first, and to the Greek."[213] But how can un-

208. Rom 8.28.
210. Gal 5.6.
212. 2 Thes 1.11.

209. 1 Cor 1.31. Cf. Jer 9.24.
211. 1 Cor 13.2–3.
213. Rom 2.10.

believers possess the glory that is given only to the justified? For "those whom God justified he also glorified."[214] "And the righteousness of God comes through the faith of Jesus Christ to all who believe."[215] Or what honor will be given to unbelievers, since blessed Peter teaches that honor is bestowed on none but believers, when he says: "Therefore, there will be honor to you who believe"?[216] Or how will peace belong to one who has not been redeemed by the blood of Christ (through which God made peace with "the things that are on earth and the things in heaven")?[217] "He is our peace, who has made both one."[218] And this peace cannot be possessed without the love and faith of Christ because, "having been justified by faith, we have peace with God through our Lord Jesus Christ, through whom we also have access through faith in this grace in which we stand, and we boast in the hope of the glory of the sons of God."[219] That hope, therefore, "does not put to shame, because God's love has been poured out in our hearts through the Holy Spirit, who has been given to us."[220] For we have in fact received "the Spirit of adoption as sons by whom we cry out, 'Abba, Father.'"[221] Therefore, in order for men to become sons of God, they receive the only Son of God by faith, and when he gives power, they receive this power both to believe in him and to belong to the number of the sons of God. "For as many as received him, to them he gave the power to become sons of God, to those who believe in his name."[222] He places his law in their hearts, and he writes it in their understanding—that is, the law of faith, which justifies when it has been breathed in; not the law of works, which does indeed doubtless condemn its practitioners.

52. (XXVII.) For surely that law (which is the law of deeds, which cannot justify man, because "by works of the law no flesh will be justified")[223] can exist naturally in the heart of the Gentiles and in the heart of unbelieving Jews. Yet without the faith

---

214. Rom 8.30.   215. Rom 3.22.
216. 1 Pt 2.7.   217. Eph 1.10.
218. Eph 2.14.   219. Rom 5.1–2.
220. Rom 5.5.   221. Rom 8.15.
222. Jn 1.12.   223. Rom 3.20.

of Christ, it in no way justifies its adherents, but it holds those who are bound by the bond of impiety. This was indeed the condition of Paul's heart when he was an unbeliever: concerning zeal, he was persecuting the Church of God; and concerning the righteousness that comes by the law, he was found blameless.[224] Nevertheless, inasmuch as he did not receive blame from God, he therefore says: "The things that were gain to me, I counted them as loss for Christ's sake. Truly, I consider all things to be loss because of the excellence of knowing Jesus Christ my Lord, for whom I have counted all things as loss, and consider them as dung so that I may gain Christ and be found in him, not having my own righteousness that is from the law, but the righteousness that comes by the faith of Christ, which is righteousness from God by faith leading to the knowledge of him."[225]

53. Who would fail to see from these words of the Apostle that the righteousness coming from the law is from man, but that the righteousness coming from the faith of Christ truly does not exist apart from God? Consequently, the former is the righteousness by which the ungodly man is set up so that he may fall into punishment, but the latter righteousness is that through which the justified man is humbled so that he may be exalted to glory. Therefore, the Apostle admits that while he was living blamelessly in that righteousness that comes from the law, he was nevertheless godless. For why else would he say: "For while we were yet weak, at the right time Christ died for the ungodly"?[226] He also truly confesses that he was an enemy of God, saying: "For if, when we were enemies, we were reconciled to God by the death of his Son, much more, now that we have been reconciled, will we be saved by his life."[227] Therefore, since our Savior himself says to the Jews: "Unless you believe that I AM, you will die in your sins,"[228] what did it profit Paul without knowledge of Christ to cling to that righteousness that comes by deeds of the law? Thus, because the Apostle testifies that the righteousness coming from the faith of Christ exists so

224. Cf. Phil 3.6.
226. Rom 5.6.
228. Jn 8.24.

225. Phil 3.7–10.
227. Rom 5.10.

that Christ may be known, it is clear that the law of faith is the law God promised he would write in their hearts.[229] That is what the context of that very passage[230] clearly points out. For there God says: "And none of them will teach his neighbor and his brother, saying: 'Know God'; for they will all know me, from the least of them to the greatest of them."[231]

54. This is the law that God writes in the hearts of them all, not because of the condition of nature, but because of the generosity of grace; not because of man's free choice, but because of the ministry of evangelical preaching; not because of the letter of the Old Testament written in stone, but because of the Spirit of the living God dwelling in the heart. This is what blessed Paul clearly indicates when he says: "You are Christ's letter, ministered through us and written not with ink but with the Spirit of the living God, not on tablets of stone, but on the fleshly tablets of the heart."[232] Therefore, this is what God writes in the hearts of men through his Spirit, and this is what the devil's hatred then destroyed, because of which hatred death entered into the world. Therefore, God writes the law of faith by which he justifies the Gentiles, with the result that he renews their nature by giving grace. Indeed, to this end he pours out love (which is the fulfillment of the law)[233] through his Spirit, so that he may cause what he commands to be fulfilled. He also bestows the grace of illumination through the Spirit of faith, precisely so that what has pleased God, namely faith, may work through love. As long as this faith is not present in man, then regardless of whatever was written through the natural law without the law of faith and has remained in man, that saves no one who works. For God justifies no one without faith, and works cannot achieve salvation for the one who works, for "without faith it is impossible to please God."[234] Thus no one attempts

---

229. This promise that God would write the law in the people's hearts comes in Jer 31.31–34. Fulgentius discusses this passage in par. 49 above, and he returns to it here.

230. By "context," Fulgentius means the whole paragraph, Jer 31.31–34.

231. Jer 31.34.   232. 2 Cor 3.3.

233. Cf. Rom 13.10.   234. Heb 11.6.

to ascribe to natural law the law God writes on the hearts of the Gentiles, not by forming their nature, but by granting them grace. For this is not the law through which man protects the bond uniting human society even without faith, but the law through which he knows and loves God by believing. It is not the law through which each proud individual lays claim for himself to good works or even to faith itself, but the law through which a man submissively attributes both his faith and his good works to God, who is working mercifully in him. For this law so reconciles and directs the heart of man that when he hears God's commands, he asks that what has been commanded be granted, and when he works in faith, he does not doubt that God's grace continually assists him.

55. (XXVIII.) And our opponents ask about God: "So why did he not cause all men to will to believe, since God is no respecter of persons?" They have to recognize that this question has been posed by those rather haughty people whom Holy Scripture urges to restrain the boldness of human curiosity, saying: "Do not try to search out things that are too difficult for you, or try to discover what is beyond your powers; but always ponder the things that the Lord has commanded you."[235] He who was caught up to the third heaven and became more terrified as he became more illumined feared these higher things.[236] For that reason he did not cease to cry out even more: "O the depth of the riches of both the wisdom and knowledge of God! How unsearchable are his judgments and his ways past finding out! For who has known the mind of the Lord? Or who has become his counselor? Or who has first given to him and it will be repaid to him? For from him and through him and in him are all things; to him be the glory into the ages of ages."[237] Thus it is enough for us to believe that God's gracious mercy is free for those who are being saved, to believe without doubting that God's justice is true for those who are being condemned, and to sing with a contrite and humble heart about the Lord's mercy

235. Sir 3.22.
236. See Paul's vision in 2 Cor 12.1–4.
237. Rom 11.33–36.

and judgment. In the case of vessels of wrath prepared for destruction, he shows that iniquity is not pleasing to his justice; and in the case of vessels of mercy, he demonstrates that his goodness is able to forgive all the sins of those whom he wishes to forgive.

56. (XXIX.) The Apostle speaks truly of God when he says: "He wills all men to be saved and to come to the knowledge of the truth."[238] Those who think that the vessels of mercy must receive this will of God in the same way as vessels of wrath do not understand as they should. They give no consideration at all to the profoundly true scriptural statement that commends the omnipotence of the divine will. It says, "The Lord has done all things that he willed in heaven and on earth, in the sea and in all the deep places."[239] It is also said of God: "For when you will, you have the power."[240] So if he wills man to be saved, but man's salvation does not begin without a good will, and if God does not begin the will itself in man but simply waits for it to be born from man, then how does God do everything he wills? O what an abysmal sin persists as long as one obstinately resists the grace of God and men deny that they are changed for the good by the work of God and would not be men had they not become men by the goodness of the God who was at work! Is it indeed true that the order of things permits a person to believe or think that God (who is the Creator of man) is able to make man but not change him? Is it true that God needs no help in order to make man but is unable to accomplish what he wills in man's will before he finds the willing itself in man? Is a person permitted to think that man possesses from God the ability to be man but possesses from himself the ability to be a better man? And so, is he permitted to think that the good will by which one believes in God is itself the work not of divine goodness, but of human evil? It is certain that every man is evil before he believes in God. And since it is written: "The crooked places will be made straight,"[241] the crooked man is made straight, the unfaithful man is made faithful. Therefore, if God does not bestow good

on an evil will but waits for it to become good by itself, then an
evil will is able to bring forth goodness from itself. The result is
that whereas the evil will possesses from God the ability to exist,
it can possess the ability to be good only from itself. All of this
would imply that our omnipotent and good God can, when he
wills, produce good from the evil wills of men only when the
wills themselves are good. In such a case, he would indeed will,
but he would be in no way able to make them good.

57. Who could be unaware that Paul had an evil will when
he was persecuting the Church of God and assaulting it? But
God put his malice to good use when, during Paul's persecution, God crowned blessed Stephen with martyrdom. Therefore, since God was able to crown Stephen through the unbelief
of Paul the persecutor, was God not able to convert Paul the
persecutor to faith? So, did Paul give his will to God previously,
and did God thus reward a willing Paul with faith? But there is a
place where Paul himself said: "Who has first given to him and it
will be repaid to him?"[242] Paul surely would not have said this if
he had known that he gave his will to God and God repaid him
with faith. Therefore, may God protect his faithful from such
foolish ideas, and may he remove such ideas from unbelievers.
For in fact, one is defiled by profane thoughts such as thinking
that either grace is not granted to an obdurate man, or it is removed from an ungrateful man. For God who converts gives life
to those whom he wills to save; God changes the wills of men so
that their wills begin to be good. Therefore, it is written: "And
I said: 'I have now begun, and this change has come from the
right hand of the Most High.'"[243] After this Scripture had been
made known, the prophet's meaning was easily understandable.
This meaning is that the change came from God's right hand,
not merely after one had begun, but even in the very fact that
he began. The Most High was not silent. Accordingly, as for
those who think that God's will (by which he wills the salvation
of all men) is equal with respect to those to be redeemed and
those to be condemned, what will they answer when they are

242. Rom 11.35.
243. Ps 76.11, following LXX (77.10 modern).

asked why God wills all men to be saved but nevertheless not all are saved?

58. (XXX.) Or when you write in your letter that "God waits" for the will of man "so that there may be a fitting reward for those who will to believe and a just condemnation for those who refuse to do so,"[244] are you testifying to what our opponents say?[245] In order to avoid unduly prolonging this letter, let us skip over all the things that can be repeated on behalf of the truth of faith in response to this perverse thought. In the meantime, let us confound and overcome such people by the testimony not of men who can talk but of children who are silent. For in children the power of Christ's cross shines brightly to make void the seeming wisdom of such people's word. This power shows that of itself it graciously accomplishes the same salvation in all men who exercise their own wills as it deigns to effect in infants who have no will. For in infants there is neither a good will (so that the reward would be fair for those who are willing), nor an evil will (so that condemnation would be just for those who are unwilling). Therefore, if God does not awaken or change men's wills so that they will be saved as they will to be, but instead waits for men's wills, how does he give eternal salvation to infants who are baptized and die in infancy, infants in whom he neither waits for nor finds a good will? Furthermore, how does he condemn to eternal torments the others who have died without baptism, since he finds in them no guilt of an evil will?

59. When these enemies of God's grace (who are not the defenders but the betrayers of human choice) see that without an intervening will either to goodness or to evil, some children obtain the kingdom and others are appointed to partake of the interminable fire, does their perversity not compel them to think God is wicked in the death of all children? In the same

244. Scythian Monks' Letter to the Bishops (= *Ep.* 16), par. 20 (Latin text in CCL 91A, 559, and CCL 85A, 168; English translation in this volume, p. 37).

245. In the passage here cited, the monks are, in fact, testifying to what their opponents say. Our translation of the passage from their letter on p. 37 makes this clear.

way, if that is their opinion, then no child ought to die before
he reaches the age when he is able to have either a good or evil
will, so that God would neither save baptized children without
a good will nor condemn unbaptized children without an evil
will. For if God's goodness does not begin to effect the salvation of a man unless he finds a good will in that man, it will
be wicked to condemn or redeem the person who is unable either to will well or not to will well. But "there is no iniquity with
God,"[246] "all of whose ways are mercy and truth."[247]

60. Therefore, because the Catholic Church truly believes
and confesses that God is just and good, one must believe most
certainly and confess confidently that one and the same grace
of God accomplishes the beginning of a good will in adults who
are to be saved and effects salvation in children without a will.
The same grace that redeems infants (who are neither willing
nor unwilling) also transforms adults from being unwilling to
being willing by illumining them. And God's operative grace
perfects this work of salvation in children without the assent of
their own will, but in adults he begins it when he establishes
the good will he has bestowed, so that the will that was evil may
become good by the work of grace alone, and so that the will
may subsequently submit by cooperative obedience to the grace
working with it. Thus God is not cruel to infants who are to be
condemned (to whom the benefit of baptism is not granted),
just as he is not unjust to adults to whom he does not give a
good will. And just as an evil will rightly causes the adults to be
punished, so a condemned origin rightly causes the infants to
be punished. But God did not form in men either the stain of
original guilt or the wickedness of their own will. Consequently,
in all those whom he saves, he does not find a good will. Instead, as the diversity of people's ages demands, God (whose
will to good no one can resist) either freely makes the evil will
he finds in adults to be good or perfects the grace of the sacrament in children without any human will, either good or evil.

246. 2 Chr 19.7.
247. Ps 24.10, following LXX (25.10 modern).

61. (XXXI.) For this reason, regarding all those whom God wishes to save, we must understand that we do not think anyone can be saved apart from God who wills it. Further, let us not imagine that the will of the omnipotent God either is not fulfilled or is in any way impeded in certain people. For all whom God wishes to save are unquestionably saved, and they cannot be saved unless God wishes them to be saved, and each person whom God does not will to be saved is not saved, since our God "has done all things that he willed."[248] Therefore, all are saved whom he wishes to be saved, for this salvation is not born of the human will but is supplied by God's good will. Nevertheless, these "all men" whom God wishes to save include not the entire human race altogether, but rather the totality of those who are to be saved. So the word "all" is mentioned because the divine kindness saves all kinds from among all men, that is, from every race, status, and age, from every language and every region.[249] In all of these people, this message of our Redeemer is fulfilled where he says, "When I have been lifted up from the earth, I will draw all things to myself."[250] Now he did not say this because he draws all men whatsoever, but because no one is saved unless he himself draws him. For he also says: "No one can come to me unless the Father who has sent me draws him."[251] He also says in another place: "Everything that the Father has given me will come to me."[252] Therefore, these are all the ones whom God wills to be saved and to come to the knowledge of the truth.[253]

62. But it is well known that sometimes when the divine words speak of "all," they nonetheless do not always intend this to mean the whole human race. For example, the Lord says through the prophet: "In the last days I will pour out a measure of my Spirit upon all flesh."[254] Blessed Peter shows that this was done in the 120 men on whom the Holy Spirit came with tongues of fire.[255] Therefore, if we think that in this passage, the phrase "all flesh" is understood to include all men, the di-

---

248. Ps 134.6 (135.6 modern).   249. Cf. Rv 5.9.
250. Jn 12.32.   251. Jn 6.44.
252. Jn 6.37.   253. Cf. 1 Tm 2.4.
254. Jl 2.28; cf. Acts 2.17.   255. Cf. Acts 2.3.

vine message will begin to be considered false. May it never be! Instead, "God is true,"[256] and, "The words of the Lord are pure words."[257] Just as God gave his word that he would pour out a measure of his Spirit upon "all flesh," so he did, so he does, so he will do until the end of the age. Truly, he pours out a measure of his Spirit "on all flesh," that is, on all men, namely, upon all those whom he wills to be saved.

63. So that we may recognize more fully who those "all" are, let us hear the words of the same blessed Peter, who (filled with the Holy Spirit) concluded his sermon with this exhortation: "Be penitent and be baptized, every one of you, in the name of Jesus Christ for the remission of your sins, and you will receive the gift of the Holy Spirit. For the promise is to you and to your children, and to all who are far off, even to whomever the Lord our God calls."[258] So he said "all," but the Lord calls "whomever." Blessed Paul also indicates that they have been called according to God's purpose, and says in another place that God has "included them all in unbelief so that he may have mercy on all."[259] Even so, God does not show mercy on absolutely everyone whom he includes in unbelief in such a way that he would mercifully give the grace of faith to all unbelievers. Rather, the merciful God gives the same grace of faith not to unbelievers but doubtless to those about whom he says to Moses: "I will be merciful to whom I am merciful, and I will show mercy to whom I will be merciful."[260] Therefore, he displays grace as a willing gift just as the Lord deigns to speak to his disciples: "To you it has been given to know the mystery of the kingdom of heaven, but to them it has not been given."[261] He also says: "He who is able to receive it, let him receive it."[262] But in order to teach that the very capacity to receive is granted by divine generosity, he says in another place: "Not all receive this saying, but those to whom it is given."[263]

256. Rom 3.4.   257. Ps 11.7 (12.6 modern).
258. Acts 2.38–39.   259. Rom 11.32.
260. Ex 33.19; cf. Rom 9.18. 261. Mt 13.11.
262. Mt 19.12.   263. Mt 19.11.

64. These are all those on whom God has mercy because they are preceded by his mercy so that they may believe and be freely saved through faith. The fact that they believe does not take its beginning from the human will, but faith is given to the will itself in accordance with the free generosity of the merciful God. Blessed Paul recorded this distinction between different senses of the word "all" (a distinction that a faithful understanding must preserve completely) at one place in his letter so that even when he says "all men" without noting any exceptions, he might still indicate all men of a certain kind while excluding others. For he says: "Just as through one man's offense all men have come under condemnation, so also by the righteousness of one man all men have come to justification of life."[264] Can it really be that when the Apostle says, "condemnation upon all men" and "justification upon all men," we must actually believe that the phrase "all men" means that those who were all surely condemned through the sin of Adam were the very same ones who are all justified by Christ? Against this interpretation stands the death of countless unbelievers who pass from this life without the grace of justification and are snatched away to the eternal punishments of the second death without the sacrament of baptism. Therefore, it remains for us to conclude that not absolutely all of those whom the Apostle places under condemnation pass over to the grace of justification, but that only these "certain all" from among those "all" do so. Therefore, all are sons of wrath through Adam leading to condemnation, and from among them, "certain all" are sons of grace through Christ. Therefore, the fact that these are all procreated sinfully (by means of carnal generation) through the first man condemns them. For all who bear the image of the earthly man are of the earth, and all who receive the image of the heavenly man leading to eternal life are of heaven. Again the prophet says: "All nations whatsoever that you have made will come and worship before you, O Lord, and they will glorify[265] your name into eternity."[266] And the Lord says to his faithful: "You will be

264. Rom 5.18.
265. Reading *glorificabunt* for *glorificabant*.
266. Ps 85.9, following LXX (86.9 modern).

hated by all nations because of my name."[267] Does divine Scripture, therefore, deny itself with contradictory thoughts? May it never be! But truly he means both "all these" and "all those," that is, both all believers in all nations who glorify the name of God and all unbelievers in all the same nations who (because of mortal godlessness) persist in hating the name of Christ and his faithful.

65. The same distinction is also found in the letter that the blessed Apostle writes to the Colossians, where he says: "For in Christ were created all things in the heavens and on earth, things visible and invisible, whether thrones or dominions or principalities or powers. All things were created through him and in him, and he himself is before all, and in him all things hold together."[268] And a little later he says that [the Father] "was pleased to make all fullness dwell in him,[269] and through him to reconcile to himself all things, whether things in the heavens or things on earth, making peace through the blood of his cross."[270] Do we really believe that all things that are in the heavens and on earth are brought to peace through him? May it never be! For the person who wishes to think this way will face the dilemma of choosing between two heresies. Either he will be forced to deny that the devil and his angels were created through Christ, or he will have to affirm that even they must be reconciled by the blood of his cross. But let whoever is involved in the wickedness of these thoughts beware lest he be condemned to the punishment of everlasting fire with the devil himself and his angels. For if anyone believes that the devil either was not created by Christ or is to be restored at some time by the reconciliation Christ effects, he is guilty of one and the same heresy. For indeed, if Christ the Lord had not created the devil, his condemnable departure from Christ would not have happened,[271] and if Christ were going to save him at some time,

267. Mt 10.22.   268. Col 1.16–17.
269. That is, in Christ.   270. Col 1.19–20.
271. Fulgentius's point here seems to be that if Christ had not created the devil, then the devil would not have existed at all, and as a result could not have departed from Christ.

Christ would never have mentioned eternal fire at all.[272] Therefore, all things were created through Christ and in Christ, because nothing exists that the Father has not created through
the Son and in the Son. And all things are being reconciled
through him and in him, because there is no man who obtains
the benefit of reconciliation apart from the cross of Christ.

66. Therefore, from this rule (which is shown to be among
the oracles of heaven) let us understand the phrase "all men
whom God wills to be saved" in such a way that we know that
all who are being saved are saved only by God's gracious will.
For truly, in the case of each person being saved, there are no
preceding meritorious deeds of the human will, but God's will
alone is the cause of human salvation. "For wrath lies in his in-
dignation, and life lies in his will."[273] Therefore, his wrath is the
reward for our iniquity, but our life is truly the gift of his will.
"For just as the Father raises the dead and gives them life, so
does the Son also give life to those whom he wills,"[274] and he
wills the same ones to be given life whom he wills to be saved.
Therefore, he saves those whom he wills just as he gives life to
those whom he wills. For there is nothing he has willed that he
has not done, as the Scripture testifies: "He has done all things
that he willed."[275] Consequently, it is appropriate to say that God
does not will to do some things he could do; but it would be
a sin for anyone to say that the Almighty is unable to do anything he wills, for "who will resist his will?"[276] Surely no one
does, because there is no nature independent of his creation.
And just as nothing exists naturally that he has not made, so
nothing happens for the salvation of men that he has not predestined to be done according to the eternal disposition of his
good will. And [by this predestination] he freely gives even that
faith by which we may walk well, and he gives that perseverance

272. That is, if the devil were not going to suffer in eternal fire, then no one
would. In that case, why would Christ have even spoken of such eternal fire in
Scripture?

273. Ps 29.6, following LXX (30.5 modern).

274. Jn 5.21. 275. Ps 134.6 (135.6 modern).

276. Rom 9.19.

by which we are able to achieve the goal. God has always possessed these gifts in his eternally and unchangeably disposed will, according to which he has predestined and prepared both the things he would give and the people to whom he would give them. By predestining, he has himself prepared the gift of grace that, once the grace is actually given, completes the effect of the predestination.

67. (Epilogue) My most beloved brothers, you now have my statement (expressed in few words) of our faith and confession, both about the Incarnation of our Lord Jesus Christ and about grace. This statement certainly combines the teaching that the Only-begotten God was begotten naturally and without beginning from God the Father, and that he was born naturally from the Virgin according to the flesh. For God the Word is one and the same, whom the eternal Father begat coeternal with himself in his first birth, and whom the virginal womb brought forth in a second birth after the Son of man was conceived temporally. He gives his grace and the beginning of a good will to us to lead us to faith, and he gives help to the will itself so that what one wishes well may also work well. For God, who himself formed man in accordance with his predestination, prepared beforehand those to whom he willed to give the gift of illumination so that they might believe, the gift of perseverance so that they might progress and endure, and the gift of glorification so that they might reign. He is also bringing his work to a conclusion in no other way than the way he has disposed it in his eternal and unchangeable will. The Apostle testifies to the truth of God's predestination, by which we were predestined in Christ before the foundation of the world.[277] If anyone refuses to receive (by believing in his heart), or to reveal (by confessing with his mouth),[278] whether he has not, before the last day of his present life, abandoned the stubbornness of his godlessness (by which he, as a rebel, resisted the living and true God), it is evident that he does not belong to the number of those whom God in Christ freely elected and predestined to the kingdom before the foun-

277. See, e.g., Eph 1.4.
278. Cf. Rom 10.9–10.

dation of the world. But on behalf of such ones,[279] the prayer of the faithful must never cease, and love must never grow weary, that God may give them the grace of his illumination, by which the seed of the divine message itself may bear fruit. This message sounds in vain in the outer ear unless God opens the hearing of the inner man in accordance with his spiritual gift.

279. That is, the ones whom God has elected but who have not yet come to Christ, although of course we do not know who they are.

FULGENTIUS'S SECOND LETTER
TO THE SCYTHIAN MONKS

Y THE GRACE of God, Datianus, Fortunatus, Boethos, Victor, Scholasticus, Horontius, Vindiciamus, Victor, Januarius, Victorianus, Fontius, Quodvultdeus,[1] servants of Christ, send greetings in the Lord to the highly esteemed holy brothers, John the elder and archimandrite, and Venerius the deacon,[2] and to the faithful men whose names are included in your letter.[3]

1. Just as through Christ's grace the bond of love preserves members of the ecclesiastical body in the unity of faith, so likewise it is necessary for the members to be concerned for one another. This concern is necessary so that after the disease of any kind of perverse dogma has been refuted, we may then give our attention not only to the preservation and restoration of health, but also to continued and unwearying preaching and prayer. For this is what happens when concern for the purity of the brothers is vigilant: the Holy Spirit himself, through whom "God's love has been poured out in our hearts,"[4] "works all things together for good for those who love God"[5] and who

---

1. This list of senders does not include Felix or the second Januarius mentioned at the head of the first letter (*Ep.* 17). Interestingly, Fulgentius also does not name himself as a sender of this letter.

2. This list of addressees does not include Peter, Leontius, and another John mentioned at the head of *Ep.* 17. This letter mentions Venerius, who is not mentioned at the head of *Ep.* 17.

3. As explained in the introduction, Fulgentius wrote this letter (*Ep.* 15 in the collection of his letters) to the monks after his return to Ruspe in 523, at the end of his second exile. The Latin critical text may be found in CCL 91A, 447–57.

4. Rom 5.5.   5. Rom 8.28.

love their neighbor in God. For just as we receive love itself by the gift of spiritual grace, so also we demonstrate that as long as we are concerned for the brothers, divine grace lives in us, and that the more we exercise pure love, the more we receive an increase in the grace of divine compensation.

2. So we have received the letter from you, beloved ones, a letter that on the one hand eased the pain of our exile[6] and on the other hand truly made it more grievous. Indeed, we rejoice because you hold to the true teaching about the grace of God, by whose gift the free choice of the human mind is enlightened, and with whose help it is governed. But a certain cloud of sadness hangs over us because you mentioned that certain brothers are not adhering to the correct path of the Catholic faith in the matter of God's grace and human choice, but want to exalt the freedom of human choice in opposition to God's grace.

3. In the first place, most beloved brothers, on this matter you must recognize (we do not at all doubt that you have recognized) that those kinds of things are divinely permitted so that henceforth the power of divine grace can be understood by a clearer proof. Grace itself is in no way recognized unless it is given. As long as it is not present in a man, he necessarily resists it by either word or deed. For he who holds thoughts contrary to the Christian faith resists the grace of God by word; and he who does not hold to the plan of the Christian life in his character resists it by deed. To be sure, divinely given grace works in a man so that his heart, upon receiving the gift of faith and love, may both bring forth worthy speech and persevere in zeal for doing good. This is divinely given to the faithful, as the blessed Apostle both shows and prays for when he says, "Now may our Lord Jesus Christ himself, and God our Father, who has loved us and given us everlasting consolation and good hope through grace, comfort your hearts and establish you in every good work and word."[7]

6. Fulgentius is writing after the end of his second exile, but he and the other North African bishops received the monks' letter while they were still in exile on Sardinia.

7. 2 Thes 2.16–17.

4. Therefore, every gracious gift of speaking good words and doing good works is a gift from God to us. He has made known to us that he is the one who also bestows on us the very ability to think worthy thoughts, so that a man may learn to glory not in himself but in the Lord. Of course, the blessed Apostle assigned man's worthy thoughts to divine grace when he said, "And such confidence we have through Christ toward God: not that we are sufficient to think that anything comes from our own power, as if it were from us; but our sufficiency is from God."[8] Hence, even though certain people who do not yet possess grace do not understand that they lack it, yet those who have received divinely given grace ought to be strengthened all the more by that declaration of grace. As a result, they understand that it is not bestowed on everybody. And those to whom it is not given must remain ignorant of the fact, and those to whom it has been given must know that it is a gift of the divine bounty. For the Apostle testifies that the gifts of the Holy Spirit are recognized as being received from the same Holy Spirit. Therefore, he says, "We have received not the spirit of the world, but the Spirit who is from God, so that we may know the things given to us by God, things we also declare, not with learned words of human wisdom, but by the teaching of the Spirit, [comparing spiritual things with spiritual things. The natural man does not perceive the things which are of the Spirit of God, for they are folly to him, and he is not able to understand that those spiritual things are discerned spiritually, and the spiritual man makes judgments concerning all things, and is himself judged by no man]."[9]

5. Therefore, we receive grace through the Holy Spirit so that, after we have received that Spirit, grace may be in us so we may know what we have received. Accordingly, most beloved brothers, we must know and profess by the correct movement of true faith both the deep poverty of the human will and the

8. 2 Cor 3.4–5.
9. 1 Cor 2.12–15. The portion enclosed in brackets is missing in the earlier manuscript (*N*) and is supplied in the margin of the later manuscript (*Port.*). It was likely added by a later copyist to complete the biblical quotation.

unfailing generosity of divine grace. "For what do you have," the Apostle asks, "that you did not receive? But if you received it, why do you boast as if you did not receive it?"[10] Indeed, before the generosity of grace, there is certainly free will in man, but it is not good, for it has not been enlightened. Accordingly, unless grace is given, the will itself is not considered to be good. For the free will of man, apart from the gift of grace, is like the eye without light. For the eye was made for seeing, but unless it receives light, it will not see. And that light is "the true light that enlightens every man who comes into this world."[11] And the true light enlightens man by giving itself through grace. Therefore, just as the eye of the body always needs to receive light so that it can look upon the light itself, so also the knowledge of grace cannot support man's free choice unless a spiritual infusion of grace itself is given.

6. Accordingly, since in your letters[12] you have brought up these things that pertain to the truth of Catholic dogma and have asked us to discuss them, we have taken care to define them briefly, one by one. In doing so, we will follow, by the gift of the same grace, what spiritual grace deigned to pour out through the hearts and tongues of the holy Fathers about the matter under discussion. Noting that Esau and Jacob were not yet born,[13] you said that Jacob was elected by freely given mercy, but that Esau was held in original sin and was hated in accordance with God's just judgment. Your opponents, on the other hand, say that Esau is truly the figure of the Jewish people who are to be condemned because of their future evil works, and that Jacob is truly the figure of the Gentiles who are to be saved because of their future good works.

10. 1 Cor 4.7.
11. Jn 1.9.
12. That Fulgentius mentions "letters" (plural) here suggests that the monks may have written to him again after they received his first letter (*Ep.* 17). Throughout the rest of this letter, Fulgentius refers to things the monks have said and questions they have asked (see pars. 7, 10, 11, 13, 14, as well as the remainder of this par.), and these references suggest that this letter was occasioned by a second letter (now lost) from the monks.
13. See Rom 9.10–13.

7. It is good for you to bring these two points, which you pro-
pose separately, into agreement with the Catholic consensus.
For these points appropriately acknowledge the grace of God
and show that you do not deny the mystery of prophecy. For
those two brothers are rightly understood to signify two nations,
especially since it was foretold to Rebecca, who was consulting
with the Lord, that two nations would be separated from her
womb. Truly, one must recognize in that separation both undeserved goodness and righteous severity. For since "every excellent gift and every perfect gift is from above, coming down from
the Father of lights,"[14] so also those who are separated by grace
are saved. In fact, what was chosen and loved in Jacob was not
human works but the divine gifts. On the contrary, since "our
wickedness highlights God's righteousness,"[15] there is no doubt
that the wickedness of human iniquity was condemned in Esau.
In that, to be sure, God shows in Jacob the free beneficence of
his mercy, by which beneficence he saw fit to adopt Jacob by his
free grace. For he did not choose him because of the merits of
any future good work, but instead he foreknew that both faith
and good works were going to be given to him.

8. From this follows what the blessed Apostle says to Abraham's descendants (who were preceded by Jacob as a figure):
"By grace you have been saved through faith."[16] And in order to
show that faith is not given to anybody in return for good merits, but that every good merit is begun by the gift of faith itself,
and to show that faith itself is a gift of God, he continued by
adding: "and this is not from yourselves, but it is a gift of God."[17]
And lest anyone dare to claim for himself the merit of any good
works whatsoever, and lest he think that he has received faith
as a reward for any works, the Apostle added: "not from works,
lest anyone should boast."[18] But in order to show that not just
faith but even good works are divinely granted, he immediately
added: "For we are his workmanship, created in Christ Jesus for
good works."[19] He testifies that God has not only given these

14. Jas 1.17.   15. Rom 3.5.
16. Eph 2.8.   17. Ibid.
18. Eph 2.9.   19. Eph 2.10.

works, but that he has also prepared them, when he says, "which God has prepared so that we may walk in them."[20] Therefore, Jacob was saved by grace through faith, and by grace he subsequently received the ability to do good works.

9. Therefore, inasmuch as it is certain that Esau was a vessel of wrath and Jacob a vessel of mercy, one must affirm even more certainly that Esau rightly deserved wrath so that he might be condemned, for God, who inflicts wrath, is not unjust. One must likewise affirm that Jacob freely received the gift of prevenient mercy so that he might be saved. So Jacob, justified freely by the grace of God, was made a vessel of mercy through a grace that God did not owe, and was mercifully prepared for glory by that very grace. But Esau was rightly prepared by just wrath for punishment: For "our wickedness highlights God's righteousness."[21] Consequently, God shows the mercy of free kindness in Jacob, but indeed the judgment of just severity in Esau. After Esau had received the sacrament of circumcision on the eighth day according to the procedure of the divine institution, he was free from the guilt of original sin, but, because of the iniquity of his heart, he remained in the antiquity of the earthly man and was abandoned to the judgment of the One who freely saves and justly condemns. In Esau's person are signified not only those who deny the faith, but also those who have been members of the Church all their lives yet persist in evil works. About them the Apostle says: "For those who do such things will not reach the kingdom of God."[22] For just as he who was circumcised perished because he loved darkness more than light, so everyone who does not put aside the old man that is being corrupted according to its erroneous desires will be condemned in judgment because he did not utilize the sacrament of baptism appropriately. To be sure, those who belong to the same old man are not only among the ones who do not know God, but also those about whom the Apostle says: "They profess that they know God, but they deny him by their deeds."[23]

20. Ibid.   21. Rom 3.5.
22. Gal 5.21.   23. Ti 1.16.

10. Concerning young children, the rule of Catholic truth
must unquestionably be adhered to. According to it, one believes that a child who is baptized is saved by God's freely bestowed goodness, but one who dies without baptism is condemned because of original sin. And one must not say that a
child who died without the grace of justification (and thus was
assigned to the company of the wicked) was delivered from future sin by God's beneficence. Whether one is a young child or
an adult, each is delivered from sin by a single remedy: if he is
redeemed by the blood of Christ. Whoever thinks grace is given
to all people truly has the wrong idea about grace, since not
only does faith not belong to all, but there are some nations
to whom the preaching of the faith still does not extend. And
the blessed Apostle says, "How then will they call upon him in
whom they have not believed, or how will they believe in him
whom they have not heard? Or how will they hear without a
preacher?"[24] So grace is not given to all, since those who are
not believers cannot be partakers of grace, nor can they believe
if the hearing of faith has not reached them. Indeed, grace is
not given equally (no matter to whom it is given), but it is given
"according to the measure of Christ's gift,"[25] even as God has
distributed a measure of faith to everyone. He does not show
partiality to people, but "one and the same Spirit accomplishes
all things, distributing his own gifts to each individually as he
wills."[26]

11. You say that a man is saved by God's mercy alone, but
our opponents say that unless a man has run and worked in accordance with his own will, he cannot be saved. One may rightly
hold to both of these assertions if he preserves the correct order
of divine mercy and human will, so that divine mercy precedes,
the human will follows, and God's mercy alone confers the beginning of salvation. In that case, man's will emerges as cooper-
ating in his salvation. The result is that God's preceding mercy
guides the direction of the human will, and the human will,
obeying by means of the same subsequent mercy, runs toward

24. Rom 10.14.   25. Eph 4.7.
26. 1 Cor 12.11.

the prize in accordance with God's purpose. Consequently, the human will, because it runs and works effectively, realizes that it possesses the gift of running and working because of God's mercy. It is thus not ungrateful for mercy, through which it receives the beginning of salvation so that, by the same mercy, it attains the full reward of eternal salvation. For then it will be good if it is preceded by God's gift, and it will remain good if it is not deprived of his help.

12. But whoever thinks that God bestows grace the way a person lends money upon receiving an acceptable security is wrong. Indeed, the fact is that God both bestows the security (that is, the Holy Spirit) on those whom he pleases and distributes his money (as if it were money sought from bankers) for the care and benefit of his slaves, as he says in the Gospel. Truly, the statement of the Apostle by which he says, "Therefore, he has mercy on whom he wills and he hardens whom he wills,"[27] is certainly received better from a believer's perspective. If an individual is unwilling to receive Paul's statement from a believer's perspective, let him subsequently consider without contention what the Apostle Paul says: "Does the potter not have power over the clay to make from the same lump one vessel for honor and another for dishonor?"[28] And when Paul acknowledges the potter's right to make both vessels, let the individual recognize in the vessel for honor the undeserved grace of the merciful God, and in the vessel for dishonor let him recognize the deserved judgment of the God who hardens, that is, the God who abandons. But we say that God hardens, not because he compels a person to commit iniquity, but because whenever he does not snatch a person away from iniquity, he is just in not doing so, because he is just. Therefore, when God is merciful, a man is saved apart from his own merits; but when God hardens, the unrighteous man justly receives what he deserves. To be sure, God saves by the gift of goodness and hardens by the judgment of severity.

27. Rom 9.18.
28. Rom 9.21.

13. This, however, is what you say: "For God is the one working in you both to will and to accomplish according to his good will."[29] But our opponents say: "If you are willing and obedient to me, you will eat the good things of the land."[30] If the heart, at peace in faith, needs both and receives both, no question will remain about God's grace and the human will. For God commands man to will, but God also brings about the fact that man wills. God commands him to work, but he also brings about the fact that he works. Therefore, the blessed Apostle demonstrates both by saying, "With fear and trembling, work out your own salvation, for God is the one working in you both to will and to accomplish according to his good will."[31] Therefore, as each one works out his own salvation with fear and trembling, it is necessary that he be willing, but God brings about this willing and working in those who are his. As a consequence man has free choice and hears the commands that he must keep, but man's free choice is in no way capable of fulfilling the commands unless it is divinely helped. As a result, man knows he must work as long as he receives the command, and he always knows he owes to God every good thing he wishes and does. He also knows from the Apostle's witness that God works in man "to will and to accomplish according to his good will." He has deigned to promise this grace to his faithful through the prophet, saying, "I will put my Spirit in you, and I will cause you to walk in my righteous ways and keep my statutes and do them."[32]

14. So once God has begun to bring about a will in a man, the man is then converted to God, and, since the man is working in himself, God is therefore pleased to work. For the Apostle says about God, "May he prepare you for every good work by working in you what is pleasing in his sight, so that you may do his will."[33] To the extent that man is even able to extend his hand to life, to that extent he will have had the Lord as his protection at his right hand. And it is quite absurd for our opponents to think that holders of secular or ecclesiastical offices are

29. Phil 2.13.   30. Is 1.19.
31. Phil 2.12–13.   32. Ezek 36.27.
33. Heb 13.21.

vessels of mercy, but clerics, monks, and lay people are vessels of shame.[34] In fact, when the Apostle mentions those vessels of mercy which God has prepared for glory (not present glory, to be sure, but future), he says to them, "When Christ, your life, appears, then you also will appear with him in glory."[35] To that point, he says a little above, "Set your minds on the things that are above, not on the things that are on earth."[36] Therefore, the vessels of mercy are those to whom it is said, "Come, you who are blessed by my Father; receive the kingdom."[37] But surely the vessels for shame are those to whom it is said, "Depart into the everlasting fire that has been prepared for the devil and his angels."[38] Therefore, what makes men vessels of mercy is neither ecclesiastical nor secular preferment, but spiritual love in the Church. For that reason, a man in any profession whatsoever who clings to a faith that works through love will be a vessel for sanctified honor and useful to the Lord, prepared for every good work.

15. It is truly a mark of great obstinacy that anyone would either argue against or dispute the idea that the saints are predestined, since in fact no one dares to oppose apostolic preaching, which not only says of God, "But those whom he foreknew he also predestined to be conformed to the image of his Son,"[39] but also, in another place, "He predestined us to himself for adoption as sons through Jesus Christ."[40] Even further, blessed Paul confidently preaches that our Head himself, the firstborn among many brothers, was predestined, by saying that the one "who was made from the seed of David according to the flesh"[41]

---

34. It appears that the opponents of this teaching on grace have tried to blunt the force of Paul's statement in Romans 9 that there are vessels of mercy/honor and vessels of shame by claiming that the phrases "vessels of mercy" and "vessels of honor" refer simply to people who hold prominent ecclesiastical and secular positions, whereas the phrase "vessels of shame" refers to those who have no such titles. Cf. Fulgentius's fuller treatment of this opinion in *The Truth about Predestination and Grace*, Bk. 2, pars. 36–46 (pp. 190–98 in this volume).

35. Col 3.4.   36. Col 3.2.
37. Mt 25.34.   38. Mt 25.41.
39. Rom 8.30.   40. Eph 1.5.
41. Rom 1.3.

was the one "who was predestined to be Son of God in power, according to the Spirit of sanctification."[42] Therefore, whoever denies that Christ and his saints were predestined is a perverse opponent of the apostolic faith. But all whom God wills to be saved and to come to the knowledge of the truth[43] have themselves been predestined. The reason they are called "all" is that they are saved from both sexes, from every race, rank, age, and social condition of men. To be sure, the will of God Almighty is always fulfilled because his power is in no way overcome, for he himself is the one who "has done all things that he willed in heaven and on earth, in the sea and in all the deep places,"[44] and whose will no one resists.[45] For it is also true that the Son bore witness concerning himself, that he makes alive those whom he wishes, and that he anticipates no beginning of a human will in those he intends to make alive, but instead he makes them alive by creating the good will itself.

16. What we have written above has to do with adults. As for little children, by the operation of grace alone, God causes them to be saved, even though a good will cannot yet exist in them. Indeed, the free choice that was healthy in the first man before he sinned is now impaired in the sons of God because of their own weakness, but is supported by the greater grace of the divine gift. As for the question of the origin of souls, to be sure, we must either leave it aside or deal with it without wrangling. For either souls originate through propagation, or they are created new in individual bodies. This is a subject that the authority of the Holy Scriptures does not specifically address, so we must inquire cautiously, all the more because the faithful can remain ignorant of this subject with no detriment to their faith. But we must particularly observe and insist on the fact that even the souls of newborn children are bound by their connection to original sin. Thus they all must receive the sacrament of holy baptism, by which the bond of original sin is broken, and the adoption of sons, which had been lost in the first man, is recovered through the Second Man.

42. Rom 1.4.
44. Ps 134.6 (135.6 modern).
43. Cf. 1 Tm 2.4.
45. Cf. Rom 9.19.

17. Therefore, you, most beloved brothers, are to be steadfast and unmovable by the grace of God. As you adhere to the true faith, show charity to the brothers who understand it differently. Do not despair about anyone, because the one who does not understand truth about something today can know it tomorrow by God's revelation. For he is near to God whenever he wishes to be. So let us pray for them, that God will work in them. Let us demonstrate toward them a good will, by which we can have a reward, since we know that in the sight of God, whoever is among the number of the predestined will not perish, and that the will of the Almighty will be fulfilled in all of them, so that they will be saved by grace and partake of the knowledge of the truth, by the illumination of the Lord.

18. Above all, pay attention to the books that Saint Augustine wrote to Prosper and Hilary,[46] and urge the above-mentioned brothers to read them. Hormisdas of blessed memory, the glorious bishop of the Apostolic See, made mention of these books, with great commendation of universal praise, in a reply letter he wrote to our holy brother and fellow priest Possessor, who was consulting him.[47] These are his words: "Yet what the Roman (that is, the Catholic) Church follows and preserves concerning free choice and the grace of God can be amply learned in the various books of the blessed Augustine and especially those to Hilary and Prosper. Moreover, short summary chapters are also contained in the ecclesiastical archives."[48]

19. So, most beloved brothers, we have preferred to answer your questions briefly in a general reply. In addition, to the ex-

46. Fulgentius is referring to Augustine's last two treatises, *On the Predestination of the Saints* (Latin text in PL 44:959–92; English translation in FOTC 86, 218–70) and *On the Gift of Perseverance* (Latin text in PL 45:993–1034; English translation in FOTC 86, 271–337).

47. As explained in the introduction, Possessor was in Constantinople and was in contact with John Maxentius after the other Scythian monks had gone to Rome. Possessor wrote to Pope Hormisdas expressing concerns about Faustus's work *On Grace*.

48. Pope Hormisdas, *Letter to Bishop Possessor* (= *Ep.* 231), Latin text in CSEL 35, 700.

tent that the Lord deigns to give his slaves the grace of accurate speech, one of us has responded to all those questions which you made known that the above-mentioned brothers either perceived or articulated against grace and predestination. He did this with sufficient argumentation in three books dedicated to you,[49] and he produced seven books[50] against Faustus the Gallican's two books. When you examine them, you will immediately discover the degree to which discussion exposes, evident reasoning refutes, divine authority rejects, and the harmonious testimony of the earlier Fathers belies the ideas of the aforenamed Faustus, ideas that are contrary to the truth and profoundly inimical to the Catholic faith.

20. Furthermore, we hope that the Lord will bestow the help of his grace so generously that he will grant an increase of holy knowledge to those who think well, and that he will give believers help to recognize truth beyond what is required. For he is the one who makes those he has predestined to life participants in his grace, so that in all their good deeds they will submit their human choice to God's grace, that they will know that every excellent and every perfect gift descends from him,[51] and so that they will also know that they must seek help from the one who gives grace and perseverance to those he has predestined, so that they will receive grace for grace,[52] the gift of everlasting life.

49. Fulgentius, *The Truth about Predestination and Grace,* translated later in this volume.
50. Fulgentius, *Seven Books against Faustus* (a lost work).
51. Cf. Jas 1.17.
52. Cf. Jn 1.16.

FULGENTIUS'S *THE TRUTH ABOUT PREDESTINATION AND GRACE*

BOOK ONE[1]

O THE HOLY BROTHERS John the elder and Venerius the deacon.[2] I thank God that by his operation, you are the kind of men who contend very courageously and fervently on behalf of that grace by which we are saved. I am, however, saddened because some of our brothers, calling themselves Christians, strive to deny the Catholic faith. That is, they attribute the gifts of God's grace to the power or merit of the human will, as if our effort, without God's help, might avail for obeying the divine command, and as if the command were God's only in the sense that he commanded us to work, but did not himself accomplish in us what he commanded. And according to them, if God bestows something good on man, he should be viewed not as giving, but as rendering.[3] They go so far as to think that the gifts of divine kindness depend on the quality of human actions and to claim even in the case of little children who are divinely foreknown and predestined that nothing in the elect may be found to be a free blessing of the heavenly counsel. Furthermore, they think that mercy does not guide anyone by its free graciousness, but that the everlasting compensation of punishment and reward depends only on the future action of each person's own will.

---

1. As explained in the introduction, Fulgentius wrote this treatise in 523, after his return to Ruspe at the end of his second exile. The standard title is *De veritate praedestinationis et gratiae*. The Latin critical text may be found in CCL 91A, 458–548.

2. Since this is a treatise rather than a letter per se, the list of people to whom it is dedicated is much shorter than the lists of addressees for *Epp.* 17 and 15.

3. That is, giving that man what he deserves.

2. Also, I greatly marvel and grieve that this anomaly has crept into some people's thought. By this anomaly, they undoubtedly become enemies of God's grace, since they go so far as to assert that children are baptized on the merit of future works. They assert this in order that they may also claim something similar about children who, on the other hand, die without baptism according to the kind divine counsel. They claim that those who are snatched away to punishment apart from the grace of sacred washing are the ones who God surely foreknew would commit future evil deeds if they were to live somewhat longer here below. So they claim that out of kindness, God prematurely took them from the course of their present life (as if someone could be exempted from everlasting punishments or gain the rewards of eternal life without the benefit of holy redemption). Therefore, as long as they obstinately contradict the truth, they wound themselves with mortal guilt. They seemingly want to distinguish the merits of Esau and Jacob (who were certainly twin brothers from a single seed and begetting) in such a way that, just as they assert that Esau was condemned because of the foreknowledge of future works, they likewise contend that Jacob could be saved not by the free gift of divine goodness, but only by the foreknowledge of future works. The result is that they acknowledge God to be just toward both, but they do not believe that God has bestowed anything on either of them because of free mercy. Here the question chiefly concerns children and thus deals not with someone's personal blot from current sins but rather with the origin of the sinful state itself. In this case, everyone who does not wish to withdraw from the truth of apostolic faith and who desires to preserve the correctness of Catholic teaching by God's enlightenment, must truly believe and affirm with unwavering faith and confession, with no shadow of doubt, that the one true and good God (that is, the lofty and ineffable Trinity of one nature and essence) fashioned the first man's whole nature as good and perfect, without natural sin, without any flaws. One must also believe that God did not create a flesh that had to die or that the soul's blot was not from any sort of implanted sin, and therefore, one must believe that human nature possessed a created goodness given by

God and that original sin in those who were born subsequently derived from the voluntary transgression of the first man. In addition, one must believe that likewise both the stain of iniquity and the punishment of death flow to all men as a result of the wicked transgression and very just condemnation of the one man. For man was made in the image of God and [initially] received righteousness both in will and in work.

3. (II) Thus man was created in such a way that he would be able either to sin or not to sin in accordance with his own will. Therefore, he was appropriately punished for his fall through a voluntary transgression, for he was not constrained to sin by any natural tendency of the flesh or by any necessity lying within the soul. Although, as the Apostle teaches, he himself was not deceived, he nonetheless consented by his sinful will to the woman, who was deceived so as to fall into transgression. Thus he thoughtlessly inflicted the mortal wound on himself, so that in the one man whose soul and body died because of sin, all—however many would be born from that first sinful man through the intercourse of a man and a woman—were initially subjected to sin and death. Therefore, after the progenitor of all men sinned by his own will, he experienced the truth of the divine precept that he had heard: "In whichever day you eat of it, you will surely die,"[4] and he also experienced the justice of the avenging God. By one taste of the forbidden tree, he gave up righteousness, fell into punishment, and of his own accord, died spiritually in his soul. He also unwillingly received the punishment of bodily death.

4. Therefore, the voluntary death of the soul produced penal death for the body, and since death from sin gained possession of the first man, death from vengeance also followed immediately. From this it came about that the offense bound all his progeny, not only those who could sin by their own choice, but also those children who were not yet exercising their own will. And because sin prevailed, the offense bound the punish-

4. Gn 2.17.

ment to itself, and death both passed into and reigned over all men. Consequently, the Apostle also says, "Through one man sin entered into this world, and death through sin, and so death passed to all men, because in him all have sinned."[5] And again he says, "Death reigned from Adam to Moses, even in those who did not sin in the likeness of Adam's transgression."[6] Therefore, in himself a sinful man subjected all his descendants to his own sin, when he lost true freedom by doing wrong: "For by whatever someone has been overcome, by that also he has been made a slave,"[7] and, "Everyone who commits sin is a slave of sin."[8]

5. The one sole mediator between God and men, Jesus Christ, was born free from that servitude which holds children in bondage from birth. Even though he was born true man (yet without the presence of the lust of the flesh and without the intercourse of a man and a woman, but begotten by the Holy Spirit), he received true flesh from the flesh of his mother in such a way that, as true God, he assumed human nature but not the guilt from humanity's original sin. Likewise, he did not receive our sins in his body in order to do them, but he bore them in order to destroy them. For the authority of apostolic preaching truly teaches that "he did not sin, and deceit was not found in his mouth,"[9] and that "he bore our sins in his body upon the tree, so that, separated from sins, we might live righteously."[10] His mother, who bore only him, was a virgin before conception and remained a virgin, inviolate after his birth, for she did not sense sexual desire when she conceived in her womb the God who was miraculously made man. Nor did she undergo any corruption while she was bearing the Redeemer of the human race in the true flesh of our race. For the true God, taking on true flesh from the virgin and assuming from her the completion of his human body, did not deprive her of the grace of virginity. It was not fitting that the Creator God should bestow the purity of virginity on human flesh at creation, and that then the same God who received human flesh should take away the virginity of

---

5. Rom 5.12.   6. Rom 5.14.
7. 2 Pt 2.19.   8. Jn 8.34.
9. 1 Pt 2.22.   10. 1 Pt 2.24.

the flesh by which he was born and which he created in order to redeem it. He is himself the Second Man from heaven, who is said to be from heaven not because he wanted to bring the substance of his body with him from there, but because the form of a slave (which he, God, who created heaven and earth, assumed into the unity of his person) could have nothing of earthly desire within it.

6. For that reason, God did not send a heavenly body to earth, but in himself he elevated the true nature of the earthly body to heaven. Receiving this true earthly body from his mother's earthly body, he bore our sins in his flesh, for he had no guilt stemming either from original sin or from his own deeds. For Isaiah says that "he himself bore our sins."[11] Therefore, in order that among men also, where sin abounds, grace might abound all the more, he not only washed away that sin by which the earthly man defiled all his offspring, but also by his grace he forgives every believer for whatever is added to original sin by men's voluntary impulses and deeds. The blessed Apostle indeed teaches this when he says, "For judgment came through one man leading to condemnation, but grace, following many offenses, led to justification."[12] This is the grace of God that frees us through Jesus Christ our Lord, the work of whose grace the Liberator himself conveys to us, as he says, "If the Son sets you free, you will be truly free,"[13] and in another place, "For the Son of man has come to seek and to save that which had perished."[14]

7. This grace of God, by which we are saved, is not given to anyone by virtue of preceding good merit, nor yet is it denied to anyone by virtue of preceding evil merit. For the first man transmitted the demerits of his sin to all men whose flesh was conceived in accordance with the law of sin. Therefore, although there is no sin in children as a result of their own will, nevertheless, the parental blot inheres carnally in the newborn sons of wrath. That blot, to be sure, does not disrupt the well-arranged

11. Is 53.11.   12. Rom 5.16.
13. Jn 8.36.   14. Lk 19.10.

order of divine creation; but by the stain of paternal transgression, it does inflict horrid filth on those born subsequently. Therefore, no one is distinguished from that condemned lump on the basis of the foreknowledge of future works, but one is separated out on the basis of the compassionate potter's help and work. For this reason, vessels of mercy (which, although they are from the same lump, are freely made into vessels for honor) are set apart from the vessels of wrath (which were created for dishonor) in accordance with the gift of free justification. But, in order to show the grace that freely justifies sinners, apostolic preaching calls them not vessels of righteousness, but vessels of mercy, as blessed Paul says: "What if God, wanting to show his wrath and to make his power known, endured with much longsuffering the vessels of wrath fitted for destruction, so that he might show the riches of his glory in the vessels of mercy, which he prepared for glory?"[15] This mercy finds no one worthy, but instead finds all people unworthy, and from among them it makes worthy those whom it wills.

8. In accordance with this mercy, God went before Jacob and chose him before he was born, not according to the merit of any past or future human work, but according to the plan of the God who predestines. For the Apostle says that "while they had not yet been born or done anything good or bad, in order that God's electing purpose might stand, not because of works, but because of him who calls, it was declared to Rebecca that the older would serve the younger."[16] So in order that God might prefer the younger brother over the older, there was no sort of merit for any past or future work, inasmuch as the guilt stemming from the same lawful and righteous act of intercourse remained equal in the case of both. Therefore, this was accomplished by the grace of divine goodness, grace that was never bestowed in such a way that it might reveal some good merits in man, but was bestowed so that grace itself might confer merits on those who did not have any. For if grace had ceased and a distinction had been made between the one to be chosen and

15. Rom 9.22–23.
16. Rom 9.11–12.

the other to be condemned solely on the basis of foreknowledge of the human works of these children, the Apostle would never have said that "not because of works, but because of him who calls, it was declared to her that the older would serve the younger." For doubtless the Apostle would have said "by works," if he had known anything about good merits of future human works. But since he knew that the only merits either possessed were the merits of condemnation, he attributed the basis of election only to the purpose of divine kindness. For this reason, of those two brothers who issued from the same begetting by our father Isaac, God received them together in the seed of conception and brought them forth together into the light of birth, but by divine mercy alone he set apart from the lump of condemnation the one whom he willed to set apart. This one's protection was the predestination of freely given gifts, not the foreknowledge of future merits. For in this way God's plan remained in compliance with election, so that free election might be in conformity with God's plan. For God's will is the cause of election; election is not the cause of his will. And in this way God was merciful in dealing with the one whom he freely elected, so that he might not be unjust in dealing with the one whom he rejected. For he accepted one freely, but the other he forsook justly. Indeed, "all the ways of the Lord are mercy and truth."[17]

9. Consequently, the free goodness of the compassionate God and the severity of God who judges justly determined that the brothers would not both receive the free gift of mercy and at the same time that they would not cast lots to determine which one should perish, although there was originally one source of both. For this reason, even before it was said through the prophet, "Jacob I have loved, but Esau I have hated,"[18] the prophetic word stipulated nothing of any past or future work, but spoke only of their birth, as Malachi said: "Was not Esau Jacob's brother?" and "Jacob I have loved, but Esau I have hated, says the Lord."[19] Why then does the prophet speak not of some

17. Ps 24.10, following LXX (25.10 modern).
18. Mal 1.2–3; cf. Rom 9.13.
19. Mal 1.2–3.

difference in works, but only of the fraternity of birth, if in fact
people were supposed to remember that good works characterized the one who was beloved and evil works characterized the
one who was hated, so that neither was there any personal favoritism toward the one who was beloved, nor was any unjust
condemnation to be thought of in the case of the one who was
condemned? Fraternity in itself signifies no difference in works,
by which one may distinguish one from another by comparing
merits. Therefore, apart from remembering works, God offers
no other reason why he loved one of the twin brothers and hated the other, except so that we might recognize through their
common bond of conception and birth, constituting them as
brothers, that each one is by equal merit bound into the lump
of condemnation, and so that merciful goodness might freely
distinguish one of them from that lump, and so that God's just
severity might not be unjust in leaving the other one in that
lump. Indeed, the condemnation of any child would be unjust
if mortal propagation had received no contagion of sin from
the paternal root. Indeed, divinely inspired Scripture testifies
not only that no one can be clean of filth even if he has lived
only one day upon earth,[20] but also that even when a member
of the human race is legitimate and conceived in wedlock, he is
still not free from the guilt of iniquity.

10. At this point, let no sensible person suppose that an un-
founded accusation needs to be set up in opposition to the
truth. For as we seek to follow the doctrine of the holy Fathers
with God's help, we say that the blot of original sin lies in the
conception of the children, not in legitimate intercourse within
marriage. For we know that marriage was established by God
as a good thing from the beginning of the human race. Consequently, there is no doubt that apostolic teaching commends
honorable matrimony in all ways, as well as the immaculate
marriage bed. Therefore, although marriage in faith and love
produces a gift praised by God and dedicated to himself—pure
offspring—nevertheless the children are tainted by the stain of
the first man's sin. Therefore, it is good and not evil when a

20. Cf. Jb 14.4.

man is born of a good marriage, but he would not be evil even if he were born of adultery or fornication. For God conferred the gift of fruitfulness on human nature. In truth, the evil of sexual desire is not a creation of God; it is the penalty for sin. Hence, even the purity of marriage does not produce a pure man, for he is begotten with the intervention of defiled sexual desire. To be sure, nuptial integrity does not love that sexual desire, but the necessity of mortal propagation in marriage tolerates it. Sexual desire itself defiled those conceived, although it cannot induce or drive believing parents to engage in forbidden intercourse. For that reason, the holy David, born of a legitimate and faithful marriage, grieved very sorrowfully over the blot of fleshly generation, in these words: "Behold, I was conceived in iniquity; and in sin did my mother nourish me in the womb."[21]

11. Since these things are so, it is impossible that anyone who is conceived in iniquity might be born without bondage to iniquity. In the decision by which God released Jacob from that bondage while rejecting Esau, no human merits were involved, but only the goodness of divine grace. To be sure, both were circumcised with a visible bodily circumcision that was divinely bestowed before the time of our fathers as a sign of the righteousness of faith. But only Jacob, who was freely justified by God, received that true circumcision of the heart that is according to the spirit, not the letter, whose praise is not from men but from God. Indeed, although Esau himself was also circumcised in the flesh, nonetheless he was not removed from the lump of perdition by the gift of divine love and election. He was certainly circumcised in the flesh, but that fact was of no advantage to him because in no way did he receive spiritual circumcision that could deliver him from the knowledge of the flesh, which is inimical to God. Therefore, before the world even existed, God hated the earthly man's iniquity that remained in Esau, and he justly relegated Esau to punishment. Moreover, in Esau's brother God did not foreknow any good works that might issue from the man and lead God to choose and love him, but God prepared the grace of justification for him before the world ex-

21. Ps 50.7, loosely following LXX (51.5 modern).

isted, so that through grace God would bestow on him not just the beginning of a good will, but also the achievement of good work. Nor did God find in Jacob good merits, but he set him free by the free blessing of mercy. "And he said to Moses, 'I will be merciful to whom I am merciful, and I will show mercy to whom I will be merciful.'"[22] "Therefore, it is not of the one who wills, nor of the one who runs, but of God, who shows mercy."[23]

12. Therefore, God granted his grace freely to the one who had been born[24] because he prepared the grace freely for him while he was still yet to be born. Indeed, God grants to the good whatever good they have in respect of will or work, and he even preserves the things he has bestowed. It is true that God could never have prepared evil works or granted them to the unjust and godless, works for which they live to their condemnation. Nor has he planted in them evil wills, by which they might culpably desire unrighteous things, but he has prepared for them the punishment of eternal fire so that they might feel his avenging justice while they are in everlasting flame. Therefore, the evil will of men is not from God, and for this reason the just Judge punishes that will in the men themselves, because the good Creator does not recognize the order of his creation in such a will. For this reason, God the avenger condemns persistence in iniquity and the stubbornness of haughty necks because these attitudes do not arise from his generosity. But for those whom God makes heirs of his kingdom, he prepares a good will freely, gives it freely, and even provides them with perseverance. For he has freely and mercifully prepared the merits to which he will grant rewards, and then to these merits he indeed justly returns the rewards the merits have earned.

13. Next, there is no doubt that in these two brothers a figure of two groups of people has been established, one group to be saved, the other to be condemned. Yet salvation is not thus bestowed on the former group because of works, just as condemnation is not rendered to the latter because of works. But

22. Ex 33.19.   23. Rom 9.15.
24. That is, Jacob.

one group received the gift of saving grace, which it did not deserve, and the other received the destruction of just condemnation according to its merit. In one group the merits of condemnation were found, and on the other group the free merits of glorification were conferred for the sake of its justification. The one group had within itself what was displeasing to God, but the other received from God himself what was pleasing to God whom it was going to please. Consequently, in all who are being handed over to the Gehenna of fire, just severity finds the sort of evil merit that it punishes. In as many people as the evil merit was originally found, in these also it is increased by the fault of their own will. Children are an exception, since their will cannot yet be free to choose righteousness and flee sin, because at their tender age reason is asleep and not yet active. But the rest, who are old enough to have the use of reason, either do not come to faith or withdraw from the faith because the fault of their own will is increased. But whatever anyone's physical age, from birth to decrepit old age, no one is found worthy of justification. In spite of being unworthy, a person is justified by free goodness, in order that he may become righteous when he had been unrighteous, may become God's friend when he had been his enemy, and may be absolved of guilt. And no person is snatched from the power of darkness and transferred into the kingdom of God's beloved Son, unless the Lord of glory, who freely saves and justly condemns, has freely deigned to go before him. The merciful and just God justly punishes the perverse will that he does not mercifully correct, for he finds in it a perversity that he himself did not make. But he himself freely prepares the good will, freely gives it, himself helps it, himself perfects it.

14. (VII.) Certainly, therefore, let us affirm that no men can attain perfection through their own efforts, nor can they lay hold of the beginning of righteousness, but let us affirm rather that all men who become good are preceded by divine righteousness. Let us affirm that God's help brings progress and perseverance to them so that after receiving a good will, they may not fall. Let us affirm that grace is given to no man be-

cause of past or future merits, but that all men's good merits are both begun and perfected by the gift and help of grace itself. Indeed, the wicked (those whom the just judgment of God abandons to their iniquity), even if they are said to be deprived of the sacrament because of the guilt of original sin, are handed over to the punishment of eternal fire because of the merit of subsequent (that is, of their own) sins. For the merciful and just God justly punishes human sins (original and voluntary), either in children or in grown people, unless he has mercifully washed these sins away. For he is himself the good and true God who made man but did not create sin in him. And he has never found in any men good merits and works on the basis of which he might save them, but he himself changes both their wills and their works when he justifies them by his free mercy. And by the certain and unchangeable steadfastness of his foreknowledge concerning the vessels of mercy, God did not foreknow any gift except the gift of his own grace, a gift he knew he had to bestow in order to produce merits that earn rewards and to give rewards to the merits. For God himself both gives free goodness to the human will and helps the good will produce works. He himself even foreknew those works of human evil that the vessels of wrath would commit, works that were certainly going to come about.

15. Therefore, according to correct faith and clear truth, in the case of a child who is taken from this life without the benefit of the second birth, we must admit that just as God foreknew the child's future death, which was actually going to happen, so also it is absurd to say that God foreknew the child's future sins which were not going to occur. For God, the author of all things, has not foreknown the things that would not be done as if they were to be done. For we know that God's foreknowledge is so true and unchangeable that the things he foreknows as going to happen will surely happen, and that he may not foreknow something that will not happen according to his foreknowledge as if it were going to happen. In fact, even a mutable creature thinks only of things that are actually going to happen, and a mutable creature's mind is nothing like that of the im-

mutable Creator. Thus nothing is past or future to God. All the things that he foreknows must happen are present to him in such a way that after they have happened, they cannot be past in his eyes, because just as he knows things past, in the same way he also knows things future. For all things that change or pass away with time still continue in his knowledge without passage of time or change. But as for the fact that God's foreknowledge does not include those things that are not going to happen, but includes only those things that must happen, the book of the prophet Daniel testifies with these words: "God, you are the one who knows all things secret, who knows all things before they happen."[25] God, therefore, knows in his eternal foreknowledge what is going to take place, so that it will take place in actuality.

16. (VIII.) It is therefore absurd to say that God has foreknown that a child, if he were to live, would be ungodly, when in fact what God foreknew was that this child was going to live no longer than he did, that the child would not reach an age at which he might live in an ungodly way, and indeed that the child was going to be removed from this world as an infant. And in such a child, there has been no foreknown sinful period of life, hence it could not have happened that the iniquity of a future period that would not come about could be foreknown, since the period of a child's life right after birth can pass without any actual sin at all, but no actual human sin can be committed without the passage of some period of time. For it is not absurd to call things foreknown about a future period of life "works," whether good or bad, but it is absurd to claim foreknowledge of any human work for a period of life in which it is shown that a man is not going to exist. And we rightly say that just as God did not foreknow the original sin of anyone except those who were going to be conceived, so also he did not foreknow the actual sins of any except those who were going to live.[26] Therefore, it is right to say that God foreknew the works of those whose life has not been prevented from coming to completion.

25. Dn 13.42.
26. That is, those who would live long enough to commit actual sins.

17. It remains simply to conclude that whoever thinks God has foreknowledge of future works that were not going to take place judges that some part of God's foreknowledge (which he acknowledges as true) is a lie because it does not exist. It is false to say that anything which will never be present is going to happen in the future. For God's knowledge cannot have anything false within it, for falsity cannot belong to truth. So by the foreknowledge of truth, which does not receive falsity in itself, God foreknows that what must happen will happen, just as he foreknows that what is not to happen will not happen. Therefore, God did not foreknow any sins in a child that the child did not commit before he died. For if he had foreknown the things that were to happen, they certainly would have happened. Nor did he know the future things that he foreknew would not happen. Accordingly, it must be admitted that, just as the child died, so God foreknew that he was going to die. God's foreknowledge is in no way in error, because just as he foreknew that the world was to be made, so also he made it just as he foreknew it was to be made. Likewise, just as individual things were made in the world itself, or are made, or must be made, so they always had to be made according to God's foreknowledge just as they followed in his work, or were definitely going to follow. Therefore, God did not foreknow any man as doing something which that man was not going to do, in the same way that his foreknowledge includes any of those things that men either have done, or do, or will do at some time. For it is right to say that the true God foreknows those works of men which are begun concerning things, persons, and times. But when neither a thing, nor a person, nor time is in question, it is sure that there is no work that one might claim to be divinely foreknown. But it is inconsistent with the truth to say that in God's foreknowledge something is going to happen, when in many ways one can prove that it will not happen. So one may show that from the perspective of the future, the present in no way is going to happen or has happened, since it is in no way possible for an event to be called "future" if that event will not be able to be called "present" at some time.

18. (IX.) Therefore, concerning a child who did nothing, God foreknew that he would do nothing. To be sure, we cannot know why God did not remove original sin from him, yet we must in no way doubt that God acted justly. For although the incomprehensible depth of God's counsel is hidden from us (who are not only created from nothing but are also bearing the blot of sin—a blot which, just as grace continually washes it from the human sons of God, so weakness produces it again in abundance), nevertheless, the fact that God acts justly has been made clear to us, because there is no iniquity in God. About this, it is written: "God is faithful, and in him there is no iniquity. The Lord God is righteous and holy,"[27] and in another place: "The judgments of God are true and righteous in themselves."[28] We also believe that even the negligence of parents and that of any people at all somehow relates to the hidden depth of these judgments (for "the judgments of God are a great deep"),[29] just as we do not doubt that the concern of parents for their child whom they bring to baptism must be ascribed to the gifts of divine grace. If indeed the parents are not gifted with godliness and a worthy manner of living, God, who also makes good use of men's evil intentions, works the benefit of grace in a child by utilizing the concern of evil parents. If indeed the believing parents are good, the good intention of the parents not only benefits the child, but also accrues to the parents themselves so that they may deserve a future reward. "For God, the one working both to will and to accomplish according to his good will,"[30] himself bestows the grace of good intention on those parents who believe in him, so that they may conduct themselves with pious concern for their child until he attains the life-giving healing of holy regeneration. Neither their action nor the pious concern of their good intention, however, would be sufficient unless God should deign to go before the child with the free gift of his mercy. Truly, the good intention that God inspires in the parents for the regeneration of the child stimulates them

27. Dt 32.4.
28. Ps 18.10, following LXX (19.9 modern).
29. Ps 35.7 (36.6 modern).
30. Phil 2.13.

to ensure that the child lives until the time he attains to the washing of saving water. But truly the effect of this regeneration does not come from any man's will or manner of living, but from God who has mercy, who both stirs up the parents' will and gives aid to the willing ones.

19. Therefore, the Redeemer works mercifully so that a child may be redeemed by the work of regeneration. He prepares opportunities, provides wills, grants persons, and arranges places. And he does this not only in the case of children, but also in the case of adults. Accordingly, we read in the book of the Acts of the Apostles that an angel suddenly instructed Philip (who was in Samaria) to go down the road that leads from Jerusalem to Gaza, where he might not only preach the mystery of the Christian faith to the visiting eunuch (who was not even inquiring about the benefit of regeneration), but might even administer the sacrament of baptism to him.[31] Notice how the Holy Spirit, going before the eunuch with his grace, favored him with a person who was a truthful preacher. He even gave Philip the occasion to preach when he mercifully stirred the eunuch's mind to read Isaiah. In his free goodness, God even provided a place by leading them to a pool. He completed the work of saving grace in the eunuch. This same eunuch, by the illumination of the Spirit, believed that Christ was the Son of God, and coming to the pool, he earnestly asked for the administration of the sacred dipping, and he departed not merely baptized but also filled with the Holy Spirit.

20. And who advised Cornelius the centurion when an angel was sent to instruct him to summon the Apostle Peter,[32] if not the one who freely imparted to the same centurion the gift of both fearing God and acting worthily? But so that God might remember Cornelius's prayers and alms, he earlier remembered Cornelius himself, not for some good work that Cornelius had done, but for his own pleasure, so that he might impart to him the gift of fearing God, by which gift he inspired in him a zeal

31. See Acts 8.26–40.
32. See Acts 10.5.

for alms and a love of holy prayer. Therefore, the one who found in Cornelius that which was pleasing in his sight was God himself, who granted Cornelius the grace to please him. For it is God himself about whom the Apostle says, "Now may the God of peace, who brought our Lord Jesus (that great shepherd of the sheep) back from the dead through the blood of the eternal covenant, prepare you for every good work by working in you what is pleasing in his sight, so that you may do his will."[33] In Cornelius there was so much divine grace that he was advised to summon Peter to himself, and the Holy Spirit also commanded Peter concerning the men Cornelius had sent who were coming to him. He not only commanded him to go with them, but he even removed every sort of fear or doubt, and he strengthened those whom he himself had sent. Finally, the Holy Spirit said to this same blessed Peter, "Behold, three men are seeking you. Arise therefore, and go down, and go with them without hesitating, for I have sent them."[34] We also read that the apostles wanted to go to Bithynia and Asia, but were forbidden by the Holy Spirit.[35] And after the Lord cast Saul prostrate on the ground by his own voice, he visited Ananias and sent him to baptize Paul.[36] And Paul, writing to the Corinthians, clearly affirms that a sacred, earnest care was divinely inspired in his disciple Titus, because of which care he was troubled about them. For he speaks this way: "But thanks be to God, who put the same earnest care for you into the heart of Titus."[37]

21. (X.) The sacred Scriptures have made it clear that no one resists God's will, that no one changes his providence, and that no one understands his judgments. Therefore, in kindness God displays the abounding riches of his grace toward all those whom he separates from the condemned lump and makes into vessels of mercy for honor and glory. While men are applying human reason [to this process], God either leads the appropriate people to salvation or denies it to them, while certainly maintaining justice for some and bestowing mercy on others. Since

33. Heb 13.20–21.
34. Acts 10.19–20.
35. See Acts 16.7.
36. See Acts 9.1–19.
37. 2 Cor 8.16.

all this is the case, why shall we not also believe very confidently that infants must be baptized, and why shall we not freely proclaim that the diligence of parents[38] is attributable to the grace of the God who redeems, and indeed that their negligence[39] is attributable to the justice of the God who judges? This does not mean that God causes one to neglect a good work, since God could never be the cause of any evil work. Rather, it means that the more a good will (itself given by God) advances in love, the more it bears a greater concern for the salvation of any soul. In truth, by its own merit an evil will either does not receive the grace of love or loses it, and since such a will does not turn away from its negligent apathy, it is abandoned in its darkness and becomes increasingly blind.

22. Therefore, as God works mercifully in men, he also provides assistance from other people and from opportune moments, and when a child is actually baptized, this act provides the occasion for the Lord to accomplish his own work of holy cleansing. For God, by the free power of the sacrament, cleanses a child who is not willing, who is not running, who is ignorant of the faith and ignorant of salvation and its usefulness, who is not asking for regeneration, and in whom there can be no confession of faith. The God who does all that himself either stirs up the minds of the parents to act on behalf of the child's redemption or stirs up the wills of some believers so that, as they work out their own salvation with fear and trembling[40] and he advances them toward the reward of a good recompense, their pious concern may also lead the infant to salvation. Even so, if the one who has given a cup of cool water to one of the least of the disciples in Christ's name (by which action only a man's body is nourished) will not lose his reward,[41] how will the one who lives with pious concern and is diligent for the salvation of the child's flesh and soul not have his reward?

---

38. That is, diligence in having their children baptized.
39. That is, negligence in the sense of not having their children baptized.
40. Cf. Phil 2.12.
41. See Mt 10.42.

23. (XI.) And for this reason, one must believe that God gives this good will to pious parents so that they will not disregard the fact that the fruit of their flesh, which they know was carnally produced and polluted by the contagion of original sin, must be cleansed by spiritual regeneration. Furthermore, God gives this will so that they will not so much desire to have a temporal heir, as they will desire and diligently work so that their son may become a co-heir of Christ with them, and also so that the son whom they now have of mortal seed who will pass away mortally may become for them an eternal brother reborn of water and the Holy Spirit under God the Father. Nevertheless, there is no doubt that God has bestowed this laudable will on those parents to whom he has imparted the grace of holy love through the Holy Spirit. They too come to eternal life, not because they, in the body of this death, give birth to children who will die, but because as they live in the fear of God, they are diligent to hasten with their children to the benefit of the second birth and, so that this second birth may be accomplished in their children by their work,[42] they, out of their Christian love, bring forth to baptism those to whom they gave birth through human fertility. Likewise, they do not permit those children who have been baptized to fall away through crime and shameful behavior, but they strive to nourish them and bring them up, as the Apostle commanded, "in the discipline and admonition of the Lord."[43] They desire more that their children be pleasing to God than that they be rich or famous in this world.

24. In fact, up to this point, it is evident that parents ought to bring the grace of baptism to their children quickly, so that not only will good believers be accustomed to doing so diligently, but so that even parents who do not belong to the number of God's children will do so—parents who, in spite of being called "believers" in name, are proven to deny the faith by their works, since they engage in practices that cannot be consistent with the faith. As a case in point—so that I may not speak of others—do we not see certain disgraceful women anxiously bringing their

42. That is, the work of having the child baptized.
43. Eph 6.4.

children (whom they acknowledge to be the result not of marriage, but of fornication) to the grace of baptism, and do we not see them taking great care lest the children who were born of them carnally be deprived of spiritual birth? Thus the women who (for the most part) conceive and bear them reluctantly hasten to the church with them willingly and with trembling. Moreover, since they do not address their sin of fornication, they remain in their iniquities, yet they eagerly desire that their children be released from the bonds of original sin. Thus our good God causes the pious will of good parents to advance toward the accomplishment of grace not only for their children but also for the parents themselves. In fact, he even causes iniquitous parents to be diligently concerned about obtaining blessings for their children, on whom God himself confers grace. Even those who annul the benefit of baptism for themselves by their evil deeds are aware of what the grace of baptism confers. And although they yield to mortal lust in their own flesh, they nonetheless yield more to recognized truth when it comes to the fruit of their flesh.

25. Indeed, some Christian parents of children, oblivious to Christian love and to their own salvation no less than their children's, are unconcerned about their children's need for regeneration. (It is, however, difficult to believe this could happen because it is far removed from religious sentiment.) Let such parents hear not our words, but the Apostle's thought about this wickedness, and let them tremble violently. He says, "If anyone has no concern for his own, and especially for those of his own household, he has denied the faith, and is worse than an infidel."[44] And just as no one's denial of the faith comes from God, so also God does not give permission for anyone to blame the divine will when he neglects any good work. And just as it is the work of divine grace when parents bear pious concern for their children's regeneration, so also is it the work of divine judgment when God abandons evil wills as parents prize the material welfare of their children to such an extent that they neglect the welfare of their children's souls. In such cases, they are con-

44. 1 Tm 5.8.

cerned about the earthly life of the children who are going to die anyway, but they do not fear whether their children should die with the guilt of eternal condemnation upon them, and as a result, they bring maximum guilt upon themselves and spiritually become the cruelest of murderers. Because of their apathy, their own acts of neglect serve the cause of diabolical gain, and as they please our most wicked enemy, they provoke the good king by their evil works. Therefore, just as we must humbly praise God ("all of whose ways are mercy and truth")[45] when he grants grace, so no man can rightly blame him when he withholds grace. In fact, such are God's goodness and righteousness that he can freely and mercifully redeem whomever he wants to redeem: "For who resists his will?"[46] Truly he is neither willing nor able to condemn anyone unjustly at any time, for "the Lord our God is upright, and there is no unrighteousness in him,"[47] and "our wickedness highlights God's righteousness," nor is "God who takes vengeance" "unrighteous."[48]

26. (XII.) Therefore, if anyone wishes to consider the wondrous and incomprehensible power of divine grace, let him consider with humble and pious heart how parents (most of whom are pious, faithful, diligent, and concerned) hasten to baptize their children, and how the children who die without baptism do so in the arms of parents hastening to baptism. So let us consider two children who have died without baptism: one whom the harmful indifference of the parents neglected; the other whose parents' pious concern was definitely not lacking but could serve no purpose because he was taken prematurely by a swift death. He actually died in the arms of those carrying him to baptism. Before he might gain the blessing for the future life, he encountered an immediate death and died before the blot was removed. He was snatched away to punishment before being led to grace. If in the case of one of these two, we tell him that his parents' negligence harmed him, let us tell the other

45. Ps 24.10, following LXX (25.10 modern).
46. Rom 9.19.
47. Ps 91.16, following LXX (92.15 modern).
48. Rom 3.5.

why the effect of salvation was denied him, to whom neither his parents' desire nor way of life could have been advantageous. Or are we to tell him that by God's decree he was foreseen to be ungodly and so we think that he was actually helped by the blessing of a lamentable death? Who would say such a thing? Or who would not understand that such a death snatched the dying child prematurely not from condemnation, but from salvation? Indeed, his condemnation was not mitigated, but he was denied redemption, and it was not decreed that he suffer less, but he was taken away lest he be set free. And in this situation, did not the parents' pious will and course of life come from God? But still, they were of no advantage because it was not God's will that the child be baptized. Because of his profound and righteous judgment, God imparted to them a God-fearing concern for their child, but he was not willing to bestow the living remedy on the child. In fact, God likewise imparted the gift of love to holy David so that he might command that his son Absalom be spared lest he die in his transgression,[49] but it was not God's will that wicked Absalom be preserved for future penitence. In this way, he showed what the holy will of an upright man was obligated to do, but divine justice worked what it knew to be necessary.

27. And if anyone considered that situation with a pious mind, would he not be delighted by the sweetness of divine mercy in the same way that he would be terrified by the depth of divine judgment? For sometimes a child is born to believers, even to those who (as we have already said) are solicitous with godly faith and love for the redemption of their child, but he dies before he is washed by the sacred water of baptism. Another child is born to unbelieving parents who do not enthusiastically or even tepidly desire his salvation; in fact, they do not even desire it at all. This child is violently taken away from his parents or kidnapped by the order of a dispensation from above and is brought to holy baptism because of the devoted love of certain believers, and soon after being baptized he departs this life. If one considers the first state of these two children, both are equally children of wrath because they are both simultane-

49. See 2 Sm 18.5.

ously bound by the same debt of original sin. And where the states of the two are completely equal, their merits surely cannot be said to be unequal. Therefore, there is no difference in the states of the children that might cause one to be elected and the other to be rejected. In fact, if one takes the will of the parents into consideration, the Christian parents earnestly desired that their child be baptized and hastened eagerly to have it done, but their child was prevented by death from being baptized and was assigned to the eternal fires. On the other hand, the one born to unbelievers and brought to the grace of baptism against the will of his parents was made an heir of God and co-heir of Christ. Why did God foresee a future in which parental love could confer nothing on the one and hostile parental cruelty was very beneficial to the other? Who can penetrate the depth of God's judgments? Nevertheless, who does not understand here both the mercy of free kindness and the justice of divine severity? For inasmuch as there are no merits in the two children's acts and no dissimilarity in their states, it is indeed clear to us that both were bound by the chains of original sin, but it is indeed hidden from us why they were not both set free from those chains.

28. (XIII.) Consequently, let us recognize that we can never understand why God, after rejecting one, should freely snatch the other from the lump of perdition. Yet we ought to know for certain "that the Lord is gracious and compassionate, long-suffering, abounding in mercy, and true."[50] He gives mercy to the one whom he sets free in such a way that he does not at all disregard justice and truth concerning the one whom he condemns. Therefore, the one who has been set free has received grace, and may he always praise it. In truth, he who has been condemned has found justice, and so he has no grounds for reproaching God, for it is written: "that every mouth may be closed, and all the world may become subject to God."[51] Thus, one recognizes the surpassing grace of God in the good things of his life, and the other finds in his condemnation not a false

50. Ps 85.15, following LXX (86.15 modern).
51. Rom 3.19.

foreknowledge of future things that he was not going to do, but the true guilt of his first parent.

29. Someone will say, "Why did God not bestow free mercy on both, since one sin bound both?" To such a person, we respond in view of the incomprehensible, but sound, depth of God's judgments, that the reason they were not both set free or both condemned is that God can never will or do evil. This God commanded with just severity that payment of a debt be required of one, and because of his free goodness, even ordered the other to be forgiven. In both we recognize with certainty God's free kindness (which can freely forgive all sin without any merits stemming from works), because one of them is absolved and the other condemned. Indeed, the justice of God (whom no sin can ever please) appears in the one who is condemned. Consequently, merciful absolution cannot be blameworthy, nor can just punishment. Goodness, which is overcome by no evil, absolves the guilty, and justice, which does not rejoice in sins, punishes the guilty. Therefore, when God saves men, he grants grace by his own good works, and when he punishes sinners for their iniquities, he renders justice for evil human works. In the former case, he indeed repairs what they have become; in the latter, he judges what they have done. "For all have sinned and come short of God's glory."[52] For even those who have not sinned by their involvement in works, all draw original sin from the transgression of the first man.

30. Moreover, let us not think that the secret counsel of the divine will is unjust because it justifies one ungodly person and condemns the other. It is hidden from us, but let no one therefore doubt that it is divine justice, for no man can search this out. Accordingly, let us simply exhibit humility of heart, and let us sing with the prophet the mercy and judgment of God,[53] while we restrain our inclination to search this out, so as to avoid discussing what we cannot understand. For he warns us by Holy Scripture, saying, "Do not try to search out things that are

52. Rom 3.23.
53. Cf. Ps 100.1, following LXX (101.1 modern).

too difficult for you, or try to discover what is beyond your powers; but always ponder the things that the Lord has commanded you, and do not be curious about his many works."[54] Truly we waste our time with unnecessary seeking, when no amount of discovery justifies it, for harmful curiosity immediately slips into sin if human weakness ever fails to take stock of its own limits. In this very deep secret of the divine will, we should rather learn that nothing else accords with our salvation except that each of us learn to say humbly with David, "Your knowledge is too wonderful for me; it is great, I cannot attain to it."[55] Likewise, let us join our God-fearing cry with that of blessed Paul, who says, "O the depth of the riches of both the wisdom and knowledge of God! How unsearchable are his judgments and his ways past finding out! For who has known the mind of the Lord? Or who has become his counselor?"[56] In this passage, before speaking of the unsearchable judgments of God, blessed Paul first speaks appropriately of the depth of his wisdom and knowledge. With those words, he has indeed stopped every complaint and rash voice whatsoever that has been raised against God's just judgment. For it is certain that the role of the person and office of a judge is not to neglect knowledge when adjudicating a case, not to abandon the straight path of wisdom when judging, lest he at any time be prone to give an ignorant judgment hastily against an unproven "fact" or be found to suppress a proven fact because of his foolish perversity. Therefore, God is not ignorant that he might judge rashly, nor is he foolish that he might condemn someone unjustly, for prophetic authority proclaims of him: "The Lord is righteous and loves righteousness: his countenance beholds uprightness."[57]

31. (XIV.) Accordingly, God is worthy of eternal praise in all his works, for he freely forgives the iniquity of all those whom he calls and justifies according to his purpose, and he remains blamelessly just toward all those he punishes. There is only one

54. Sir 3.22.
55. Ps 138.6, following LXX (139.6 modern).
56. Rom 11.33–34.
57. Ps 10.8, following LXX (11.7 modern).

state for adults and children who finish the course of their present lives without baptism, in unbelief. Because of their great association with original sin, both adults and children will go together into the eternal fire that has been prepared for the devil and his angels,[58] because the grace of the Savior did not destroy in them the contract by which the deceiver's wickedness subjected them to himself. But on this point the condition of the adults is worse because, after enjoying the faculty of reason, they still reject or neglect the saving remedy of regeneration, without which not only will they be unable to possess the kingdom, but they will also be subject to graver punishments. For those who despise the kindness of God, "in accordance with their hard and impenitent heart, treasure up for themselves wrath for the day of wrath and of the revelation of the just judgments of God, who will render to each one according to his works."[59] Consequently, they will burn in the eternal fires (fires in which those who die without baptism will burn, even children who have done nothing good or bad) not only because of original sin, but they will also be tormented much worse because of their evil will, in proportion as they add yet more of their own wickedness. In this matter of original sin, to be sure, eternal death embraces both, but the punishment for the wickedness of wills and acts increases. For it is worse to refuse to seek the benefit of redemption because of an ungodly will than to be incapable of coming to that benefit because one is hindered by a truly tender age. And he who adds his own burden to the burden received from our first parents is even harder pressed than the one who bears only the burden of another.

32. A Christian should not doubt at all that the grace of God goes before those who are cleansed of the burdens of original or even personal sins. Concerning the generosity of his grace, certain people—after giving slight consideration to the situation—greatly err in thinking that grace is given to all men equally, even to those who woefully lack the benefits of that same grace. Indeed, those who think in this way lack grace themselves, as

58. Cf. Mt 25.41.
59. Rom 2.5–6.

long as they do not believe that the grace itself is necessary for a man to receive that grace. God does not give the grace unless he first produces a good will in the man. And may each one who receives grace gain as much as God, in accordance with his free mercy, pours into the heart of the one who accepts it.

33. (XV.) Therefore, dearest brothers, in certain particular matters on which we raise questions because of some cloud of obscurity, we should hold to the statements of the holy Fathers, for the prevenient mercy of God freely illuminated them so that they might believe, and subsequently instructed them spiritually so that they might teach. For these men who held the truth of the apostolic preaching in all things most certainly knew and wrote down in books and letters what we must recognize: that the grace of God is not given indiscriminately to all men. To be sure, grace is God's free gift. For this reason, the Apostle says that "each one has his own gift from God, one in this way, and another in that."[60] The grace that God gives freely to vessels of mercy begins when he illumines the heart; it does not find the will of man to be good, but makes it good. And so that the will may be chosen, grace chooses it first, and the will is not received or highly esteemed unless grace is at work in a man's heart. Therefore, both the reception of grace and even the desire for grace are the work of grace itself. No one will be able to desire or seek that grace, nor even to recognize it, unless he first receives grace from the one who (apart from any preceding works or good desires) bestows it for the very purpose that grace may itself prepare, give, illumine, enliven, preserve, and perfect the will in which it will always remain.

34. (XVI.) Therefore, so that we may know, love, and earnestly seek God's grace, he gives it beforehand to a man who does not know, love, desire, or seek it earnestly. Therefore, grace makes itself known, loved, desired, and earnestly sought. Just as the Lord said through the prophet Ezekiel, when the Lord removes from men their stony heart and gives them a heart of flesh,[61] he does indeed change the human will by the

---

60. 1 Cor 7.7.   61. See Ezek 36.26.

illumination of his grace. This change comes about not from human choice, but from the right hand of the Most High.[62] The sons of men, whose hearts are burdened, who love what is vain and seek what is false,[63] do not themselves bring forth a good will to love and seek after truth, but instead they receive from the Lord the gift of a good will. For it is written that "the will is prepared by the Lord."[64] A good will is given by "the true light that illumines every man who comes into this world"[65] so that a man may believe in God and love God faithfully. God governs and rules the will continually so that a man's faith will not fail or his love grow cold. That is why our Savior says to Peter, "I have prayed for you, Peter, that your faith may not fail,"[66] for "faith that works through love"[67] characterizes the saints. Therefore, just as no one can possess the beginning of a good will unless he has been illuminated by the prevenient mercy of God (for "the will is prepared by the Lord," and again it is written: "My God, his mercy will come before me"),[68] so also no one will be able to maintain the same good will until the end unless he has been continually preserved by the same continuing mercy. For blessed David says to God, "Your mercy follows me all the days of my life."[69] Therefore, the mercy that freely goes before an evil man so that he will be changed for the better, also continues to guide the one whom it makes good so that he will not be changed for the worse.

35. Therefore, every good thing pertaining to the will and to work can belong to a man if it is given by the generosity of prevenient grace and is preserved by the assistance of the same continuing grace. Grace precedes the evil man so that he may, through the gracious God, begin to have a good will, which he previously did not have because he could not acquire it by his own effort. But grace also follows the good man so that he will

62. See Ps 76.11 (77.10 modern).
63. Ps 4.3, following LXX (4.2 modern).
64. Prv 8.35, following LXX.   65. Jn 1.9.
66. Lk 22.32.   67. Gal 5.6.
68. Prv 8.35, following LXX; Ps 58.11 (59.10 modern).
69. Ps 22.6, following LXX (23.6 modern).

persevere and increase in a good will, which he could not produce on his own, but has received freely. Therefore, it precedes by directing the man's perverse heart, for it is written: "But the Lord directs the hearts."[70] But it follows by keeping the heart right, because it is likewise written: "My just help is from the Lord, who saves those who are upright of heart."[71] Therefore, grace works in both situations: both in the erring man, that he may live once he has been corrected, and in the corrected man, that he may not fall back into depravity.

36. (XVII.) But whoever seeks conscientiously learns from the testimony of the saints' words that this grace is not given to all, and among those to whom it is given, it is not given equally. For what prior good thing could a man possess (by which he might aim for eternal life) other than a good will? About such a good will, it says in Proverbs: "The will is prepared by the Lord."[72] Therefore, the Lord, who prepares a good will in us, does himself bestow on us the beginning of a good will. Furthermore, God works in us not only so that we may will, but also so that we may perform well that which we will. The Apostle teaches this when he says, "With fear and trembling, work out your own salvation, for God is the one working in you both to will and to accomplish according to his good will."[73] The book Song of Songs points out that the beginning of a good will is rooted firmly in faith. There Christ says to the Church: "You will come and pass as a result of the beginning of faith."[74] But blessed Paul asserts that faith is not given to all when he says, "For not all have faith,"[75] and again, "For they do not all obey the Gospel."[76] We also know from the teaching of the same Apostle that faith is not given equally to those to whom it is given. He says, "For through the grace given to me, I tell each one among you not to think more highly than it is appropriate to think, but to think soberly, to the degree that God has dealt to each one a measure of faith."[77]

70. Prv 21.2.
71. Ps 7.11, following LXX (7.10 modern).
72. Prv 8.35, following LXX.   73. Phil 2.12–13.
74. Song 4.8, following LXX.   75. 2 Thes 3.2.
76. Rom 10.16.   77. Rom 12.3.

37. Because of this, the chorus of the apostles itself received not the spirit of the world but the Spirit who is from God so that the apostles might know the things given to them by God.[78] Since they knew that the beginning of faith was conferred on them by the Lord, they kept beseeching him to increase that same faith in them. For Luke the evangelist remembers that the disciples said to the Lord, "Lord, increase our faith."[79] If the will of any man could have made a beginning on its own, it would in fact have increased on its own. But the blessed apostles knew whence they had received the beginning of faith, and knew that they were not holding onto it, and thus they were earnestly seeking its increase for themselves. The same grace that had conferred on them the beginning of faith was itself awakening in them the desire for increased faith. Nevertheless, even if the will were already faithful in desiring that growth, it still would in no way be sufficient in itself, unless he who had given the beginning of faith to those who were not seeking it would also, in kindness and mercy, bestow the increase upon those who were seeking it. Therefore, so that the apostles would believe, a will was not lacking, for the Lord prepared a will within them. For on his own a man possesses only unbelief, and the result is that he does not believe; but when he receives faith from God, the result is that he believes in God, and that faith may be perfected in him by its subsequent increase. Divine grace, not the power of the human will, accomplishes this. For just as God by grace prepares the will to believe, so he also completes that will by the operation of grace. And just as he himself gives faith to those who do not have it, so he himself also multiplies it in those who do have it. For this reason, it is written thus in the letter to the Hebrews: "Therefore, laying aside every weight and the sin that surrounds us, let us run with patience the race set before us, looking to Jesus, the author and perfecter of our faith."[80] Accordingly, if a man has faith from himself, Jesus is not the author of faith, and if a man completes his faith by his own strength, Jesus is not the perfecter of his faith. But apostolic authority confesses that the Lord Jesus is the author and perfecter

78. See 1 Cor 2.12.   79. Lk 17.5.
80. Heb 12.1–2.

of our faith. Therefore, it is certain that faith cannot come to be in us or increase in us unless the one whom apostolic authority confesses to be the author and perfecter of faith gives it to us, increases the gift, and completes its growth. For this reason, the Apostle Paul has written in his letter to the Ephesians, just as he preaches that grace is given by God, so he testifies that it is not given equally to all, but in accordance with his custom God gives mercifully, not in response to merits, but freely. Therefore, the same Apostle says, "Each one of us has been given grace according to the measure of Christ's gift."[81] These and similar testimonies show that grace is not given to all or given equally to those to whom it is given, but in accordance with the measure of the gift of Christ. Hence, when the blessed Apostle Paul concludes the same letter, he wishes that peace, love, and faith may be granted by God. He says, "Peace be to the brothers, and love with faith, from God the Father and the Lord Jesus Christ."[82]

38. (XVIII.) Therefore, God has conferred upon us a good will so that we might want to believe in him, and he himself has given us faith so that we might believe in him; and this same God has poured the grace of his love into our hearts by the Holy Spirit so that we might also love him. Therefore, we have received grace not because we wanted to, but because grace was given to us while we were not yet desiring it. We have been able to possess that very grace so that we might receive [additional] grace, but faith was given to us by grace while we were unbelievers. That is what the chosen vessel[83] testifies with clear words, when he says, "By grace you have been saved through faith; and this is not from yourselves. It is a gift of God."[84] Therefore, grace alone produces a good will in us and alone grants faith to that will. But since a good will possesses faith, it cannot be good without faith, for "without faith it is impossible to please God."[85] A good will begins to accomplish good if the working of grace remains always present to help. Therefore, God's grace produces in us a good will so that it may have something to help

81. Eph 4.7.   82. Eph 6.23.
83. That is, Paul.   84. Eph 2.8.
85. Heb 11.6.

in us, not only as it wills but also as it works. As a result, grace imparts the gift of believing to our will so that it remains available to that same will as it believes and works. Therefore, grace knows that it possesses within itself the generosity of faith, so that the human will may possess good merits through faith, not from itself but from the grace of God.

39. But it is not enough for us to know that faith is divinely given to each of us, unless we know for certain that God bestows as much faith upon each of us as he deigns to bestow, not as much as the human will deserves. Before the human will receives faith, it is able of itself to acquire [only] punishment, not faith. For "everything that is not of faith is sin,"[86] and, "without faith it is impossible to please God."[87] For there is no doubting that whoever does not please God displeases him, and that whoever displeases God does not appease him, but rather provokes him. Therefore, a will that does not possess faith cannot deserve to receive faith. For not having faith displeases God, and the evil of unbelief merits not justification but damnation. Therefore, the distribution of faith is free, for faith is bestowed on each person not in accordance with the faith of unbelievers (because they have none), but in accordance with the voluntary generosity of the God who justifies. Indeed, the teacher of the Gentiles[88] teaches this by advising us "not to think more highly than it is appropriate to think, but to think soberly, to the degree that God has dealt to each one a measure of faith."[89] Blessed Peter also testifies that the grace of God is manifold. For this reason, he charges each believer to work in accordance with the nature of the grace he has received, when he says, "Practice hospitality one toward another without grumbling. As every man has received such grace, minister it to one another as good stewards of the manifold grace of God."[90] Blessed Paul likewise says, "We, being many, are one body in Christ, and individually we are members one of another, possessing gifts that differ according to the grace that has been given to us."[91]

86. Rom 14.23.　　　　　　87. Heb 11.6.
88. That is, Paul.　　　　　 89. Rom 12.3.
90. 1 Pt 4.9–10.　　　　　　91. Rom 12.5–6.

40. (XIX.) Furthermore, lest anyone strive to attribute the difference between the various gifts to any kind of human works or merits, the same blessed Paul shows that the free gifts are bestowed through the abundance of spiritual grace, which finds no merit on the basis of which it might confer a gift, but does itself give the beginning of good merits. Thus, he says, "There are varieties of gifts, but the same Spirit. And there are varieties of ministries, but the same Lord. And there are varieties of operations, but the same God, who accomplishes all things in everyone."[92] And after enumerating the spiritual gifts, he says, "But one and the same Spirit accomplishes all these things, distributing to each individually as he wills."[93] Accordingly, each and every Christian must know that the beginning of saving grace consists not in human nature, nor in legal commands, but in the enlightenment of the heart and in the free gift of divine goodness. By means of this grace, we can not only know what is divinely commanded, but also love and perform it. For human nature itself cannot at any time, by its own efforts, recover the good will by which it might please God. Human nature lost this will in the first man, when he consented to the devil by means of a will that he had received uncorrupted from God but that had become corrupted. He then lost the good will in such a way that no one afterward could possess it as a result of his own efforts, unless each person receives it freely from him from whom the first man received it when he was created. If the first man had not lost the good will, every man since then would have possessed such a good will naturally.

41. Also, the commands of the law can be heard externally with carnal ears, but no one ever perceives them salvifically with the interior hearing of the heart unless he has inwardly received the gift of spiritual grace. For the letter of the law increases sin by prohibiting it, if the listener lacks the aid of spiritual grace. And when a man knows the law, he becomes a transgressor unless the Lord prepares his will for fulfilling the law: "For the law brings about wrath, and where there is no law there is no trans-

92. 1 Cor 12.4–6.
93. 1 Cor 12.11.

gression,"[94] and: "Scripture has shut up all things under sin so that justification might be given to believers by the faith of Jesus Christ."[95] Therefore, the law without grace can point to the sickness, but it cannot heal it. It shows the wounds, but it does not administer the medicine. But grace inwardly administers help so that one may fulfill the precept of the law. And just as the law reveals guilt, grace grants forgiveness. Therefore, the role of the law is to make us aware of our sins; the role of grace is to make us avoid sin. For the Apostle says, "I would not have known sin except through the law. And I would not have known covetousness, unless the law had said, 'You shall not covet.'"[96] Concerning grace, he also says, "Who will deliver me from the body of this death? The grace of God through Jesus Christ our Lord."[97] Wickedness derives from a corrupted nature, with the result that a man sins. The role of the law is to show and declare to man his own sin of which he is ignorant. But the role of the gift of grace is to heal man's wickedness, which nature has inflicted upon him and which the knowledge of the law has increased. Therefore, grace accomplishes in a man both enlightenment and salvation. This happens so that, after being preceded by the aid of grace, not only may a man know that the commands of the law (which, while he was unable to fulfill them, he heard to no avail and in fact to his condemnation) are holy and just and good, but also that he may receive love, by which he will be able to love and to fulfill what he learns.

42. (XX.) Therefore, let us not think that God's grace is given to all men. For not all have faith, nor do all receive the kind of love for God that results in their salvation. Instead, they have a corruption of the human will that keeps them from either believing or loving God. As long as the human will is not changed by the grace of the divine gift, it either does not understand the commands or despises the insights that come from understanding. In other words, the man sins in ignorance, or his sin increases because of the corruption stemming from the transgression. Therefore, concerning these men whom the darkness of

94. Rom 4.15.
96. Rom 7.7.
95. Gal 3.22.
97. Rom 7.24–25.

ignorance surrounds, it is written that "they did not know, nor did they understand; they walk in darkness."[98] As the Apostle says, they "walk in the vanity of their mind because their understanding is obscured by darkness, and they have been alienated from the life of God through their ignorance, because of the blindness of their heart."[99] In fact, about those who know, he says that "although they knew God, they did not glorify him as God, or give thanks, but became vain in their speculations."[100] And it is said about the disdainful slave that "the obstinate slave will not be corrected by words, and even though he understands, he will not obey."[101] What, then, does the phrase "he will not be corrected by words" mean, except that if grace is lacking, he will not be converted solely by the command of the law? For God converts us and gives us life, so that his people may rejoice in him. He shows us his mercy and gives us his salvation.[102] Therefore, a man has the wickedness of unbelief (which originates from within himself) that keeps him from believing in God. But the purpose of the gift of divine generosity is that each one may believe and love God. For if grace is even sought, it finds such men as the Apostle has in mind, that is, those who are "foolish, unbelieving, disobedient, serving various desires and pleasures, living in malice and envy, hateful, and hating one another."[103] He preaches that we are saved from such vices neither by any capacity inherent in the nature of all men, nor by a mere knowledge of the law, but by the kindness of God our Savior.[104] It is by his work "that we deny ungodliness and worldly lusts so as to live sober, righteous, and godly lives in this present world."[105]

43. (XXI.) God's grace through Jesus Christ our Lord works in such a way that it makes the unwise wise, grants faith to the unbelieving, calls the disobedient to life and even calls them back again after their worldly desires have been cast out, and

98. Ps 81.5, following LXX (82.5 modern).
99. Eph 4.17–18.
100. Rom 1.21.
101. Cf. Prv 29.19.
102. Cf. Ps 84.7–8 (85.6–7 modern).
103. Ti 3.3.
104. Cf. Ti 3.4.
105. Ti 2.12.

inspires in them a desire for the heavenly kingdom. His grace works further so that after their various carnal lusts have been removed, it bestows on them the gift of spiritual pleasure and will, roots out their evil will by replacing it with goodness, drives out envy with the gift of kindness, and imparts the gift of holy love to the hateful and to those who hate one another. Therefore, these things are begun in us by the work of spiritual grace and completed in us by its action, so that we may forsake evil deeds, be good, and burn with the fire of holy love. For "the fruit of the Spirit is love, joy, peace, longsuffering, goodness, kindness,"[106] and other things that the apostolic teaching commends. We recognize this because the Spirit accomplishes in us the things that must be done for our salvation, for he himself works in us so that we may do the things we have learned. For "we have received not the spirit of the world, but the Spirit who is from God, so that we may know the things given to us by God."[107] We are led by the same Spirit so that by leading good lives we may be sons of God. For "as many as are led by the Spirit of God, these are sons of God."[108]

44. Therefore, in obedience to the heavenly words, let us hold most firmly that the beginning of all good things in us is granted by divine generosity. But in order to continue, we must not do evil, and in order to begin to will and to do good, we cannot possess from ourselves either the beginning or the increase. For just as it is written concerning self-control, that "no one can be self-controlled unless God grants him to be,"[109] and just as the Apostle lists it as a fruit of the Spirit,[110] so also does he list love, which "does not act falsely,"[111] because it is related to self-control. Love, through good works, "covers a multitude of sins,"[112] and through love God works in us not only so that we will turn away from evil but also so that we will do good. And by exercising love, let us love not merely our neighbors but even our enemies, and let us do good to those who hate us, and let

---

106. Gal 5.22–23.
107. 1 Cor 2.12.
108. Rom 8.14.
109. Wis 8.21.
110. See Gal 5.23.
111. 1 Cor 13.4.
112. 1 Pt 4.8.

us pray for those who persecute us and speak ill of us.[113] Therefore, this love does not originate or increase in us as a result of our will. But by the action of God's grace, it is poured out into our hearts by the Holy Spirit, who has been given to us.[114]

45. (XXII.) Therefore, whoever does not wish to be deceived or to deceive in the name of grace, let him hear the Apostle, who restrains the pride of human pretentiousness, which strives to claim for itself the beginning of a good will. He says, "For who makes you different? And what do you have that you did not receive? But if you received it, why do you boast as if you did not receive it?"[115] Let that person also humbly and wholeheartedly follow James' advice, by which he calls us away from error and leads us into the way of truth, when he says, "Do not be deceived, my brothers. Every excellent gift and every perfect gift is from above, coming down from the Father of lights."[116] And when our Maker and Redeemer himself was speaking to the crowd in parables and the disciples asked him why he did so,[117] he showed that the faculty of inner knowledge inheres only in those to whom the Lord himself has willed to grant it (because he himself is the one "who teaches man knowledge").[118] In a clear response to their question he revealed the gift of heavenly grace, saying, "To you it has been given to know the mystery of the kingdom of God, but to the others I speak in parables."[119] Also, his direct confession to his Father plainly indicates that every bit of the wisdom of the human mind for understanding divine preaching is weak unless God (who teaches outwardly by using men who speak) also illumines and aids the listener by teaching inwardly on his own. For Jesus says, "I thank you, Father, Lord of heaven and earth, because you have hidden these things from the wise and prudent, and have revealed them to children."[120] How can one claim that grace has been given to all when the witness of the Giver himself shows that it has been hid-

---

113. Cf. Mt 5.44.   114. Cf. Rom 5.5.
115. 1 Cor 4.7.   116. Jas 1.16–17.
117. See Mt 13.10.
118. Ps 93.10, following LXX (94.10 modern).
119. Mt 13.11, 13.   120. Mt 11.25.

den from the wise and the prudent? For does he not show later that the knowledge of God consists not in human power, but in divine revelation, when he says, "No one knows the Son except the Father; and no one knows the Father except the Son, and the one to whom the Son has willed to reveal him"?[121] On this point, who would fail to see that when one hears a message of heavenly instruction from a man, he hears in vain unless God the teacher speaks mercifully to him in his heart by revelation?

46. (XXIII) And this is a special revelation of the sons of God, by which they receive the gift not only of knowledge but also of divine love. For this revelation or knowledge is not the kind that belongs to those of whom the Apostle speaks: "Because that which is known of God is manifest in them, for God has manifested it to them,"[122] that is, "so that they may be without excuse, because although they knew God, they did not glorify him as God or give thanks."[123] Therefore, that manifestation (by which those who knew God did not love him) did not possess the grace by which one who knows God may also love him. Therefore, inasmuch as they did not receive grace, on that account, even though they knew God, they did not give thanks. Likewise, inasmuch as they had been prepared to be vessels of wrath for destruction, that manifestation by which they knew God worked in them in such a way that they would be proud because of their knowledge, not in such a way that they would love him by humbling themselves. Therefore, by such knowledge their excuse was removed; their salvation was not conferred. But in this revelation (which God's grace accomplishes in the vessels of mercy), the knowledge and love of God are at once divinely conferred on a man. For those who are not elect are without excuse, but the elect are made blameless. For the Apostle says, "Who will make any charge against God's elect? It is God who justifies. Who is the one who condemns? Christ Jesus who died, rather, who arose, who is at the right hand of God, who also makes intercession for us?"[124]

121. Mt 11.27.   122. Rom 1.19.
123. Rom 1.20–21.   124. Rom 8.33–34.

47. Spiritual grace grants mercy to one who is humble. Therefore, in the vessels of mercy, natural guilt is absolved by faith
and love, but in the vessels of wrath, natural guilt is fostered by
haughty knowledge. Through this knowledge, a blind heart puffs
itself up unto death, but through divine mercy the blind heart
is illuminated and humbled unto life. By [haughty] knowledge
the unwise heart is darkened, while the proud man arrogates to
himself what is God's. But by mercy, one receives light so that he
may not doubt that the very fact that he knows and loves God derives not from the capacity of nature, or from hearing the law, or
from his own will, but from God's gift. And he will always remember to be humble, lest he lose through pride what he received
when he was unworthy. Therefore, the first kind of knowledge[125]
adds to sin the guilt of transgression, but the latter[126] removes the
punishment from the sinner. The former rightly condemns; the
latter freely justifies. In the former case, knowledge fosters and
increases sin by puffing one up; but in the latter case, love covers
a multitude of sins by building one up.[127]

BOOK TWO

1. (I.) In the preceding book, I discussed Jacob and Esau
enough and more than enough. I did so with the help of God's
grace, which alone can pour into the human heart the gift of
holy knowledge and grant the mouth the unwavering ability to
speak, for we and our words are both in God's hands. I proved
by apostolic teaching that the holy Jacob was elected before he
was born without any merits from either previous or subsequent
works, but he was set apart solely in accordance with the beneficence of the divine purpose. We know that blessed Paul asserted
as much in the passage in which he says, "For while they had
not yet been born or done anything good or bad, in order that
God's electing purpose might stand."[128] The Apostle said this
in order to show that God's purpose would stand not accord-

---

125. That is, knowledge that does not lead one to love God.
126. That is, a knowledge produced by mercy leading to love.
127. Cf. 1 Cor 8.1, 1 Pt 4.8.
128. Rom 9.11.

ing to a man's choice, but according to the choice of the one who was calling the man, and in order to make known that the choice depended not on any merit of the person to be born, but on the will of God. Indeed, if some good or evil action were to be found in the children, then God's call would be the result of a man's merit; it would not be election resulting from God's grace. But because the two were not yet born and were even conceived through one act of intercourse, they had no merits deriving from their own works such that the diversity of works could have been the basis for God's choosing one and rejecting the other. If there had been such diverse merits, then God's purpose would have stood on the basis of human works, not on the basis of his own election. Therefore, there was no difference between the brothers in terms of their own good or bad work, which might confer on one the merit of election and inflict upon the other the punishment of condemnation. For this reason, God's purpose stood according to election, inasmuch as the will of the one who elected did not remain because of the merit of the one being elected, but instead the free separation of the elected was in accordance with the plan of the one who elected. For this reason, the Apostle followed up and added: "Not because of works, but because of him who calls, it was declared to her[129] that the older would serve the younger."[130]

2. After we dealt with this question of the twin brothers as much as the Lord granted us to, we then digressed from the general inquiry of this work to deal with the question of children who die without baptism. Then after we discussed and, I think, conclusively resolved that question, we at last took up with a careful inquiry the question of grace itself (which freely goes before whoever is saved). As a result, it was evident that grace is not given universally to all men, nor is it given equally to those to whom it is given. For it is God's prerogative to whom he will give it and how much to give. He does not give grace as a reward that he owes for human intentions or works, but since he is merciful and kind, he imparts it freely to hearts that need

129. That is, to Rebecca.
130. Rom 9.12.

to be enlightened. For this reason, he does in fact bestow as much of his grace as he pleases on whom he pleases, because a person is not brought to God because of any beginning of a good will or the accomplishment of any good work before God grants him grace.

3. (II.) Nevertheless, we know that on the question of God's grace and human choice, most people do not maintain a balance, but they defend one of them in such a way that they try to disallow the other. Or when they hear someone defend one of them, they think he is disallowing the other. But the grace of piety does not permit one to deny either of them, but advises one to maintain a proper balance by confessing both. As a result, in this second little book, we have taken care (supported by divine grace, which both illumines and guides human choice) to affirm God's grace and man's choice in such a way that, while we defend both, we do not disallow either. Instead, we intend to show that one of these is lacking something that the other possesses, and one expands upon the other in accordance with the free gift of kindness. We also intend to show why one is always looking for healing and from what source the benefit of medicine is continually abundant. For the Creator and Savior of mortals says that it is not the healthy who need a doctor, but the sick, and he says that he did not come to call the righteous, but sinners to penitence.[131] Therefore, from this we know what the doctor finds in the sick and what he himself provides for those who need to be healed. For he finds that human choice (insofar as one has reached an age when he is able to use reason) is either completely ignorant of its own infirmity or is puffed up by the disease of detrimental knowledge.[132] To be sure, whether it does or does not know what must be done, it is confident that it is sufficient with its own resources. Or similarly, a man embraces death without knowing it or grows sicker while not asking for a doctor, and tries to administer the medicine to himself. Hence, it follows that since he is weighed down by the fatal disease of ignorance or pride, the man neither seeks a doctor nor finds in

131. Cf. Mt 9.12–13.
132. Cf. 1 Cor 8.1.

himself the power of true healing. Therefore, there is no free will in a man before he is healed by the work of divine conversion because he prefers to yield to the disease rather than to a doctor. But by the very fact that the man yields or does not yield, he shows that he evidently possesses free choice.

4. (III.) Therefore, free choice exists both in righteous and in ungodly men. In the righteous, God the Redeemer supports and directs that free choice by his kindness, but in the ungodly, God the Avenger forsakes and punishes in accordance with his justice. Thus, in the righteous, the free choice adheres to the truth not only in what it needs to know, but also in what it needs to love. But in the ungodly, doubtless either free choice is ignorant of the command and does not recognize its sin to be sin, or even when it can know what sin is apart from the help of God's grace, it still presumes that it is able by its own effort to fulfill the commands of the divine will. The result is that the free choice does not yield humbly to God's will, but by making good out to be evil, serves its own error instead. In other words, as long as free choice does not know God's righteousness and wants to establish its own, it has not submitted to God's righteousness,[133] "for Christ is the end of the law for righteousness to every one who believes."[134]

5. Therefore, our skilled and kind doctor, as he prepared freely to bring the dead back to life and restore the sick to health, had great concern for those whom he would make alive in himself and whom he would heal by his incomparable goodness. He himself is the salvation of the weak and the resurrection of the dead. This same doctor made himself medicine for us. But so that the wisdom of God might wisely fulfill the order of the healing, the doctor first gave the command through the law of righteousness, by which the sick person might know his own infirmity. He intended then to give love through grace, by which love the sick person might become savingly aware of his own sickness, rather than being proudly confident in his own

133. Cf. Rom 10.3.
134. Rom 10.4.

strength. In this way, the doctor intended that the patient might recognize that the doctor himself was the very fountain of life and health, so that the patient might beseech him for the benefit of health. The doctor did not intend the patient to fancy he could produce his own righteousness from his haughty heart, and consequently to think that he was a stranger to disease, as if he did not need help to accomplish his own healing. (Such is the Pharisee's thinking: "God, I thank you that I am not as other men, extortioners, unjust, adulterers, or even as this tax collector.")[135] Instead, the doctor intended the patient to look upon his wounds with the humility that comes from a contrite heart and truthfully to exclaim, "I said, 'Lord, be merciful to me; heal my soul, for I have sinned against you.'"[136] Yet if the doctor had not given free choice to man, that doctor from heaven would not have healed our infirmity by knowledge of or love for the commandment. As it was, the infirmity was increased by the mere knowledge of the command, to the end that grace might begin to bring about the health whose source is faith and love. Accordingly, infirmity is combined with knowledge of the command for the proper working of man's free choice, not so much because man can (by his own will or by his own power) fulfill what the law demands of him, but so that he, through knowledge of the command, may become aware of his own infirmity and then earnestly request the help of healing grace. After acquiring grace, the patient is able to love and perform and recognize what is commanded (which he may or may not be able to do), so that he may indeed be able to seek earnestly both to attribute the misery of his infirmity to himself and to entrust the grace of health to the benefits of the medicine.

6. (IV.) It is proper that we verify by using heavenly words all those matters that we set forth above. God speaks thus through Isaiah: "If you are willing and obedient to me, you will eat the good things of the land; but if you refuse and rebel, you will be devoured by the sword."[137] It is beyond doubt that the prophet declares the freedom of human choice with the phrases "if you

135. Lk 18.11.
136. Ps 40.5 (41.4 modern).
137. Is 1.19.

are willing" and "if you refuse." Everyone knows that willing and
refusing have to do with the will. Therefore, our will is in accord
with the words of the prophet: "If you are willing and obedient
to me." Consequently, we must always will the good and must
continuously and willingly persist in good works. Indeed, when
the Apostle says that "God is the one working in us both to will
and to accomplish according to his good will,"[138] he in fact
shows that man's will is not directed toward willing the good
apart from the divine gift and that the will is divinely helped to
do good works. Therefore, since we are commanded to will, we
are shown what we must possess. But because we cannot possess
it by our efforts, we are informed that the one who gives us the
command is himself the one from whom we must seek help. Yet
we cannot even earnestly ask for it unless God works in us so
that we desire it, for the will in us that the gift of the merciful
God makes good is the same will in us that God helps so that
we may be able to do good works. The will rises from the evils
in which it lies prior to justification and renounces them with
delight, not by its own power, but because of God's prevenient
work. And after it awakens so that it not fall, it cannot be sufficient to itself alone; but just as it is awakened by the blessing
of prevenient mercy, so is it protected by the aid of subsequent
mercy so that it can persevere.

7. (V.) Therefore, blessed David, recognizing both the will
of human choice and the power of divine grace, agrees with us
that we should do good. But what he commands us to do, he
does not doubt that from the moment he requests it, we can
have it. Therefore, arousing human choice to conversion, he
terrifies us with saving preaching, saying, "If you do not convert, he has brandished his sword, stretched his bow, and made
it ready."[139] But in order to show the work we are commanded
to do, he indicates with the gift of a heavenly work the conversion that he preaches to us, saying, "God, by converting us, you
will give us life, and your people will rejoice in you."[140] So that

138. Phil 2.13.
139. Ps 7.13, following LXX (7.12 modern).
140. Ps 84.7 (85.6 modern).

each person may have pity on his own soul and may please God, human choice is thus admonished with a divine word: "Have compassion on your soul, and please God."[141] But indeed, no one can have compassion on his own soul unless he is anticipated by God's mercy and receives it so he can be merciful. To show this, the Lord himself, the giver of mercy, instructs him, saying, "I will be merciful to whom I am merciful, and I will show mercy to whom I will be merciful."[142] Therefore, blessed David says, "My God, his mercy will come before me."[143] And it has been clearly stated in the letter to the Hebrews that no one can please God unless God works in him what is pleasing in his sight. There indeed it is said: "Now may the God of peace, who brought our Lord Jesus (that great shepherd of the sheep) back from the dead through the blood of the eternal covenant, prepare you for every good work by working in you what is pleasing in his sight, so that you may do his will."[144]

8. Consequently, we do not please God unless we will to do so, but he is the one who grants us the power to will. If he does not change a man's will so that it is good, man either always desires evil or never desires good in the right way. Consequently, as long as he does not hold to the right order in good works, he displeases the true and good God in every respect. Therefore, we do not please God except by a good will, but so that we may please him, he equips us for every good work. Similarly, when we do his will, we do it willingly. But so that we may do it, he does for us that which is pleasing in his sight. For David says, "I have longed to do your will, O my God."[145] But in order to do his will, David prays for the help of spiritual grace, by which he may be taught so that he may know and be guided to work. To this end, he prays in another place to the Author of knowledge and ability: "Teach me to do your will, for you are my God,"[146] and he immediately adds: "Your good Spirit will lead me into the right path."[147] Isaiah teaches the same when he says, "Let the

---

141. Sir 30.24.   142. Ex 33.19.

143. Ps 58.11 (59.10 modern).   144. Heb 13.20–21.

145. Ps 39.9, following LXX (40.8 modern).

146. Ps 142.10 (143.10 modern).   147. Ibid.

wicked forsake his way, and the unrighteous man his thoughts, and let him turn to the Lord."[148] Paul the apostle also urges us to be renewed in the spirit of our mind and to put on the new man, who has been created according to God in righteousness and the holiness of truth.[149]

9. (VI.) Nevertheless, lest we attribute our conversion, or renewal, to human choice, the holy Jeremiah beseeches the Lord on our behalf with these words: "Convert us to yourself, and we will be converted. Renew our days as of old."[150] Again, the psalmist says, "Open your mouth, and I will fill it."[151] Here we understand that he means the mouth of the heart, not the mouth of the body. In another place he says about the mouth of the heart, "When the Lord brought to an end the captivity of Zion, we were like people who had been consoled. Then our mouth was filled with joy."[152] And then, lest some proud person think the open mouth belongs to him, the book of the Acts of the Apostles shows that by the divine gift the mouth of the human heart is opened to receive the word of Christian preaching. For there a certain woman named Lydia, a seller of purple, is mentioned: "Whose heart the Lord opened to be attentive to the things Paul was saying."[153] Again it is written that "Wisdom opened the mouth of the dumb and gave speech to the tongues of babes."[154] For he opened the mouths of the dumb so that unbelievers might believe, and he gave speech to the tongues of babes so that they might speak what they had come to believe. For this reason, Paul deservedly attributes his faith and eloquence to the gift of the Holy Spirit, when he says, "Since we have the same Spirit of faith as the one who wrote, 'I believed and therefore I have spoken,' we too believe and speak."[155] Man believes voluntarily and speaks voluntarily, but man's will cannot do so on its own, unless God grants it. For Wisdom opens the mouth of the dumb so that the unbeliever may believe, and

148. Is 55.7.   149. Cf. Eph 4.23–24.
150. Lam 5.21.   151. Ps 80.11 (81.10 modern).
152. Ps 125.1–2, following LXX (126.1–2 modern).
153. Acts 16.14.   154. Wis 10.21.
155. 2 Cor 4.13. Cf. Ps 115.10 (116.10 modern).

Wisdom gives speech to the tongues of babes, so that the believer may speak.

10. Therefore, the precepts by which the prophets and apostles advise us what we must seek and what we must avoid instruct our choice so that we may serve the Lord's commands willingly. But the prophets and apostles (who were filled with the Holy Spirit) lived holy lives, taught holy things, and never stopped asking for divine help. (To be sure, what they were seeking from God was help for fulfilling the things he had commanded.) Since they asked for divine help, they doubtless believed that man possesses a will that has free choice, and they likewise testified that free choice without the help of God's grace is insufficient and ineffective, not only for doing those holy things that must be done, but even for contemplating them. As a result, the holy Apostle[156] shows that man possesses a will that has free choice when he exhorts the Philippians both to think about those holy and just things that must be thought about and to do those things that must be done in accordance with wholesome precepts. He says, "Whatever things are true, whatever things are honorable, whatever things are holy, whatever things are just, whatever things are of good report, if there is any excellence, if anything is praiseworthy, think on these things that you have learned and received and heard and seen in me; do these things, and the God of peace will be with you."[157] Did he not command them both to think about and to do the things that are holy, and did he not also clearly show us where that ability to think and to act comes from? He says about thinking: "Not that we are sufficient to think that anything comes from our own power, as if it were from us."[158] What does "from us" mean if not "from the will of free choice"? Where then does the will of free choice come from if not from us? "But," he says, "our sufficiency is from God."[159] Similarly, he proclaims that we are led to act in accordance with the Spirit of God when he says, "For as many as are led by the Spirit of God, these are sons of God."[160]

156. That is, Paul.
157. Phil 4.8–9.
158. 2 Cor 3.5.
159. Ibid.
160. Rom 8.14.

11. (VII.) There is, therefore, a distance between the letter that gives orders and the spirit that gives life, that is, between law and grace, for the law summons the will of man, but grace converts it, and the law speaks so that we may will the good, but grace grants us to do the good. In the case of the law, divine justice strikes terror into man's will, but in the case of grace, mercy bestows love. In the former, the will receives "a spirit of servitude in fear"; in the latter, it receives "the Spirit of adoption as sons by whom we cry out, 'Abba, Father.'"[161] Consequently, this free will of ours has that property naturally within itself so that it can willingly seek good or evil, and it seeks the good by prevailing, but the evil by failing. But on its own, it is sufficient only to fail, and so in order to prevail, it always needs the help of divine mercy. For unless it is lifted up by God's prevenient grace, it in no way rises, for "the Lord lifts up the downtrodden."[162] Unless our will is helped by prevenient grace leading it, it in no way runs [the course of one's life], for it is said of God, "He has led me in the paths of righteousness for his name's sake,"[163] and it is said to him, "Lead me, Lord, in your righteousness, because of my enemies."[164] Unless the will is led with the protection of grace, it does not arrive at its goal, for the holy David says, "Send out your light and your truth; they have led me and brought me to your holy mountain and into your tabernacle."[165] And the human will, after rejecting evil deeds, will not be able to choose or love the good things that lead to eternal life unless it receives from God the grace of discernment and love. For when speaking of spiritual gifts, blessed Paul says this about discernment: "Indeed, to one is given the word of wisdom through the Spirit, but to another a word of knowledge by the same Spirit, to another faith by the same Spirit, to another grace of healing by the one Spirit, to another mighty deeds, to another prophecy, to another discernment of spirits."[166] But when God

161. Rom 8.15.
162. Ps 145.8 (146.8 modern).
163. Ps 22.3, following LXX (23.3 modern).
164. Ps 5.9, following LXX (5.8 modern).
165. Ps 42.3, following LXX (43.3 modern).
166. 1 Cor 12.8–10.

grants discernment of spirits through his spiritual generosity, which spirits does he mean, if not the spirits of good and evil? Of course, he gives this discernment so that, once we have been enlightened and aided by the Holy Spirit's grace, we may know how to preserve, and be able to preserve, the Holy Spirit's gifts with fear and trembling, and so that we may be able to repulse the promptings of diabolical wickedness with saving discernment. The blessed Apostle John commands us with these words: "Beloved, do not believe every spirit, but test the spirits to see whether they are from God."[167]

12. (VIII.) But in order for us to know the things that God gives us, the Spirit at work in us must be not the spirit of the world, but the Spirit of God; not the spirit that man has so that he may be born in the world, but the Spirit whom he has received so that he may be reborn from God. The Apostle clearly teaches this when he says, "Now we have received not the spirit of the world, but the Spirit who is from God, so that we may know the things given to us by God."[168] The Apostle testifies that the divine gift is given not only so that we may know, but also so that we may understand, as he writes to Timothy: "Understand the things I say."[169] According to that statement, human choice is indeed appropriate for understanding, because if a man did not have human choice, he could in no way understand the things that are said. But so that the Apostle may show the source from which understanding is given to human choice, he adds (after saying, "Understand the things I say"), "For the Lord will give you understanding in all things."[170] So also the most holy David, when he asks God for understanding so that he may learn God's commandments, says, "Your hands have made me and fashioned me. Give me understanding so that I may learn your commandments."[171] Proverbs also bears witness that "the Lord gives wisdom, and from his face proceed knowledge and understanding."[172] And the Apostle James com-

167. 1 Jn 4.1.　　168. 1 Cor 2.12.
169. 2 Tm 2.7.　　170. Ibid.
171. Ps 118.73, following LXX (119.73 modern).
172. Prv 2.6.

mands, "If anyone lacks wisdom, let him ask of God, who gives to all liberally and does not reproach."[173] And in order to show that the will to ask is itself divinely given, he adds, "But let him ask in faith, not doubting in anything."[174] For without faith, it is impossible to call upon God, as Paul points out when he says, "How then will they call upon him in whom they have not believed?"[175] So because no one calls upon him before believing, no one believes in God unless he receives faith. It is thus certain that the one who enlightens us so that we may believe also awakens us so that we may ask for wisdom.

13. (IX.) Consequently, a man wills the good by his will, and he does the good by his will, but without God's gift and help he can never will or do the good. Indeed, he is called upon to know and admonished to act because he always has the free choice of will. But he cannot have holy knowledge unless he receives it from above as a gift of grace from the Father of lights, from whom every excellent and perfect gift comes.[176] And once he has this knowledge, either he does not do what he now knows he must do, or he is crushed by the weight of his own pride while he strives to take credit for what he does. In fact, this is the reason I mentioned holy knowledge above, for knowledge that makes man proud and does not build him up in love is not holy. That is the kind of "knowledge" with which some who knew God did not glorify him as God or give him thanks. That is the kind of "knowledge" about which it is written, "If anyone thinks he knows something, he does not yet know anything as he ought to know it."[177]

14. Therefore, knowledge of a certain commandment is never sufficient to enable anyone to live a good life, unless love has become the guardian of the commandment and unless a person (in order to love) does not love by his own will. For this reason, each of us is commanded to love God and his neighbor, according to the lawful saying: "You will love the Lord your God with

173. Jas 1.5.
174. Jas 1.6.
175. Rom 10.14.
176. Cf. Jas 1.17.
177. 1 Cor 8.2.

your whole heart, and with your whole soul, and with your whole mind,"[178] and, "You will love your neighbor as yourself."[179] Our Savior says that the whole law and the prophets hang on these two commandments. But the love by which we may love God with our whole heart is not a love that comes from within our heart, but it comes from God. For "God's love has been poured out in our hearts through the Holy Spirit, who has been given to us."[180] And God has bestowed love upon us so that we may love one another. For the blessed John says, "Beloved, let us love one another, for love is from God, and everyone who loves his brother is born of God and knows God. He who does not love does not know God, for God is love."[181]

15. Therefore, because it is evident from the divine words that God is love,[182] it is in fact clear that no one can have God, who is love, if God himself has not given himself to that man. Therefore, God brings it about that our free choice is to love him and our neighbor as appropriate, because in God love is divinely given to a person. For without love, one can love neither God nor one's neighbor at any time. But God bestows himself on us so that we may love him. Because God is love, we do not love God except by this love. Therefore, unless we receive God, we cannot love God. Likewise, fire and water, life and death have been placed before a man so that he may extend his hand with free choice of will to whichever he wishes.[183] If free will is lacking, the hand reaches nowhere. But man never extends the same hand to grasp life unless God preserves that hand by his free goodness. For this reason, the prophet tells him, "You have held my right hand, and you have led me in your will."[184] Also, David says in another place that our right hand is itself preserved by divine protection, for he says, "The Lord is your keeper. The Lord is the protection of your right hand."[185] He implores him again to direct the works of our hands for us, after

178. Mt 22.37. 179. Mt 22.39.
180. Rom 5.5. 181. 1 Jn 4.7–8.
182. Cf. 1 Jn 4.16. 183. Cf. Sir 15.17–18.
184. Ps 72.24, following LXX (73.23 modern).
185. Ps 120.5 (121.5 modern).

he has granted illumination. So he says, "May the splendor of the Lord our God be upon us, and may he direct the works of our hands for us."[186]

16. (X.) And because there are so many passages of this kind in both the Old and New Testaments, it is very well demonstrated that divine grace continuously assists a man's choice, for either that choice is helpless to initiate good deeds without prevenient divine grace, or it can in no way be adequate on its own for performing them without the grace that goes before it. Nevertheless, one may not say that the choice does not exist just because it needs help. Nor may one say that because the choice exists, one must believe that it can suffice on its own to begin or to complete a good action. Accordingly, if the humble and meek heart assents to the divine words (because it can do so, if the gift of humility and meekness is divinely conferred upon it), wisdom and knowledge are granted to the contrite and humble heart because the veil has been lifted from the inner and higher understanding. For it is written, "The Lord gives wisdom, and from his face proceed knowledge and understanding."[187]

17. Therefore, there are no commandments except those God has given to man so that they may be useful in training a man to work voluntarily and humbly. Nevertheless, the good will does not begin without faith, and it is not perfected without love. But instead, faith and love are gifts of divine kindness. If a man did not voluntarily take to himself these gifts, he would not possess them or profit from them. (For God prepares a man's will in such a way that he may pour the gift of faith and love into him.) One must then admit that what we are taught by the holy words is true, namely, that a man is saved by God's mercy alone. For it is written: "Save me in your mercy."[188] One must also admit that man achieves everlasting salvation by the use of reason, if he runs and works in accordance with his own will. For the Apostle does not say in vain, "Run in such a way that you will grasp [the prize]";[189]

186. Ps 89.17, following LXX (90.17 modern).
187. Prv 2.6.   188. Ps 30.17 (31.16 modern).
189. 1 Cor 9.24.

and, "Each one will receive his own reward according to his labor";[190] and, "Labor as a good soldier of Christ Jesus";[191] and in another passage, "Therefore, brothers, be steadfast and immovable, always abounding in the work of the Lord, knowing that your labor is not in vain in the Lord."[192] In the book of Wisdom, someone seeks help for that kind of work, crying out with his whole heart, "God of our fathers and Lord of mercy, you made all things by your word, and in accordance with your wisdom you established man to rule over the creation that you made, to rule the world with equity and justice, and to dispense judgment with uprightness of spirit. Grant me wisdom, the consort of your throne."[193] And a little later he adds, "Send wisdom from your holy heaven, and send it from the seat of your greatness, so that it may be with me and labor with me, that I may know what is acceptable in your sight. For wisdom knows and understands all those things, and it will lead me prudently in my works and protect me by its power, and my works will be accepted."[194]

18. (XI.) Nevertheless, lest anyone think that even this desire to pray for wisdom for oneself is not divinely bestowed, the writer says just above that he knew that he could not have possessed the desire if God had not given it,[195] and he says that this very desire, in response to which wisdom was given, was itself a gift. Therefore, he was instructed to learn from what source he was stirred to pray. Nevertheless, he both knew willingly[196] and prayed willingly, because Christ's prevenient grace instructed and stirred his human choice, while it was yet ignorant and indolent, to know and to pray. Therefore, it is the role of divine mercy to enlighten man's free choice, for it is by free choice that a man both knows the things pleasing to God and combines the service of his work and God's assisting grace in voluntary devotion. The purpose of man's choice is said to be for his enlightenment: "My God, his mercy will come before me,"[197]

190. 1 Cor 3.8.
191. 2 Tm 2.3.
192. 1 Cor 15.58.
193. Wis 9.1–4.
194. Wis 9.10–12.
195. See Wis 8.21.
196. That is, he knew that he needed wisdom.
197. Ps 58.11 (59.10 modern).

and mercy is referred to for help: "Your mercy will follow me all the days of my life."[198] If this were not the case, choice would not be enlightened by prevenient grace. Nor could choice be helped by subsequent grace if its enlightenment were not suitable for some good thought or work. Divine revelation shows that this would be impossible when it says, "Who among men can know the mind of God? Or who can know what the Lord intends? The thoughts of mortals are fearful, and our plans are uncertain."[199] Therefore, the thoughts of mortals are fearful, not with a praiseworthy fear, but with a reprehensible one; not a good fear, but a bad one. From that fear God has freed us, he who "by death destroyed the one who had the power of death, that is, the devil, so that he might free those who through fear of death were subject to slavery all their lives."[200]

19. (XII.) Our Redeemer clearly identified this slavery from which he snatched us and this freedom that he freely conferred on us when he said, "If you remain in my word, you will truly be my disciples, and you will know the truth, and the truth will set you free."[201] And when the Jews claimed that they were the seed of Abraham and had never been slaves to anyone, he immediately in his response pointed out to them both their condition of deadly slavery and the true freedom that he was going to confer on his own followers. He said, "Truly, truly I say to you, whoever commits sin is a slave of sin. A slave does not remain in the house forever, but a son remains for ever. So if the Son sets you free, you will be truly free."[202] Therefore, he certainly establishes that those thoughts of mortals are fearful, thoughts by which they are slaves of sin and "subject to slavery all their lives."[203] Paul emphasizes that we have been freed from that slavery by God's grace, when he says, "For when you were slaves of sin, you were free of righteousness. But what fruits did you then bear that you are now ashamed of? Those things result in death. But now, since you have been set free from sin and have

---

198. Ps 22.6 (23.6 modern).   199. Wis 9.13–14.
200. Heb 2.14–15.   201. Jn 8.31–32.
202. Jn 8.34–36.   203. Heb 2.15.

become slaves of God, you have your fruit leading to sanctification, the outcome of which is truly eternal life."[204]

20. Behold what God's grace has bestowed on us! He has set
fearful people (about whom Scripture says, "The thoughts of
mortals are fearful")[205] free. Without doubt their thoughts were
subject to that fear, for which the divine word rebukes those
who are subject. It says, "There they were in great fear, where
there was no fear."[206] This is a fear begun by desire for things
of the world, a fear that causes guilt and increases punishment. This fear takes possession of its captives and keeps their
thoughts entangled in uncertain and unstable matters. For this
reason, the one who says, "The thoughts of mortals are fearful,"
immediately adds: "And our plans are uncertain."[207] For plans
that are devoted to uncertain things are uncertain, and uncertain things cannot be possessed certainly. Every day we can, in
spite of ourselves, lose whatever we cannot carry with us into
eternity. Consequently, the plans of mortals are uncertain precisely when the heart is entangled and gripped by love for either things that can be taken from the possessor against his will,
or possessions from which the possessor can be taken against
his will. A little later, Scripture shows us the source from which
the uncertainty of man's plans arises. It says, "A body that per-
ishes oppresses the soul, and an earthly dwelling depresses the
mind with its many thoughts, and it is with difficulty that we as-
sess the worth of things of the earth, and we discover with great
effort the things that are in front of our eyes."[208]

21. (XIII.) Therefore, after Holy Scripture has shown us the
affliction of our mortality, it then teaches us the grace of divine
kindness so that we may understand the source of the knowledge given to us and so that the advantage of rebuke and spiritual health may be conferred. As a result, one who can scarcely

204. Rom 6.20–22.
205. Wis 9.14.
206. Ps 13.5, following LXX (Ps 14.5 modern).
207. Wis 9.14.
208. Wis 9.15–16.

set a value on the things of earth and with great effort discover the things that "are in front of our eyes"[209] asks of God: "Who will search out what is in the heavens? Who will understand your mind, unless you confer your wisdom and send your Holy Spirit from on high? Were the paths of those who live on earth thus corrected? Did men learn what pleases you? Were they healed by your wisdom?"[210] What do the phrases "did they learn" and "were they healed" mean? They can mean nothing else but what he says is granted to men through the Holy Spirit and God's Wisdom (who is doubtless Christ). This is that we may learn what we must do for our spiritual health when God's prevenient mercy enlightens and heals us, so that what we learn through the prevenient grace we may do through the same subsequent grace. For indeed grace precedes us when the Lord forgives all our iniquities.[211] It follows us when the Lord heals all our diseases. Mercy precedes a man's free choice when through its own benevolence it brings about the beginning of a good will that did not yet exist. But mercy follows when it administers help to the person who has received that good will, so that he, by doing well, may achieve the result of a good will.

22. Therefore, prevenient mercy alone prepares a man's will to cooperate with it, and subsequent mercy helps the will to cooperate with it. Therefore, prevenient mercy freely leads a man who had been in darkness into the light, not only by admonishing from the outside, but also by bestowing the grace of enlightenment from the inside. For "the Lord gives sight to the blind,"[212] actually making an unbeliever into a believer, a proud man into a humble one, a harsh man into a meek one, a fornicator into a chaste man, a malicious man into a kind one, a ferocious man into a peaceful one, a lover of the world into a lover of God and his neighbor, a plunderer of others' property into a liberal giver. Thus, because God's mercy comes first and works wondrously in a man's heart, a man who was carnally arrogant because of temporal wealth willingly becomes a humble man who fears God and is poor in spirit. A harsh, disobedient

209. Wis 9.16.   210. Wis 9.16–19.
211. Cf. Ps 102.3 (103.3 modern).   212. Ps 145.8 (Ps 146.8 modern).

man who formerly fought against divine instruction becomes one who gently and peacefully submits to hearing and obeying the word. And a man who shortly before was drunk with a confusion of perversities and spewed forth iniquitous barbarities comes earnestly hungering and thirsting to be filled with righteousness. So it comes about that such a man even mourns for sins that he previously rejoiced in with fatal delight, and he then persists ceaselessly in works of mercy, and as he pursues mercy, he thereby achieves a crown. Finally, as his faith performs holy works laudably through love, he whose heart was some time ago filled with obscene thoughts achieves purity of heart so that he may see God.[213]

23. The right hand of the Most High brings about this change,[214] by which human choice is enlightened. These works of the Lord are great[215] and deftly crafted for all his plans. Thus does God prepare his plans in us, for he prepares in us what he finds in us. While he makes the bow of the powerful weak, he also girds the weak with strength.[216] That is, he weakens the presumptuousness of human strength in those men whom he saves freely, so that they may acknowledge their weakness and accept the help of divine strength. God mercifully does these things in us while he bestows good things for bad (that is, while he gives good things for bad by prevenient mercy), in order that he may preserve those good things in us by his subsequent mercy. For when he provides help to those who are justified and have a good will, he definitely furnishes an increase by his gifts, and in this way he strengthens what he has accomplished in us, while not allowing the good will (which he granted) to become inactive and fail us.

24. (XIV.) Thus, according to the Apostle's precept, with fear and trembling let us work out our own salvation, knowing that

213. The reader has undoubtedly noticed various allusions to the Beatitudes (Mt 5.3–11) in the latter half of this paragraph.
214. Cf. Ps 76.11, following LXX (77.10 modern).
215. Cf. Ps 110.2 (111.2 modern).
216. Cf. 1 Sm 2.4.

God is the one working in us both to will and to accomplish according to his good will.[217] And let us not think that because of the benefits of grace, we may neglect the precept and thus become careless about good works. For in fact, grace withdraws from those whose love grows cold. So let us listen to the Apostle (himself a participant in grace) as he shows us the works of grace. He says, "What then shall we say? Shall we continue in sin so that grace may abound?"[218] He immediately responds: "May it never be! For since we have died to sin, how shall we continue to live in it?"[219] Thus grace works in us so that we, being dead to sin, may live to righteousness. For this reason the same Apostle says again that we are to consider ourselves dead to sin, but alive to God in Christ Jesus our Lord.[220] Consequently, divine grace works salvifically through human choice with respect to both death and life: that is, with respect to the death of sins and the life of virtues. Therefore, God says, "It is I who will kill and will make alive."[221] When we lived to sin, corrupt works followed our corrupt will. In the same way, now that we have received the benefit of grace and therefore have a will changed for the better, let us live not to sin but to God. In order that this would come about, when we were indifferent because of the sentence of death upon us, we received a fervor for life from the Holy Spirit, who was freely given to us, so that we can, by the grace of God, both will and do the good. For this reason, the Apostle commands us to be "fervent in the Spirit, serving the Lord."[222] We must not cease from holy labor, for we are not only promised the reward of divine grace, but also provided with help. Since "each one will receive his own reward according to his labor,"[223] we must not, while doing good, be lacking in works and prayer,[224] nor must we ascribe any of these good things that we do to the strength of our will or capacity. If we were to do that, we would rightly be numbered among the proud, who, "being ignorant of God's righteousness and wanting to establish their own, have not submitted to God's righteousness."[225] For the wis-

217. Cf. Phil 2.12–13.
219. Rom 6.2.
221. Dt 32.39.
223. 1 Cor 3.8.
225. Rom 10.3.

218. Rom 6.1.
220. Cf. Rom 6.11.
222. Rom 12.11.
224. Cf. Gal 6.9.

dom of the flesh is in fact inimical to God, for it is not subject to the law of God, nor can it be.[226]

25. (XV.) Therefore, let the humble man's will follow the Redeemer's prevenient mercy and accompany his subsequent mercy. When mercy precedes us, we set aside those things that are behind; and when mercy follows us, we reach for the things that are ahead. Thus grace itself guides us by bestowing a hunger for things before us and removing the record of things past, and in doing so, it does not permit us to abandon the way of life we have laid hold of. Grace comes first so that we may pursue "the prize of the high calling of God."[227] Grace also follows so that we may glory in tribulations, "knowing that tribulation produces perseverance; and perseverance, character; and character, hope; and hope does not put to shame, because God's love has been poured out in our hearts through the Holy Spirit who has been given to us."[228] Grace keeps us from being seduced and captivated by the desires of the world or from yielding against our will in the face of adversities. Thus, because of subsequent mercy, we die to the world to the extent that we are more and more renewed in the spirit of our mind.

26. Therefore, to the extent that a man is divinely helped, let him make diligent efforts to obey the heavenly commands. Let him not assign to his own voluntary efforts the fact that he does not fail under hardship, that he steadfastly runs his course, that he fights the good fight, that he keeps the faith,[229] but let him attribute all these things to the gift of grace working in him and with him. Let him expend the effort of his good will on holy pursuits, for his will is good, if he does not doubt that his effort is the gift of divine generosity. In fact, the Apostle exhorts Timothy to excellence in this endeavor by saying, "Labor as a good soldier of Christ Jesus."[230] For he testifies that he has worked more than all others when he says, "I have worked more than all of them."[231] But in order to show that he had obtained the

226. Cf. Rom 8.7.
227. Phil 3.14.
228. Rom 5.3–5.
229. Cf. 2 Tm 4.7.
230. 2 Tm 2.3.
231. 1 Cor 15.10.

gift of faith and the power of working by the gift and help of divine grace, he continues, "I was formerly a blasphemer and a persecutor and an aggressor, but I obtained mercy."[232] And he shows the work of that same mercy when he says, "But I give my opinion as one who has obtained mercy from the Lord to be faithful."[233] Accordingly, after saying that he was not worthy to be called an apostle because he persecuted the Church of God, he shows the work of prevenient mercy in himself by saying, "But by the grace of God I am what I am."[234] And in order to show that the gift of working has been bestowed on him by the generosity of grace, he continues, "And his grace in me was not in vain."[235] And what does "vain" mean, if not useless? So he adds, "But I have worked more than all of them. Yet not I, but the grace of God labored with me."[236]

27. (XVI.) Grace alone worked in Paul to change him from an unbeliever into a believer. It converted an enemy and bestowed faith upon an unbeliever at a time when, because of his unbelief, he did not deserve to receive faith. As a result, Paul believed by his will and labored more abundantly by his will than all the others. But he could not have believed and labored had he not received from above the gift of grace that worked in him and with him. Therefore, when Paul was unwilling and unbelieving, grace went before him so that he might have a good will. In just the same way, the grace that had conferred that good will worked with the cooperation of Paul himself to help that good will in all ways. As a result, for this reason Paul's labor was fruitful, because he attributed his labor not to his own strength, but to the grace of God, whose help strengthened him. He knew he would not have had the incentive for that labor, nor would it be effective, if he had not had the help of prevenient and subsequent mercy. Therefore, the laborer did not lack a will, since grace gave that will, unceasingly helped the will it had given, and strengthened the one who possessed the will so that Paul would not fail in his work. Therefore, such a good will was wor-

232. 1 Tm 1.13.   233. 1 Cor 7.25.
234. 1 Cor 15.10.   235. Ibid.
236. Ibid.

thy of a reward for itself and for its labor, because both in its very existence and in its work, it relied not on its own strength, but on the generosity of divine grace. Finally, for this reason, Paul always truly and humbly attributed all the good he was able to think and to do not to himself but to God who strengthened him. (Thus, of course, he enjoyed success with restraint, and he also resisted adversities courageously.) For he said in a certain place, "Wherever and in whatever situation I may be found, I know how to be humbled and I know how to be exalted, to be full and to be hungry, to have an abundance and to suffer lack. I can do all things in him who strengthens me."[237] Therefore, Paul was able to do all things by his free choice, but only in him who had clothed him with strength from on high. About this he says, "In the work I need to accomplish, I labor according to his work that he accomplishes powerfully in me."[238] Therefore, blessed Paul was not silent about the mercy that preceded him so that he might be faithful, nor did he use the operative grace of Christ in himself as an excuse to cease from his holy work. For grace worked in him in such a way that he neither failed by becoming slothful nor became haughty by being ungrateful for the grace itself.

28. Accordingly, just as the Psalm admonishes us for our good, let us serve the Lord with fear, and let us exult in him with trembling,[239] since we know that "God is the one working in us both to will and to accomplish according to his good will."[240] The help of divine grace is very great and a great blessing. It enlightens the mind of a man so that he can always consider that he has been preceded by free grace and must be continuously supported by divine power. The result is that the man appropriately humbles himself before God (the giver and guardian of all good things), unceasingly gives thanks, and does not cease praying. Let him give thanks that grace has gone before him so that he, an enemy, might be converted, that he, a blind man, might receive sight, that he, an unbeliever, might receive faith. And let him pray that he, a sick man, may be healed, and that

237. Phil 4.12–13.
238. Col 1.29.
239. Cf. Ps 2.11.
240. Phil 2.13.

he, a feeble man, may be strengthened by the help of grace. So let him ask with his whole will, so that he may receive; let him seek, so that he may find; let him knock, so that it may be opened to him; for he will in no way act if he does not have the will to receive, to find, and to enter.[241] And when he receives by asking, finds by seeking, and enters by knocking, let him not attribute to his own power the task of asking, seeking, and knocking. For although a man asks, knocks, and seeks willingly, he will never be able to receive when asking, or to find when seeking, or to enter when knocking, unless he first receives a holy will. For, as the Apostle James says, some ask and do not receive because they ask amiss, intending to use what they receive for their covetous ends.[242] Regarding those seekers, Wisdom says of itself, "Evil men will seek me and will not find me."[243] For this reason, those who ask do not receive and those who seek do not find because they have a will that is dedicated to the delights of the world, "for their wisdom does not descend from above, but is earthly, unspiritual, of the devil."[244] And in order that a man may ask for and seek that highest and immutable good, the Lord prepares and gives his will. When the will is given, the beginning of asking, seeking, and knocking arises out of the heart of the man because God produces this very effect. For it is written, "Guard your heart in every way, for from it are the wellsprings of life."[245]

29. (XVII.) We guard our heart, if it guards us for the one to whom it is said, "Preserve me, O Lord, for in you I hope."[246] For this reason, after the Only-begotten God had assumed the humility of flesh, he showed compassion for our infirmities and deigned to pray earnestly for us, saying, "Father, in your name guard those whom you have given to me,"[247] and again: "I do not ask that you take them from the world, but that you guard them from the evil one."[248] Consequently, a man never guards

241. Cf. Mt 7.7–8.   242. Cf. Jas 4.3.
243. Cf. Prv 1.28.   244. Jas 3.15.
245. Prv 4.23.
246. Ps 15.1, following LXX (16.1 modern).
247. Jn 17.11.   248. Jn 17.15.

his heart with a corresponding protection unless his heart is watched over by the protecting God. For "unless the Lord watches over the city, those who watch over it watch in vain."[249] For this reason, the Apostle Paul desires divine protection for our hearts, saying: "May the peace of God, which surpasses all understanding, watch over your hearts and your minds in Christ Jesus."[250] And when God says to us through Jeremiah, "Watch over your lives,"[251] blessed David knows that he cannot fulfill this command, so he pleads for God to watch over his life, saying, "Watch over my life and deliver me."[252] He says again, "You, O Lord, will guard us, and you will protect us forever from that generation."[253] Also, since David desires divine protection to be extended to each of the faithful, he says, "The Lord protects you from all evil. May the Lord protect your life."[254] And so that we may know that we continually need the protection of divine grace, he continues, saying, "May the Lord watch over your coming in and your going out from this time forth and into the age."[255] To this end, it is said that the grace of God unceasingly watches over us because it says in the same Psalm, "Behold, the one who watches over Israel will neither slumber nor sleep."[256] Therefore, just as we receive all good things (including our good will) only from God's generosity, so we preserve all that we receive only as God watches over us. For whatever gifts of a good life a man may possess, God then preserves these good things if a good will should persevere in the man. And then the will itself, by whose goodness other good things are acquired well and preserved rightly, perseveres in a man as good and just if divine grace does not stop protecting it. For just as it can have no good thought of itself unless it is made good with the help of grace, so it can in no way be sufficient by its own power to protect the things it receives unless the one who freely makes it good preserves it with the help of his grace. Truly, he is certain

---

249. Ps 126.1 (127.1 modern).   250. Phil 4.7.
251. Jer 17.21.   252. Ps 24.20 (25.20 modern).
253. Ps 11.8, following LXX (12.7 modern).
254. Ps 120.7, following LXX (121.7 modern).
255. Ps 120.8, following LXX (121.8 modern).
256. Ps 120.4, following LXX (121.4 modern).

of the progress of a good will if he carefully and vigilantly protects the things he receives from God, with the result that he pleads earnestly for the help of divine protection with frequent prayer and eagerness for good work. Thus it will come about that as long as the one who is praying receives help, he will not be deprived of the reward for good work.

30. Truly, God will grant perseverance in praying for and doing what is good to those whom he has predestined to life. To be sure, "every excellent gift and every perfect gift is from above, coming down from the Father of lights."[257] Since he had eternal foreknowledge of his own works, he prepared not only the things he would give but also the rewards he would render, in accordance with the immutable counsel of his own good pleasure. For this reason, he accomplishes the things he has arranged exactly as he arranged for them to be accomplished. For just as the decree of divine providence has always held true, so also does the order of things run its course in divine actions. In that order of things, all of his ways are mercy and truth.[258] The one bestows good things on the evil; the other repays the good and the evil with things they deserve. The one crowns justly and condemns justly; the other justifies in accordance with free goodness. Each person receives justice by prevenient grace unless he does not attain the crown by the same supporting grace. If our brothers, with God's help, grasp these points according to healthy teaching, they will never try in their discussions to defend the weak power of human choice in such a way that they will be convinced to believe arguments against God's grace. On the contrary, all who desire to become sharers in eternal life must be divinely informed by and adhere to the inspired thoughts of the holy Fathers. These Fathers were enlightened by the gift of divine grace to such a degree that they doubtless asserted that no good thought arises in a man's will except what is imparted by the benefit of prevenient grace, that nothing increases for the better except what is strengthened by the help

257. Jas 1.17.
258. Ps 24.10, following LXX (25.10 modern).

of subsequent grace, and that man accomplishes nothing good that is not perfected by the same operative and assisting grace.

31. (XVIII.) There is no doubt that this teaching of the Catholic Fathers, which has been passed on to apostolic institutions, remains in the churches. The Greek and Latin bishops, shaped by the outpouring of the Holy Spirit, have always held it by a unified and indissoluble consent. On behalf of this teaching, blessed Augustine, endowed with power from on high, labored harder than all of them, although it was not he, but the grace of God with him.[259] For through his ministry the Lord provided very fruitful instruction on this matter to his faithful ones. To be sure, in Augustine's lifetime, the Pelagian heresy revolted against the grace of God with bold and fatal teachings.[260] And the invincible kindness of the merciful God never failed to surround his soldier with the weapons of spiritual grace, no matter how violently the devil incited vessels of wrath against that same grace. Accordingly, Augustine, the celebrated and renowned bishop of God who possessed the fortress of strength, the very grace of God, shattered all the intrigues of the hostile crowds with the power of heaven's help, and he triumphed not only by winning a complete victory over the enemy but also by showing posterity a way to fight and win, if the vanquished evil should ever try to rear its monstrous head in a daring comeback. Indeed, having the mind of Christ, Augustine distinguished between the functions and merits of God's grace and those of human choice, and he always subjected the human to the divine and truthfully taught that the gift of righteousness is divinely and freely given to man, just as are the beginning of a good will and the full effect of glorification. Let everyone who desires to achieve eternal salvation read this man, and let every-

259. Cf. 1 Cor 15.10.
260. Here Fulgentius has in mind both what modern scholars call the Pelagian Controversy (in which Augustine was involved from 412 until he secured Pelagius's condemnation in 418, and in which he continued to write against Pelagius's follower Julian of Eclanum into the 420s) and what we call the Semi-Pelagian Controversy (to which Augustine contributed four treatises in 428–429). These two were considered by ancient writers to be a single controversy.

one pray humbly to the merciful God, so that when he reads he may receive the same Spirit of understanding whom Augustine received so that he might write, and let him pray that he may obtain the same grace of enlightenment so that he may learn, which Augustine obtained so that he might teach.

32. And we marvel, not without great sadness, that those brothers of ours who in their ignorance strive to impoverish the grace of God (insofar as it is given in order to be understood) have invented for themselves an absurd illustration, according to which they say that the gift of God's grace is exactly like someone who lends money after receiving a suitable guarantee, which he could not accept for the debt unless he had it in hand. But whoever applies this illustration to God is doubtless trying to deceive or is himself deceived. For according to the parable as we actually have it,[261] our God said that the kingdom of heaven is like a householder who, setting out on a journey, entrusted to his servants money to be increased by suitable investments.[262] And here he shows that he gave his money without receiving any guarantee. Indeed, blessed Paul, who was bearing Christ, who spoke in him, knew who gave us the money and testifies that the one who gave the money also granted the privilege of a guarantee. He says, "For we who are burdened in this tabernacle groan because we do not wish to be unclothed, but to be clothed, so that what is mortal may be swallowed up by life. And he who is preparing us for this very thing is God, who has given us the Spirit as a guarantee."[263] Similarly, when writing to the Ephesians, Paul teaches about the same guarantee with these words: "You have been sealed by the Holy Spirit of promise, who is the guarantee of our inheritance."[264] We have been strengthened beforehand by a spiritual guarantee so that we might be not lazy but prudent in protecting and increasing our Lord's money. There is no doubt that the servant who ne-

261. Here Fulgentius is distinguishing the parable as found in Scripture, in which no guarantee was produced, from another version of the parable that apparently circulated in oral or written tradition, a version in which the lending of the money was preceded by a form of collateral.

262. See Lk 19.11–27.   263. 2 Cor 5.4–5.

264. Eph 1.13–14.

glected to increase the Lord's money which he had received did not have this guarantee.[265] Consequently, God bestows his money and the guarantee upon whom he pleases as a free gift. Besides, we ourselves did not give him anything in return for the guarantee we received (for "who has first given to him and it will be repaid to him?").[266] And we did not give him a guarantee for money, but we have both the guarantee and the money that God bestowed upon us. Because that guarantee protects us, we do not lose what we have, and the guarantee continuously helps us so that we can, by suitable investments, increase the money we have received.

33. (XIX.) We indeed are more apt to accept the passage of the Apostle Paul where he says of God, "Therefore, he has mercy on whom he wills, and hardens whom he wills,"[267] if we do not take it with an argumentative attitude but relate it to the conclusion of the thought. For the blessed Apostle was talking both about free mercy (by which, apart from merits, God saves those whom he wishes to save) and about just judgment (by which he condemns the others with blameless justice). As soon as he speaks of the children Esau and Jacob, he asks himself a question about them. For they had no merits (at any rate none deriving from their own works) because as long as they were not yet born, they had done nothing good or bad, although the guilt of original sin was holding them both bound. Since that was the case, earnest love was freely extended to the one through undeserved mercy, but condemnation was justly rendered to the other through deserved judgment. So in this matter, Paul anticipated the charge his adversaries might bring against him and said, "What therefore shall we say? There is no injustice in God, is there?" His immediate response was, "May it never be!"[268] And he strengthened his response with a pronouncement of legal testimony when he said, "And he said to Moses, I will be merciful to whom I am merciful, and I will show mercy to whom I will be merciful."[269] And in order to explain the meaning of

265. See Lk 19.20–21.   266. Rom 11.35.
267. Rom 9.18.   268. Rom 9.14.
269. Rom 9.15. Cf. Ex 33.19.

his promise, he concluded thus: "Therefore, it is not of the one who wills or of the one who runs, but of God, who shows mercy."[270] Therefore, after resolving the question he had proposed about the children, he used Pharaoh as an example to show that even in the case of people who are old enough to have the use of reason, their wills could be converted only by God's compassion. He said, "For Scripture says to Pharaoh, 'I have raised you up for this very purpose, that I may show my power in you, and that my name may be proclaimed in all the earth.'"[271] So he established the double example (concerning the free salvation of both children and adults) that he had laid out with one conclusion, when he said, "Therefore, he has mercy on whom he wishes, and he hardens whom he wishes."[272] He was able to say this because he knew that he was supported by the words of the law that God had also spoken to Moses: "I will have mercy on whom I have mercy,"[273] and he knew that these words included God's statement that he would harden Pharaoh's heart.

34. (XX.) Finally, after he reaches this conclusion, the blessed Apostle counters an opponent's claim. He does this not simply because the potential objection has been put forward, but also to make known the conclusion of his preceding argument. He says, "So you say to me, 'Why does he still find fault? For who resists his will?'"[274] The answer is that those who resist his will are men who wander about in the darkness of their own blindness, and they resist when they hear that God's grace goes before and changes the wills of men, and thus when they see that they are faulted for the perversity of their dark heart. When this happens, they are accustomed to excuse themselves by seeking unjust approval from the just will of God, but the result is that they receive an even greater punishment. They blame God for not granting them grace, and they excuse themselves for offending the just God with their iniquity. They inflict wounds upon themselves with their own hands and are not hesitant to make false accusations against the doctor, as if the cause of a person's own suicide

270. Rom 9.16.   271. Rom 9.17. Cf. Ex 9.16.
272. Rom 9.18.   273. Ex 33.19.
274. Rom 9.19.

lies not in the one who commits suicide, but in the one who did not come to his aid with a healthful cure. To be sure, medicine is not the cause of death, but its cure. So one is certainly not right to blame the medicine for a death if it is not provided for a very bad wound that a man inflicted on himself. It is indeed an example of justice if the wounded man is abandoned so that the death that he brought upon himself by his voluntary acts befalls him. And it is an example of mercy if the doctor keeps him from deadly destruction by the freely given benefit of a cure.

35. Therefore, it is even more iniquitous to defame the doctor's kindness when one considers that the destruction of a man who wounds himself is voluntary; as, for example, when the complaining sinner who looks within himself learns not to set the divine will in opposition to his attempts to excuse himself for his sin, but to ask humbly for mercy. In response, the Apostle says, "O man, who are you that you should talk back to God?"[275] Contrary to what some think, blessed Paul has not failed to respond to the complaining sinner, but has beneficially restrained the arrogance of his hardened heart with a sufficient reproof. When he says, "O man, who are you?" he is speaking to the arrogant sinner who examines himself and does not find anything in his works that pleases God. As a result of this question, the sinner has understood that the command remained necessary for him to live a good life. Through this question, Paul admonishes the sinner to pray for help earnestly and with the humility of a contrite heart, and to realize that he ought to be angry only with himself for whatever sins he committed in thought or deed. Consequently, he should know that a man never receives the will and ability to live in a just and holy manner in faith and love by birth from his human parents, but these are divinely granted by God's free generosity. This generosity precedes those evil wills of men and changes them into good ones, so that it may forgive the ungodly and iniquitous their sins. And the generosity also follows the same good wills by helping them, so that it may give a crown of righteousness to those who live a good life, a crown that God will grant to his faithful, not in the

275. Rom 9.20.

present age but at that future time when he will bestow glory on the vessels of mercy and condemn the vessels of shame to burn forever in eternal fire.

36. The opinion of certain brothers about these vessels of mercy and vessels of shame varies greatly from the truth. These brothers think that the vessels of mercy are those who hold positions in the ecclesiastical or secular armies of this age and that the vessels of shame are clerics and monks or laymen of any sort. They do not think that God's goodness (which makes a distinction based on freely bestowed love between vessels of mercy, which he prepared for glory, and vessels of wrath and shame) consists of the enlightenment of the heart, that is, of faith, hope, and love. By these the one "who perseveres to the end will be saved."[276]

37. (XXI.) For this reason, blessed Paul testifies that glory, honor, and peace can be given not to anyone endowed with a secular or ecclesiastical position, but to everyone who does good.[277] And speaking of vessels that are in a great house, he does not say that a greater position will produce a vessel of honor, but he claims that any true honor will be bestowed on those who have been cleansed. This is what he says: "But in a great house there are not only vessels of gold and silver, but also of wood and clay, some for noble use, some for ignoble. And if anyone purifies himself of the ignoble, he will be a vessel sanctified for honorable use and useful to the Lord, ready for any good work."[278] And again he says about God: "He will render to each one according to his works: to those who by patience in doing good work seek glory and honor and immortality, he will render eternal life; but to those who are contentious and do not obey the truth but trust in wickedness, he will render wrath and fury. There will be tribulation and anguish for every human soul who does evil, to the Jew first and to the Greek; but there will be glory and honor and peace to everyone who does good, to the Jew first and to the Greek."[279] Blessed Peter also shows

276. Mt 10.22.
278. 2 Tm 2.20–21.

277. Cf. Rom 2.10.
279. Rom 2.6–10.

that it is by the mercy of God that those who are saved are called vessels of mercy, not that they receive a temporal position in this life, but that the gift of regeneration is conferred on them in faith, hope, and love. He says,

Blessed is the God and Father of our Lord Jesus Christ. Through his great mercy he has begotten us anew into a living hope through the resurrection of Jesus Christ from the dead, and into an inheritance that is imperishable, undefiled, and unfading, preserved in heaven for you who are kept by the power of God through faith for a salvation prepared to be revealed in the last time. In this you will rejoice, though now for a little while you may have to suffer various trials so that your faith, which is much more precious than gold tested by fire, will be found to result in praise and honor and glory at the revelation of Jesus Christ. Although you do not see him you love him, and although you do not see him you believe in him. And as you believe, you rejoice with unutterable and exalted joy, and receive the end of your faith, the salvation of your souls.[280]

38. You see that the holy shepherd is providing the saving food of spiritual teaching for his sheep, which he received from the Prince and Lord of shepherds so that he might nourish them. He certainly shows what this God accomplishes "through his great mercy"[281] in his faithful ones, namely, rebirth, not into a hope of a secular or transitory ecclesiastical position, but into the hope of eternal life. This rebirth is not into an inheritance of service in the imperial or ecclesiastical army, but "into an inheritance that is imperishable, undefiled, and unfading."[282] This rebirth is not into a hope to be pursued on earth, but one that is "preserved in heaven."[283] The sheep [are born] not among those who achieve temporal heights of a secular or ecclesiastical position, but among those "who are kept by the power of God through faith for a salvation" that is not yet granted in its perfection in this age, but "prepared to be revealed in the last time."[284] He says that "you will rejoice" in this salvation and immediately adds as a way of indicating the character of the present life, "though now for a little while you may have to suffer various trials."[285] He then indicates that things happen to the

280. 1 Pt 1.3–9.
282. 1 Pt 1.4.
284. Ibid.

281. 1 Pt 1.3.
283. Ibid.
285. 1 Pt 1.6.

faithful for a useful purpose: "So that your faith, which is much more precious than gold tested by fire, will be found to result in praise and honor and glory."[286] He reveals that this hoped-for honor and glory are to be expected soon, "at the revelation of Jesus Christ."[287] The chosen vessel[288] also indicates this by saying, "For you have died, and your life is hidden with Christ in God. When Christ, your life, appears, then you also will appear with him in glory."[289]

39. (XXII.) Therefore, as this relates to life in this age, it is certain that no one is more powerful in the Church than the bishop or nobler in the secular world than the Christian emperor. But for this reason let no bishop whatsoever be considered to be a vessel of mercy prepared for glory simply because he serves in the ecclesiastical army. But he is a vessel of mercy if he is always diligent and watches over the flock entrusted to him, preaches the word, is ready in season and out of season, rebukes, implores, chides, with great patience and instruction,[290] and if he is not arrogant and does not strive to assert dominance, but shows himself to be a slave shaped by the apostles' words and examples, and if he does not rejoice that such a high position has been conferred on him in the temporal realm, but with a humble heart shows the faithful a good example of conduct.[291] Likewise, the most merciful emperor is not a vessel of mercy prepared for glory simply because he has received the summit of earthly sovereignty, but he is a vessel of mercy if he lives in his imperial height by the correct faith, and if he, endowed with a truly humble heart, submits the high position of his regal dignity to the holy religion. He is a vessel of mercy if he takes greater delight in fearing and serving God than in ruling arrogantly over the people, and if meekness restrains his wrath, and if gentleness adorns his power. He is a vessel of mercy if he shows himself to be more beloved than feared by everybody, and if he constructively favors the interests of his subjects. He is a vessel of mercy if he exercises judgment so as not to forsake

---

286. 1 Pt 1.7.
288. That is, Paul.
290. Cf. 2 Tm 4.2.

287. Ibid.
289. Col 3.3–4.
291. Cf. Ti 2.7.

mercy, and above all, if he remembers that he is a son of his holy mother, the Catholic Church, and, as a result, contributes through his reign to her peace and tranquility throughout the whole world. For the Christian state is governed and extended much more when its ruler consults the interests of the ecclesiastical station in every part of the earth than when he resists the Church merely for the sake of temporal security.

40. Therefore, each individual becomes a vessel for honor by the gift of the merciful God, not by some secular or ecclesiastical position, but by the faith that works through love.[292] The ones our Savior wanted to be called "blessed" were not those holding secular or ecclesiastical position, but the poor in spirit, the meek, the mourning, those hungering and thirsting for righteousness, the merciful, the pure in heart, the peacemakers, and those who endure persecution for righteousness' sake.[293] And neither temporal honors nor riches led our father Abraham to friendship with God. Instead, "because he believed God, it was credited to him as righteousness, and he was called God's friend."[294] Nor did want and temporal obscurity exclude the poor man Lazarus (who was tried by the affliction of poverty and hunger) from eternal rest. Rather, the power that the rich man Abraham divinely received (so that he might be poor in spirit and live a holy life in wealth) was the same power that the poor man Lazarus received (so that he might bear fruit with endurance and be carried over by angels and arrive in the bosom of wealthy Abraham). Thus, it came about that from the world's perspective, rich Abraham's abundance was one thing and poor Lazarus's want was something entirely different. But from God's perspective, rich Abraham had a sacred poverty in common with Lazarus, and poor Lazarus possessed a sacred wealth in undivided commonality with Abraham. For "God has chosen the poor in the world to be rich in faith and heirs of the kingdom that he promised to those who love him."[295] By means of that faith, all

292. Cf. Gal 5.6.
293. See Mt 5.3–10.
294. Jas 2.23. Cf. Gn 15.6, Rom 4.3, Gal 3.6.
295. Jas 2.5.

those who, with the Apostle, boast not in a temporal position, but "in the cross of our Lord Jesus Christ,"[296] become rich because they know that "the form of this world is passing away,"[297] and thus they have died to sin and live to God.[298] Both vessels of mercy and vessels of shame can, to be sure, acquire ecclesiastical and secular positions for themselves, because those positions are open to the good and the evil alike. But only the vessels of mercy truly "boast in the cross of our Lord Jesus Christ," for God "prepared them for glory ... and called them not only from the Jews, but also from the Gentiles."[299] As the blessed Apostle makes known, these vessels truly belong to Christ. He says, "Those who belong to Christ have crucified their flesh with its passions and desires."[300]

41. In no way will anyone who has been enlightened by divine mercy and reflects on this matter dare to place laypeople (however great a secular position they have been granted) above those who scorn the world (that is, clergy and monks who live holy lives), or to call such holy men vessels of shame. For by a gift of divine grace, these holy men have despised and scorned the world itself. Nor will anyone who reflects on this matter think that the others (those who have been established at the peak of secular power, that is, the princes of this world who are religious men) are vessels of mercy simply because they wield temporal power, when in fact they have merely worn the guise of Christian religion but have not truly and laudably subjected themselves to those who despise the world (both bishops and monks).

42. Therefore, can any Christian say that the emperor Constantine was a vessel of mercy in such a way that he calls Antony and Paul vessels of shame?[301] If Constantine Augustus of blessed

296. Gal 6.14.   297. 1 Cor 7.31.
298. Cf. Rom 6.11.   299. Rom 9.23–24.
300. Gal 5.24.

301. In the early fourth century Constantine was the first Christian Roman emperor. Antony, whose long life stretched from the mid-third to the mid-fourth century, was an Egyptian solitary monk and is considered to be the father of monasticism. The point of Fulgentius's comparison is that Antony and the Apostle

memory were still taking an interest in earthly matters, would
he not count such noxious praise of his name among the most
shameful acts? Or can anyone say that blessed emperor Theodosius was a vessel of mercy prepared for glory in such a way that
he excludes John Thebaeus the monk from the vessels of mercy
and perversely claims that he was a vessel made for shame?[302]
For the most glorious emperor Theodosius (to whom God, by
the merit of faith, which God himself had given, even subjected
the unconquered nations) is said to have brought so much hon-
or to John Thebaeus, that man of God, that he in no way pre-
sumed to attack those nations before being confirmed by John's
prophetic response. So did the most religious emperor believe
that such a man was a vessel of shame? No, because Theodosius
humbly consulted God in the person of this man, and through
him he immediately recognized that God was truly giving him
a response, since John testified to the outcome of the events.[303]

43. Who would deny that the following were blessed bishops: Innocent of Rome, Athanasius of Alexandria, Eustathius
of Antioch, Gregory of Nazianzus, Basil of Caesarea, Hilary of
Poitiers, Ambrose of Milan, John of Constantinople, Aurelius
of Carthage, Augustine of Hippo, and other bishops? They governed the churches of God very vigilantly and (with the Holy
Spirit dwelling in them) resisted those heretics who were emerg-
ing or had already emerged. They did not permit old wolves
to creep into the ecclesiastical flock or permit new ones to lie
perniciously hidden in the Lord's sheepfold. Who, I ask, would
deny that they are vessels of mercy that God has prepared for

---

Paul were clearly even more saintly than Constantine, although they held no
ecclesiastical or civil office.

302. The Theodosius whom Fulgentius mentions here is Theodosius I, Roman emperor in the closing decades of the fourth century. John Thebaeus was
an Egyptian solitary monk of the same time period. Again, the point is that the
latter had no official position but was at least as saintly as the former.

303. The story of Emperor Theodosius's consulting John Thebaeus before
going to battle is related in Rufinus, *Continuation of Eusebius's Ecclesiastical History*,
11.19, 11.32 (Latin text in Die Griechischen Christlichen Schriftsteller 9, 1024
and 1036; English translation in *The* Church History *of Rufinus of Aquileia, Books
10 and 11,* trans. Philip Amidon [Oxford: University Press, 1997], 77 and 87).

glory? But who is such an enemy of divine faith and love that he is not afraid of calling Paul, Antony, John, Hilary, Macarius, and other monks of similar life and holiness vessels of shame? For in them the truth of the correct faith and the integrity of a holy lifestyle shone forth. May it never be that any Christians might believe such things about God's worthy slaves.

44. (XXIII.) For any who are led by the Spirit of God are suspicious of such unworthy attitudes, not only about monks "who castrated themselves for the sake of the kingdom of heaven,"[304] but even about married laypeople who believe correctly and live uprightly. Certainly the seed sown by the Son of man that the good earth receives to be nourished in its fertile bosom produces different kinds of fruit. Since God now grants an abundant inward increase, the fruit increases not just a hundredfold, but also sixtyfold and thirtyfold, so that it may be gathered into the storehouse. For God says through the prophet that he will give the eunuchs, that is, the virgins, honor and a place in his city and within his walls that is better than the place of sons and daughters.[305] But because of the liberality of his goodness, he also speaks through his apostle to grant fitting honor to the abstinence of widows and to conjugal purity, as Paul says: "Honor widows who are truly widows";[306] and again: "Marriage is honorable among all, and the marriage bed undefiled."[307] Can it be that the Apostle, who says that in a great house there are some vessels for honor and others for shame,[308] would teach that widows and married couples were to be honored if he numbered them among the vessels of shame? Surely none of the faithful dare to deny that all who are devoted in faith and love to the virtues unbelievers have despised are vessels for honor. But who will dare to say that those who have been set at the Lord's right hand and to whom he is going to give the kingdom are vessels for shame? They fed him as he hungered and thirsted in the person of the least of his own, clothed him when he was naked, showed him hospitality when he was a wanderer, visited him

304. Mt 19.12.   305. See Is 56.5.
306. 1 Tm 5.3.   307. Heb 13.4.
308. Cf. 2 Tm 2.20.

when he was sick and in prison.[309] Who, pray tell, would dare to say that all those who the potter himself testifies are going to enter into eternal life are vessels prepared for shame?

45. Or perhaps, are those people saying that monks and lay-people who serve the Lord devoutly in their positions and professions are vessels of shame only in this age, because they themselves see clearly that the monks and laypeople suffer affronts and tribulations? But absurdity will immediately follow those who think such things, since they would be compelled first of all to call the blessed apostles (that is, the most glorious rams of the Lord's flock, the most vigilant shepherds) vessels of shame. Will brothers of that sort really say that, in their opinion, certain members of Christ's household are vessels of shame because (as Scripture testifies) they suffered shame for the name of Christ? Let such brothers hear blessed Paul as he speaks these words to the Thessalonians: "For you yourselves know, brothers, that our coming to you was not in vain, but although we had already suffered and been shamefully treated at Philippi, as you know, we were bold in our God to speak God's good news to you amid great opposition."[310] Likewise, while writing to the Corinthians he says, "I will gladly boast in my weaknesses so that the power of Christ may dwell in me. Therefore, I delight in weaknesses, in insults, in hardships, in persecutions, in distresses, for Christ's sake."[311] And so that they may know that it is common for all the saints to endure insults in this age, let them also hear what the book that Luke the evangelist wrote testifies concerning the other apostles and their acts. There he relates that after the apostles had been sent to prison and had been freed when an angel opened the doors of the prison, the Jews brought those apostles forward again and beat them murderously and threatened them with floggings so they would not speak in the name of Jesus, and then released them. Then Saint Luke tells us in these words that they joyfully suffered shame: "Then they left the council, rejoicing that they were counted worthy to suffer shame for the name of Christ."[312]

309. See Mt 25.34–36.   310. 1 Thes 2.1–2.
311. 2 Cor 12.9–10.   312. Acts 5.41.

46. (XXIV.) But perhaps the reason they will not say that the blessed apostles were vessels of shame is that those abuses the apostles bore for the name of Christ were seeds of future honor and glory, inasmuch as those abuses did not deprive them of the truth of faith or the virtue of holy living. So the brothers who think this should know that the vessels of shame are not those who bear abuses in this age, but rather, those who have been placed within the corporate body of the Church (which the Apostle calls "a great house")[313] and yet obstinately hold opinions contrary to the correct faith until the end [of their lives], or cast off the instructions for holy living. And at the same time let such brothers learn, according to blessed Paul's thought, that "if anyone purifies himself of those things,"[314] whatever his position, whatever his honor, whatever his profession, "he will be a vessel sanctified for honorable use and useful to the Lord, ready for any good work."[315] He will receive the eternal blessing of future reward from that Judge who in this age gives free justification to whom he pleases, and who supplies the assistance of grace to whom he has justified by faith, and who leads these people into the blessing of the kingdom of heaven as he gives them glory equal to that of the angels.

BOOK THREE

1. (I.) Now we must discuss the order of the work that is undertaken concerning those whom God has predestined to adoption as sons. These have been predestined in Christ according to the standard of true faith fixed by the authority of the Holy Scriptures. They have been predestined in Christ before the foundation of the world by God's free goodness, not only for the reward of glorification but also for the grace of justification, not only for the eternal blessedness that does not change but indeed also for the faith "that works through love,"[316] not only

---

313. 2 Tm 2.20.
314. That is, the ignoble things about which the vessels of shame are concerned.
315. 2 Tm 2.21. Cf. 1 Tm 3.17.
316. Gal 5.6.

for eternal rewards but also for good merits. No Christian is to doubt that by virtue of this predestination, these have been called and justified according to God's purpose. There is no doubt that whoever tries to deny the truth of divine predestination preaches a changeable God and perversely attributes to him merely temporal knowledge of temporal human deeds. For if God is immutable (a fact that one must not doubt), he has known all future events immutably from eternity, and he has ordered all his works according to his unchangeable decree. And at no time could there be any change in the arrangement by which his eternal knowledge of the things he has arranged remains without beginning. Accordingly, just as God's foreknowledge of future events has never been lacking, so also an eternal and immutable predestination of future works and gifts has never been lacking. To be sure, since God is both eternally immutable and immutably eternal, his knowledge of things that had not yet begun must nevertheless have always been present, and likewise, his eternal arrangement of changeable works has never been able to change. Therefore, just as God has never been ignorant of future events, so also has he not been unaware of his mercy and judgment. But just as he has always foreknown all future events, both good and bad, so also has he arranged all the works of his grace and justice in accordance with immutable predestination.

2. (II.) Great indeed is the depth of God's wisdom and knowledge! Full of these riches, he consciously knew all future things because he was wise, and he foreordained them wisely because he knew them. Indeed, it is not inappropriate to say to him, "Behold, you, O Lord, have known all things past and future."[317] And blessed Isaiah truthfully preaches that he has already made all future works, saying, "He made the things that are going to be."[318] To be sure, to the extent that he has already made all his future works, to that extent he has arranged all the things that must immutably come about. As a result, one may say rightly that

317. Ps 138.5, following LXX (139.4 modern).
318. Is 45.11, following LXX.

God has already done whatever he is going to do, and the eternal and immutable arrangement is found in the works he is to do. God's power and wisdom have immutably known from eternity all future things. He has irreproachably arranged all his future works, and thus everything that he has arranged he does invincibly. God does not change the things he has predestined, because one cannot deceive his wisdom or find fault with the way he has arranged things. And God accomplishes the things he has predestined, because no one can impede or overcome his power to accomplish these things. This constitutes the foreknowledge of our God, "all of whose ways are mercy and truth"[319] and to whom the Church truthfully sings on account of his mercy and judgment.[320] Because God is immutable and eternal, he foreknew with immutable and everlasting knowledge not only all his works (which are definitely good and "sought out in all his wishes"),[321] but also evil works of angels and of men that had to be carried out in time. He foreknew not only the things he arranged to give freely to those to whom he willed (so as to show that he is good), but also the things with which he intended to repay the good and the evil (so as to show that he is just).

3. Therefore, he freely predestined the ungodly to be justified and the just to be glorified so that he might precede and follow these people with his mercy. These are the ones who have been called according to his purpose; these are the ones "whom God foreknew and predestined to be conformed to the image of his Son."[322] But by whom were they to be conformed, if not by the one who promised them to Abraham? Abraham, strengthened by faith, gave that one[323] the glory, "being fully convinced that whatever he promised he was also able to do."[324] Therefore, God, who was "faithful in his words and holy in all his works,"[325] made and still makes those whom he has predestined to be conformed to the image of his Son. About them the

319. Cf. Ps 24.10, following LXX (25.10 modern).
320. Cf. Ps 100.1 (101.1 modern).
321. Ps 110.2, following LXX (111.2 modern).
322. Rom 8.29.   323. That is, God.
324. Rom 4.21.
325. Ps 144.13, following LXX (145.13 modern).

Apostle says, "Those whom he predestined he also called, and those whom he called he also justified, and those whom he justified he also glorified."[326] All those who have been predestined are thus called so that they may be justified, and they are thus justified so that they may be glorified by God. And, as a consequence, he predestined whom he pleased both to good works and to eternal rewards. He predestined them to a good life and predestined them to eternal life. He predestined them to faith and predestined them to splendor. He predestined them to be adopted in this age and predestined them to be glorified in the kingdom. He predestined them by grace to be made brothers of the Firstborn and predestined them by grace to be made perfect as co-heirs of the same Only-begotten.

4. (III.) Just as eternal predestination contains within itself all these things, so the mercy of God who predestines and his righteous majesty fill all things. For he could never have been unaware of future sons. Through his only Son (whom he begat without beginning and who was coeternal with him), he prepared for us from eternity the grace of predestination itself. He prepared grace freely, gave grace freely, chose whom he would justify in himself before the foundation of the world, not because of human merits, but because of the free purpose of his will. Thus he made his good will the origin of our justification, instead of finding our righteousness to be the origin of his will. For the Apostle testifies that God chose us in Christ "before the foundation of the world."[327] And in order to show that we did not deserve to be chosen as a result of works, but that we have gained good merits as a result of the gift of election, he added immediately: "That we might be holy and spotless in his sight."[328] This election existed in God's eternal preparation, which by his grace was to be brought to completion in time. This eternal preparation of election is itself divine predestination, in which everything is fitly attributed to the free benefit of divine goodness, because there alone the love of the merciful God toward us is found. For this reason, the Apostle impressed this point upon us to the point of saturation

326. Rom 8.30.   327. Eph 1.4.
328. Ibid.

by continuing, "In love he predestined us for adoption as sons in and through Jesus Christ."[329] And in order to teach that everything comes down solely from the purpose of God's good will, he added, "In accordance with the purpose of his will."[330] And in order to show that this purpose of God's good will is free, he continued by adding: "To the praise of his glorious grace, by which he has graced us in his beloved Son."[331]

5. Therefore, it is profitable not only to recognize that the sons of God are predestined to this, but also to preach this fact, so that, just as we recognize that in all good aspects of the human will and work, divine predestination is working through the eternal preparation of grace, we may likewise recognize that the same predestination is working in the gift of grace itself. For this reason, we may glorify and praise God's grace in the very adoption of the sons of God that God prepared from eternity by predestining and that he now bestows by calling and justifying in time. For "God chose us in Christ before the foundation of the world that we might be holy and spotless in his sight."[332]

(IV.) Therefore, he did not find holy or spotless people so that he might choose them, nor did he foreknow that they were to be found, but he chose them before the foundation of the world so that he might make them holy and spotless. Therefore, he did not choose us because we were going to be holy and spotless, but so that we might be holy and spotless. Consequently, he predestined us "in love" in the sense that he applied to us the effect of his free love so that he might predestine us. Thus "he predestined us for adoption as sons in and through Jesus Christ,"[333] not according to the merit of our will or our work, but according to the purpose of his will. And inasmuch as we have freely received this adoption as sons from God, by whom we have been freely elected to be holy and spotless, blessed Paul makes known to us in all these things the praise of God's glorious grace. He intends everyone who is enlightened by this gift of grace both to understand that the true gift of grace derives

329. Eph 1.5.   330. Ibid.
331. Eph 1.6.   332. Eph 1.4.
333. Eph 1.5.

from eternal predestination, and to acknowledge that God's eternal predestination derives from the gift of spiritual grace.

6. This predestination remains eternally steadfast and steadfastly eternal, not only in its arrangement of the works, but also in the number of persons [it has chosen]. Thus, no one from the plenitude of that number will lose the grace of eternal salvation, and no one who is not of that number will attain the gift of eternal salvation. Since God knows all things before they come about, just as he is certain about the number of the predestined, so also there is no doubt about the outcome of works he has planned. The number of the predestined is most certain in the mind of the one who predestined them to adoption as sons through Christ, for he has ordered all things by measure, number, and weight.[334] For God promised them to Abraham, saying, "'Look into the heavens and count the stars, if you are able to number them'; and he said, 'So shall your seed be.' And Abraham believed God, and it was accounted to him as righteousness."[335] Concerning them it is said to the prophet Daniel: "And at that time your people, everyone who is found written in the book, will be saved."[336] Indeed, our Savior says to them: "Rejoice, because your names are written in heaven."[337] About them it is written in holy Daniel's book: "Those who instruct many in righteousness will be like stars forever and ever."[338] They are understood spiritually in the Psalm where it is said of God: "He counts the multitude of the stars and calls them all by name."[339] Hence, he who numbers the multitude of the stars cannot be ignorant of the number of his sons.

7. (V.) No one is added to or removed from that number, because the number itself is being completed according to the purpose of God who predestines. For in fact God predestined his saints in accordance with the purpose established by his will, and it is written about him that "he has done all things that he willed."[340] Just as no one can change God's predestination, so no

334. Cf. Wis 11.21.
335. Gn 15.5–6.
336. Dn 12.1.
337. Lk 10.20.
338. Dn 12.3.
339. Ps 146.4, following LXX (147.4 modern).
340. Ps 134.6 (135.6 modern).

one can bind his will. For if that number is not certain in God's
mind, then either divine knowledge is in error, or the divine will
is found to be mutable, or divine power is overcome by some
kind of opposition. Moreover, if only the ungodly can say any of
those things just above, or if perchance not even an ungodly person would be bold enough to say any of those things, then let no
one deny divine predestination, because we declare God's predestination to be unequivocally true, his knowledge blameless,
his will immutable, and his power unconquerable. To this predestination belong both the Redeemer's free justification and
the Judge's righteous retribution. To this predestination belong
both the mercy that Paul pursued in order to be faithful[341] and
the crown of righteousness which the Lord, the righteous Judge,
will grant to him in that day, and not only to Paul, but also to all
those who love his coming.[342] For all those whom God predestined for adoption are here freely justified from among the ungodly, since "Christ died for the ungodly,"[343] and since "all have
sinned and come short of God's glory, being justified freely by
his grace."[344] Just as he has prepared for them the free gift of justification by his mercy, so has he prepared the reward of eternal
justification by his righteousness. Therefore, the work of grace
begins with the free gift of mercy to all who are predestined, and
it is brought to completion by a just reward.

8. Thus God predestined his saints both to the grace of a
good life and to the grace of eternal life. Thus, "God's grace
is eternal life in Christ Jesus our Lord."[345] Consequently, the
ungodly are justified by the grace of God so that they may "re-
nounce ungodliness and worldly lusts so as to live sober, righteous, and godly lives in this present world,"[346] and so that "having been justified by his grace, they may be heirs of the hope of
eternal life."[347] Therefore, God gives the grace he has prepared
so that men may be justified and live good lives and receive eternal life in return for the upright things they have done. And for

341. Cf. 1 Cor 7.25.
343. Rom 5.6.
345. Rom 6.23.
347. Ti 3.7.

342. Cf. 2 Tm 4.8.
344. Rom 3.23.
346. Ti 2.12.

this reason the Apostle says that eternal life itself is the grace of God,[348] for men freely receive the gift of the good life, for which eternal life may be justly rendered. But God also prepared eternal fire for the wicked, whom indeed he justly prepared to pay their penalties while still not predestining them to commit sins. For God predestined what divine justice repays, not what human injustice allows. Therefore, he did not predestine a guilty man to sin, which he hates, but he predestined such a man to judgment, which he loves. For it is written that the Lord "loves mercy and judgment."[349] Consequently, God is going to punish not only original sin, but also every actual sin present in the wicked, because he does not provide a beginning for evil works, and never does he engage in any agreement with them. So evil works do not please God because they do not come from him. If in fact they came from him, they would not be evil. Accordingly, God justly crowns the good works that he mercifully gives; and he justly punishes the [evil] works that he does not himself give. In the former case, he crowns his own divine generosity, but in the latter case, he condemns human transgression. Therefore, what man has received from God is salvific for him, but what has come from himself is destructive.

9. (VI.) It is very reprehensible to say that if there is predestination, we need not pray or be watchful, but that we may yield to all the desires of the flesh because we have already been predestined. But certainly, since that grace that was prepared for us by divine predestination is divinely given to us so that we may watch and pray and "walk uprightly as in the day, not in reveling and drunkenness, not in debauchery and licentiousness, not in quarrelling and jealousy, but let us put on the Lord Jesus Christ and not make provision for the flesh in its desires."[350] For how can it be that someone receives grace and yet does not do the works of grace when grace itself works in him? To be sure, grace is given by the Holy Spirit: but "the fruit of the Spirit is love, joy, peace, longsuffering, goodness, kindness, faithfulness, gentle-

348. Cf. Rom 6.23.
349. Ps 32.5, following LXX (33.5 modern).
350. Rom 13.13–14.

ness, self-control."[351] Therefore, after receiving the grace of the Spirit, what person does not pray, is not vigilant, does not resist the desires of the flesh by using the support and help of grace itself? Indeed, our Savior instructs us to watch and pray,[352] and blessed Paul testifies that "those who belong to Christ have crucified their flesh with its passions and desires."[353]

10. Thus, if anyone should say, "If a man has been predestined, he need not pray or watch," it would be like saying that one who has been promised life by God should not seek the things necessary for life. We read that fifteen years were added to the life of King Hezekiah as a gift of divine compassion.[354] Therefore, since Hezekiah received what he considered to be an unequivocal divine promise, should he have said that he ought not accept food or drink, or even give any attention to the things necessary for life? Indeed it is because these things are given that a person perseveres in his desire to live, and that he loves his life and does not reject those things necessary for life. From experience we know that we think anxiously about the conditions of life. Accordingly, God's grace, which he predestined (that is, prepared from eternity for his faithful), accomplishes this in us because we received grace so that we might ask that this grace be preserved in us in accordance with the divine gift, and so that what we received in accordance with the generosity of grace might also produce good works in us. And in those people the gifts of grace (that were prepared for them as a benefit of divine predestination) continue. Therefore, let no one ever say, "If we have been predestined, let us not be vigilant or pray." When we watch and pray, let us realize the benefits of God's grace. And let us not deny that those good things that we see in ourselves originate from God's generosity. In the same way that we cannot doubt that those gifts have been predestined, so we know that they were eternally prepared. This is why the Apostle says, "For we are his workmanship, created in Christ Jesus for good works that God has prepared so that we may walk in them."[355]

---

351. Gal 5.22–23.
353. Gal 5.24.
355. Eph 2.10.

352. Mt 26.41.
354. Cf. 2 Kgs 20.6.

11. (VII.) And may it never be said that the evangelical and apostolic commands do not apply if one claims that predestination is in effect. Since Jesus knew from the beginning those who were going to believe and who was going to betray him,[356] the Creator's knowledge cannot have been false. For this reason, just as he foreknew his betrayer, no one betrayed him except the one whom he foreknew. In just the same way, he knew those who had been predestined to faith by his preparation, so he knew from the beginning those who would believe. But how do we explain the apostolic statements about predestination, since we know from the Apostle's preaching that not only were those who are members of Christ predestined, but so was Christ himself? Blessed Paul says about Christ, "He was made from the seed of David according to the flesh; he was predestined to be Son of God in power, according to the Spirit of sanctification."[357] He also says in another passage, "But we speak wisdom among the mature, wisdom that truly is not of this age or of the rulers of this age, who are being destroyed. But we speak God's wisdom in a mystery, wisdom that was hidden, that God predestined before the ages for our glory."[358] So what is one doing when one disputes the claim of predestination, if not finding fault with the apostolic teaching by a fatal impiety? To be sure, Paul had learned and was teaching divine predestination, which he knew in his head and did not deny in his body. He knew that the eternal and immutable God had, in accordance with his eternal and immutable will, foreknown all things that he himself was planning to do and had predestined all things that he foreknew he himself was going to do mercifully and justly among his saints.

12. (VIII.) Therefore, let anyone who denies predestination first delete it from the apostolic letters, and then when he has sufficiently shown that he has refuted the Apostle Paul, let him then demonstrate to men that he himself doubtless deserves to be heard. The blessed Apostle Paul did not want what he desired to write to be kept silent, but instead, just as he argued [for the truth] in his letters whenever he knew that there was some error

356. See Jn 6.65 (6.64 modern).   357. Rom 1.3.
358. 1 Cor 2.6–7.

in men, so also he wanted the truth he wrote in his letters to be preached to all men. Therefore, there is no doubt that whoever strives to refute or fight against the apostolic words denies the apostolic commands. For the blessed Apostle preached predestination faithfully and truthfully, and in the same way he commanded that it be preached faithfully and truthfully to us. And he was not afraid of being seen as introducing something like a horoscope or fate or astrology. For this reason, those brothers of yours are needlessly afraid, trembling with fear where there is no fear.[359] And while they are afraid of being censured by the ungodly, they do not hesitate to have impious feelings about God. For who can feel more antagonistic toward the eternal God, the true God, the good and blessed God, than one who denies that God has known from eternity what was going to happen in time, or who ascribes chance events to divine works while still denying that the eternal counsel of God's future work remains in the eternal will of the immutable God? This assertion is truly inimical to the divine counsel, because when it completely denies that men's good intentions and works have been held in God's eternal predestination, it thus affirms that God's knowledge depends on human intentions and actions. For there is no doubt that if God foreknew all his future works from eternity, he also prepared those works in accordance with the purpose of his good will, and he arranged what he was going to perform in accordance with the constancy of his immutable counsel. The order of the divine works cannot run its course except by remaining true to what is found among the things prepared in his immutable knowledge.

13. (IX.) For anything done in time (which is consequently mutable) is found to be eternal and immutable by nature in the depth of the riches of God's wisdom and knowledge. God knew all future events because of the fullness of his knowledge, and before the events took place he prepared all his works in wondrous order in accordance with the depth of his wisdom. Otherwise, human thought and action would precede divine wisdom

359. Cf. Ps 13.5, following LXX (14.5 modern).

PREDESTINATION AND GRACE 209

if divine knowledge did not understand it from eternity. And if God is immutable and eternal, his knowledge must be immutable and eternal. And nothing of his immutable and eternal knowledge happens in time, because if he knows that anything has happened in time, it is necessarily subject to a beginning and to mutability, and nature cannot exist without a beginning. Consequently, one finds that knowledge about nature has a beginning. In other words, whatever had not existed came into existence, and consequently non-existent knowledge about it also came into existence. And one who could possibly not know something at some time could not at the same time encompass all things in the fullness of his knowledge. Therefore, if someone did not comprehend some event that was going to happen, or if he did not comprehend what that event was going to accomplish in his eternal ordering and predestination, then that someone was actually devoid of the fullness of knowledge and thus was himself always mutable. One could not then say of him that his wisdom "applies all things powerfully from one end of the earth to the other and arranges them sweetly,"[360] nor could one say that his wisdom "applies them everywhere because of the wisdom's purity."[361] His immutability, then, does not remain intact if he cannot use his eternal counsel for his temporal works, but is able to use only his temporal counsel.

14. Therefore, since we know that God is immutable and eternal and perfect, the omnipotent Creator of all creatures, the eternal Knower and Arranger of all things that he was going to make, let us confess that he foreknew all his works from eternity, that he foreordained them from eternity, and that he prepared his gifts and ordinances from eternity. He to whom the prophet said, "In wisdom you have made all things,"[362] established all things in that same wisdom and arranged all the things that he had known from all eternity he was going to do, for he was aware of everything he was going to do. Therefore, "before the foundation of the world"[363] God has chosen

360. Wis 8.1.
361. Wis 7.24.
362. Ps 103.24 (104.24 modern).
363. Eph 1.4.

and predestined all those whom he calls and justifies "accord-ing to his will,"[364] of whatever age and at whatever time. He also gives them perseverance and leads them all to eternal life. For "he wills all to be saved and to come to the knowledge of the truth."[365] The will of the omnipotent One, however, must neces-sarily be fulfilled in all things. Therefore, whatever he has willed to happen happens, and no one resists his will. For the power of God is not less than his will, and as a result, there is nothing he might will that he cannot perform. To be sure, there are certain things that God does not will to do, although he is able to do them. Yet there is nothing he wills to happen at any time that he does not do: "The Lord has done all things that he willed in heaven and on earth, in the sea and in all the deep places."[366] Accordingly, everything he has willed to do in men, he does. He saves all those he wills to be saved, and because the Truth him-self truly says, "No one comes to me unless the Father who sent me draws him forth,"[367] he causes to come to the knowledge of the truth all whom he mercifully deigns to draw forth.

15. (X.) But the word "all" is used because they are brought together from every race of human beings, that is, from all na-tions, all stations in life, all masters, all servants, all kings, all sol-diers, from all provinces, all languages, all ages, and all ranks. Thus, all whom God wills to be saved are saved, because no one is saved unless God wills to save him by free justification. For when our Savior says, "No one knows the Son except the Father; and no one knows the Father except the Son, and the one to whom the Son has willed to reveal him,"[368] he is indeed showing that he wishes to be revealed to certain persons and does not wish to be revealed to certain others. How could he wish those to be saved if he does not wish to reveal his Father and himself to them? To be sure, it is clear in the Gospel that he spoke in parables precisely because he wanted his words to be heard but did not want them to be understood. There is no doubt that the Lord himself revealed this fact, because when the disciples

---

364. Eph 1.11.
365. 1 Tm 2.4.
366. Ps 134.6 (135.6 modern).
367. Jn 6.44.
368. Mt 11.27.

asked,[369] Matthew remembers that he said these things to them: "To you it has been given to know the mystery of the kingdom of heaven; to them it has not been given."[370] Mark also teaches that the Savior gave a similar response, testifying that these were his words: "To you it has been given to know the mystery of the kingdom of God; but to those who are outside, everything is in parables, so that those who see may see but not perceive, and that those who hear may hear but not understand, lest they be converted and their sins be forgiven."[371] Luke, too, confirms that the Lord responded similarly: "To you it has been given to know the mystery of the kingdom of God, but to others [I speak] in parables, so that those who see may not perceive and that those who hear may not understand."[372]

16. To be sure, it appears that the Lord spoke to the crowds in such a way because he did not want to reveal the mystery of the kingdom of heaven to them. In doing this, he did not want his words to be understood because he did not want them to recognize that the mystery was about him. The Apostle Paul testifies that the knowledge in question was about the mystery of Christ, saying: "Having been instructed in love so as to obtain all the riches belonging to the fullness of understanding, in the knowledge of the mystery of Christ Jesus, in whom all the treasures of wisdom and knowledge have been hidden."[373] He also says in another passage, "so that God will open for us a door for his word to declare the mystery of Christ."[374] And also, when he teaches the faithful about his perseverance in prayer, he says, "I do not cease to give thanks for you, remembering you in my prayers, that the God of our Lord Jesus Christ, the Father of glory, may give you the Spirit of wisdom and of revelation in the knowledge of him."[375] Therefore, if in general God wills all men to be saved and to come to the knowledge of the truth, why does the Truth himself hide from some people the mystery of knowledge of himself? And to those to whom he denies knowledge of himself, he

369. That is, they asked why he spoke in parables.
370. Mt 13.11.   371. Mk 4.11–12.
372. Lk 8.10.   373. Col 2.2–3.
374. Col 4.3.   375. Eph 1.16–17.

also denies salvation. For men are saved simply by coming to the knowledge of the Truth.[376] Of Christ it is truly said that "he will save his people from their sins."[377] Even blessed Peter says of him that "there is no other name under heaven given among men by which we must be saved."[378] So how could God have willed that those people be saved, when he hid the very knowledge of the Truth from them?

17. (XI.) Or does it possibly mean that because they were hardening their hearts, our Savior did not wish to reveal the mystery of knowledge of himself? About this we could answer more broadly, but let us summarize for the sake of brevity. If people want to say that the reason the Truth himself did not want to reveal the mystery of knowledge of himself was "because of the hardness of their hearts,"[379] such people must recognize at the same time that the affirmation that God "wills all men to be saved and to come to the knowledge of the truth" does not apply to absolutely all men. We know this precisely because Christ did not want to save those whom he saw as hard of heart and to whom, because of their hard hearts, he kept refusing to uncover the mystery of knowledge of himself. [So such people are logically compelled to do one of two things:] First, they are compelled to deny that God "wills all men to be saved and to come to the knowledge of the truth," since they know that our Savior did not want to give the knowledge of the mystery of the kingdom of heaven to certain people. In that case, they would be calling the Apostle Paul a liar. Or, second, they are compelled to call the holy evangelists liars, if the Apostle's statement does refer universally to all people. For how did one who "wills all people to be saved and to come to the knowledge of the truth" refuse to grant to certain people to know the mystery of the kingdom of heaven? For if he really does will to save all men whatsoever, there is no one whom he does not so will. And if he wills all to come to knowledge of himself, he is obliged to reveal to all people the mystery of knowledge of himself. But there were some to whom he did not grant the knowledge of the mystery itself.

376. Cf. 1 Tm 2.4.   377. Mt 1.21.
378. Acts 4.12.   379. Mt 19.8.

18. What, then, does it mean to will to save yet not to will to reveal the mystery of salvation? What, I ask, did it mean when he said that the Truth willed all men to come to knowledge of him and that he did not will to reveal to them the means by which they might come? What does it mean that he denies life to those he invites to his Father's domain? He said, "I am the way, the truth, and the life. No one comes to the Father except through me."[380] How, then, does he want those to whom he refuses the knowledge of himself to come to the knowledge of himself? What does it mean, then, to refuse to reveal the mystery of knowledge of himself, if it does not mean to refuse to save? Therefore, one who refuses to open the mystery of knowledge of himself to some people because of the hardness of their hearts does not will all people to be saved, for without that knowledge of him no one attains to salvation. But the Apostle could not be lying when he said that God "wills all men to be saved and to come to the knowledge of the truth."[381] Nor did the Evangelists lie when they said that the Lord himself had granted the disciples, but not others, to know the mystery of the kingdom of heaven. And there is no doubt that they knew that he granted this to those to whom he willed to grant it, and did not grant it to those to whom he did not will to grant it. The evangelists also knew that this was why he granted such knowledge to the former so they would be saved and did not grant it to the latter so they would not be saved. Therefore, he willed to save those to whom he granted the knowledge of the mystery of salvation, but he did not will to save those to whom he denied the knowledge of the saving mystery. For if he had willed to save both groups, he would have granted both groups the knowledge of the saving mystery.

19. (XII.) Therefore, both passages of Scripture are true, both are holy, both are divinely inspired; and for this reason both must be treated reverently, heard and accepted without doubting. Thus let all those whom Christ did not grant to know the mystery of the kingdom of heaven be separated from all the

380. Jn 14.6.
381. 1 Tm 2.4.

others, and let all those whom God "wills to be saved and to come to the knowledge of the truth" understand rightly that the will of the saving God is in truth known [only] to those to whom the grace of knowing the Truth is granted. In this way, God, since he has accomplished all things that he has willed, fulfills his will in all things, for he gives the correct knowledge of the mystery of salvation, along with love, to all whom he "wills to be saved and to come to the knowledge of the truth." Blessed Peter shows that the word "all" is to be understood as meaning "all those whom God deigns to call." These are his words as he speaks to the Jews: "For the promise is to you and to your children, and to all who are far off, even to whomever the Lord our God calls."[382]

20. For blessed Paul also uses the word "all" in a certain passage without intending it to be understood as referring to all people indiscriminately. Writing to the Philippians, he says: "All are seeking their own interests, not those of Jesus Christ."[383] If, in that passage, no one is excluded from that "all," then all the apostles and the other believers of that time must indeed be counted among the "all," because no ungodly person will be considered. Therefore, it remains that we must understand "all" to mean "certain ones," that is, not all people without exception, but all who seek their own interests, not the interests of Jesus Christ. Earlier in the same letter he indicates some good people: "But some preach Christ from a good will, some from love, for they know that I have been placed here for the defense of the Gospel."[384] Therefore, those who were preaching Christ from a good will out of love were not seeking their own interests, but Jesus Christ's, because "love does not seek its own interests."[385] Thus, they were not among all those who were seeking their own interests instead of Jesus Christ's. At the end of his letter, he calls these good people "saints." And just as he calls all the others evil, so he also calls all the former ones good, for he says, "All the saints greet you."[386] Consider this: In one and the

382. Acts 2.39.
383. Phil 2.21.
384. Phil 1.15–16.
385. 1 Cor 13.5.
386. Phil 4.22.

same letter, blessed Paul mentions all the saints and all those who seek their own interests instead of Jesus Christ's, for in truth all who were not seeking their own interests were saints, and all those who were seeking their own interests were not saints. So one must consider all the former and all the latter not as a single entity, but as separate entities. In other words, both are designated as "all" in such a way that all the former may be distinguished from all the latter, and all the latter from all the former, in accordance with the right ordering of the truth.

21. We find this same understanding of the word "all" in all the tribes that God promised to the seed of Abraham, as well as in the one in whom God indicates the tribes are to be blessed. God says, "And in you will all the tribes of the earth be blessed."[387] Blessed Peter also confirmed this, saying to the Jews: "You are the sons of the prophets and of the covenant that God made with our fathers, saying to Abraham: 'In your seed will all the nations of the earth be blessed.'"[388] And in order to show that Christ was the seed of Abraham, in whom the promised blessing of every tribe would be found, he immediately added these words: "God first raised up his Son for you and sent him to bless you."[389] Christ, therefore, is the seed of Abraham, in whom all the tribes of the earth will be blessed. God's promise is indeed true, for "the Lord is faithful in his words, and holy in all his works."[390] Concerning God's promise, Abraham "did not waver in distrust, but he was strengthened in faith, giving glory to God and being fully convinced that whatever he promised he was also able to do."[391]

(XIII.) Therefore, although no Christian doubts that all the tribes of the earth are blessed in Christ, nevertheless blessed John, speaking in the Apocalypse about Christ (that is, about the very seed of Abraham, in whom all the tribes of the earth will be blessed), says truthfully, "Behold, he will come with the clouds,

---

387. Gn 22.18. Cf. Gn 12.3.   388. Acts 3.25.
389. Acts 3.26.
390. Ps 144.13, following LXX (145.13 modern).
391. Rom 4.20–21.

and every eye will see him, as well as those who pierced him, and all the tribes of the earth will see and lament over him."[392] Behold, all the tribes of the earth will be blessed in Christ, and all the tribes of the earth will lament when he comes.

22. So how will we hold both of these ideas together in our minds if we understand the universal fullness of all the tribes as consisting either [completely] in goodness or [completely] in evil, such that nothing is left for the other side? Instead, the same blessed John (who drank in the abundance of true preaching from the breast of truth) represented all the tribes that would lament at Christ's coming so as to make clear that the true God promised that all the tribes that would be blessed through the seed of Abraham were being gathered from all the other tribes. In the same book, he introduces those who have been redeemed by the blood of the Lamb as they sing a new song, saying: "Worthy are you to take the scroll and to open its seals, for you were slain, and by your blood you have redeemed us for our God, from every tribe and tongue and people and nation, and you have made us a kingdom and priests for our God, and they will rule over all the earth."[393] In another passage of the book just cited, when each of the twelve tribes of the sons of Israel is known to represent thousands of witnesses, so that each tribe also represents an innumerable multitude of believers from all the tribes of the earth, the text says, "After this, I saw a great multitude that no one could number, from all the nations and tribes and peoples and tongues, standing before the throne and before the Lamb, dressed in white robes, with palm branches in their hands."[394] These constitute all the tribes gathered together from all the tribes. They are all the tribes that believe in Christ and are blessed, as distinct from all those tribes that lament because they had not believed in Christ. Thus the tribes are understood to comprise all believers and all unbelievers, all the good and all the evil, all whom God saves in accordance with his most merciful kindness, and all whom he condemns in

392. Rv 1.7.
394. Rv 7.9.

393. Rv 5.9–10.

accordance with his most just severity. While he justly withholds the knowledge of truth from some, he also mercifully reveals the knowledge of truth to others, and he accomplishes in all peoples his most omnipotent will.

23. (XIV.) Furthermore, according to the very useful rule of this understanding, whoever is willing to examine the divine Scriptures with the simple eyes of the heart will be able to find witnesses in the divine words. When one discusses the things that pertain to the beginning or the accomplishment of salvation with respect to the human will, it is indeed true that among those old enough to use reason, those who will are saved and those who do not will are not saved. But those who are being saved gain the will to be saved at the moment when they are preceded by divine grace so that they may will. Indeed, they will to be saved at the moment when they receive the will in accordance with the gift of divine generosity. For holy Scripture can in no way lie, and it says: "The will is prepared by the Lord."[395] With Christ speaking within him, the Apostle also says truly, "With fear and trembling, work out your own salvation, for God is the one working in you both to will and to accomplish according to his good will."[396] Not only does the Apostle attribute the beginning of the good will and work to God, but he also testifies that God brings both to pass: "So that our God may make you worthy of his calling and fulfill by his power every act of your good will and the work of your faith."[397] And in order to show that this comes about through grace, he continued by adding, "So that the name of our Lord Jesus Christ may be glorified in you, and you in him, according to the grace of our God and Lord, Jesus Christ."[398] Therefore, divine grace works in those who are willingly being saved with the result that they will, and human hardness perseveres in those who are unwilling, with the result that they do not will. Nevertheless, a man will not have that hardness when God is pleased to remove it. To be sure, God can, without difficulty, accomplish what he has promised,

---

395. Prv 8.35, following LXX.
396. Phil 2.12–13.
397. 2 Thes 1.11.
398. 2 Thes 1.12.

for he says about certain people, "I will remove from them their heart of stone and give them a heart of flesh."[399] Consequently, he removes their heart of stone by removing their hardness of heart, and he gives a heart of flesh by imparting the grace of holy belief. Thus he softens the heart that had been hard and grants the beginning of holy faith in it.

24. (XV.) Certainly God created the free choice of the human mind faultless in the first man, yet even then that choice was faultless only with the help of grace. Indeed, by means of that grace, free choice was able (if it so willed) to remain in that same state of righteousness; and it was also able (if it so willed) to depart from that grace through a malevolent will. But now prevenient grace works in a man to set right the freedom of his choice. To the extent that a man's choice is set right, to that extent it is free; but to whatever extent it is led captive, to that extent it is still entangled in the bonds of servitude to evil. Those bonds do not merely press lethally upon the children of this age, but they also afflict them frequently. This is the very law of sin, which tenaciously held the Apostle Paul in the clutches of concupiscence, as it lived in his members and resisted the law of his mind. Even though he was a resolute soldier who delighted in the law of God according to the inner man, he was not able to subject the law of sin effectively to himself. Nevertheless, he actively made suggestions for subduing sinful desire. Hence the same Apostle says, "For I delight in the law of God in my inner man, but I see another law in my members battling against the law of my mind and holding me captive to the law of sin that is in my members."[400] He was not silent about the fact that he could be set free only by the help of grace, so he continues by saying, "Wretched man that I am! Who will deliver me from the body of this death? The grace of God through Jesus Christ our Lord."[401] Therefore, he possessed the strength of grace in his mind, but he felt the weakness of choice in his body, a weakness that Adam did not possess before he was corrupted by willingly violating the command. As a result, although he was

399. Ezek 36.26.   400. Rom 7.22–23.
401. Rom 7.24–25.

already established as an apostle (and thus not under law but under grace), and although he served the law of God with his mind, he was nonetheless compelled to serve the law of sin with his flesh. For the fact that he served the law of God with his will had been divinely given to him, and the fact that he served the law of sin had remained in him of necessity. To be sure, he was unwillingly burdened by those bonds, from which every saint both chooses and asks to be delivered, saying to God: "Free me from my bonds."[402] Feeling within himself the affliction of these bonds, the Apostle said: "For I do not do the good that I want, but I do the evil that I hate. But if I do the evil that I hate, it is no longer I that do it, but sin that dwells within me."[403]

25. (XVI.) The saints who live mortally in the body of this death still possess these bonds, and indeed they are unfortunately vexed by them. God allows this so that the saints will know that because of sin, they have lost the grace both of holy freedom and of the initial peace present in the first man, and so that they will know that they cannot receive it again except through the grace of Christ. This will happen only in that life in which the saints will have no anxiety related to strife, but rather the perfect security of peace. Then, to be sure, after [this life] has trampled on death, every struggle with sin will be rooted out of the members of the body. Then it will be truly said of that peace, "Death has been swallowed up in victory. O death, where is your victory? O death, where is your sting? For the sting of death is sin,"[404] into which we have fallen because of the first man's transgression, which none of us can escape in this life. For "if we say that we have no sin, we deceive ourselves, and the truth is not in us."[405] We must be watchful in the struggle so that we may rest in peace. We must always be mindful of the weakness of free choice that the iniquity of the first man has generated in us. We must humbly beseech the Divine Majesty to replace it with the help of his power, so that he may grant power to us who labor and lead us who conquer to peace. This will happen so that we may

402. Ps 24.17, following LXX (25.17 modern).
403. Rom 7.19–20.   404. 1 Cor 15.54–56.
405. 1 Jn 1.8.

have perfect freedom of choice, completely free from every sin. Then, to be sure, every creature who is now being renewed in Christ "will be set free from bondage to decay into the glorious freedom of God's sons."[406] And when each one is set free, he will without doubt fully enjoy the gift of free peace and peaceful freedom. For if that kind of peace and freedom were even now present in a man to the extent that the first man had peace and freedom before his sin, such a man would not see in his members another law fighting relentlessly against the law of his mind and leading him captive forcibly in the way of the law of sin.

26. Therefore, before the first man sinned, the free choice of the human mind was truly free to such a degree that the man sensed nothing conflicting within himself. Consequently, he was whole and happy, and he did not sense within himself any wretchedness, for he retained righteousness with steadfast freedom. He indeed served righteousness[407] freely, and therefore he rejoiced in true freedom.

(XVII.) Therefore, as long as the first man served righteousness, he had no sin whatsoever. But as for us, although we have been "freed from sin and made slaves to God,"[408] yet "if we say that we have no sin, we deceive ourselves, and the truth is not in us."[409] Adam, before sin, bore no heavy burden such as that which is upon his descendants "from the day they leave their mother's womb until the day they are buried in the mother of us all."[410] In Adam before sin, the flesh had no desire that resisted the spirit. The spirit easily ruled over the body in such a way that the man faithfully obeyed the Creator. The soul possessed the body in subjection, and, in turn, pure devotion subjected the soul to God. Now, however, we do not learn to obey God perfectly in body and soul, so in us the flesh desires things contrary to the spirit, and the spirit desires things contrary to the flesh, so that we do not do the things that we wish to do.

---

406. Rom 8.21.
407. Reading *iustitiae* instead of *iustitia*.
408. Rom 6.18.   409. 1 Jn 1.8.
410. Sir 40.1.

27. Therefore, the freedom of the first man contained greater peace, but now the freedom of believers receives greater love through grace. He enjoyed a completely restful righteousness in a state of peace; believers are given a glorious victory in conflict. Consequently, the grace given now is greater, because while faith restores free choice, God also restores the freedom of our choice by the infused gift of faith and love, just as he also brings about strength in our weakness. For ruin through sin robbed the first man of his sound choice, so greater grace has been given after sin so that human choice may be restored. So it happened that "where sin abounded, grace abounded even more,"[411] and thus choice was restored by the gift of faith. Even though man does not possess as much wholeness and peace as he did at first, he nonetheless receives more power from [God's] generosity. As a result, man's will, which had abandoned God solely as a result of the deceiver's deception, is now supported by the help of grace and is not separated from Christ either by deceptions or by sufferings. In a wonderful way, God shows what both human strength and divine strength are able to accomplish, so that man, whose health was overcome through his own will, is not overcome and weak after receiving greater grace. Therefore, man's strength, supported by less grace, fell because his will was overcome with his own permission. But man's weakness, with the greater help of grace, receives the victory that he lost before. Therefore, power to do good or evil can be present in any man who is old enough to use reason. The power to do evil springs only from the choice of a free will, but the power to do good belongs to free choice the moment God gives it. Blessed John the Evangelist testifies that this power is divinely given when he says: "But as many as received him, to them he gave the power to become sons of God, to those who believe in his name."[412]

28. (XVIII.) In your letter you placed your question about the soul next to last, but in this response I have addressed it last because I think it is more likely to lead to conflict among you

411. Rom 5.20.
412. Jn 1.12.

than to find a satisfactory answer. Dealing with this question has a greater chance of increasing strife than of producing knowledge. Each side leans on its own arguments so much that it may in no way be convinced by contrary arguments. When blessed Augustine probed for himself the impenetrable depths of this question, he did not want to offer a definitive opinion concerning this matter, since he thought he wished to affirm without doubt something wholly inappropriate, something that someone else might be able to shatter with a contrary response. He shed light on this subject with argumentation no less abundant than profound—the more praiseworthy because of its appropriate, moderate temper—in the tenth book of *A Literal Interpretation of Genesis*,[413] in the books he wrote to Vincentius Victor, *On the Origin of the Soul*,[414] in the first of the two books he wrote to Saint Jerome,[415] and also in three letters that he composed to Bishop Optatus[416] on this question. After considering the nature of the intellectual acumen needed, the order of reasoning, and the relative importance of the matters to be inquired about and discussed, he then dealt with them individually and

413. *De Genesi ad litteram;* Latin text in CSEL 28, 1–435; English translation in ACW 41 and 42.

414. Vincentius Victor was a North African layman who wrote elegantly in opposition to Augustine's view of the origin of the soul. Here Fulgentius mentions Augustine's response to Vincentius. The Latin title is *De natura et origine animae* (Latin text in CSEL 60, 301–419).

415. Jerome, a Roman of the fourth and fifth centuries who spent the latter part of his life in Bethlehem, was the greatest biblical scholar of the early Church. He is best known as the translator and compiler of the Vulgate, which would become the standard Latin Bible by the ninth century. Augustine's letter to Jerome that Fulgentius calls a "book" here is *Ep.* 166 (Latin text in CSEL 44, 545–85; English translation in FOTC 30, 6–31).

416. Optatus was bishop of Milevis in North Africa in the late fourth century. He wrote extensively against the Donatists (a rigorist group in North Africa that tied the efficacy of the sacraments to the sanctity of the priest performing them), and his work was the starting point for Augustine's polemic against that group. The first of Augustine's three letters to Optatus is preserved as *Ep.* 144 in the collection of Jerome's letters (Latin text in CSEL 56, 294–305; English translation in NPNF, second series, 6, 283–87). The other two letters to Optatus are in the collection of Augustine's letters: *Ep.* 190 (Latin text in CSEL 57, 137–62; English translation in FOTC 30, 271–88); *Ep.* 202A (Latin text in CSEL 57, 302–15; English translation in FOTC 30, 407–20).

pleaded his case. He retained, however, the consensus from each pronouncement so that he would not be undertaking the labor of such a great controversy in vain, since an ill-considered pronouncement on any issue would empty his discussion of meaning. He examined both viewpoints, the one that affirms that soul is propagated by soul just as body is propagated by body, and the other that asserts that souls are created anew with each person being born. He saw that either could be disputed by contrary responses. So as not to draw this matter out unduly, this work will include only certain selected responses.

29. (XIX.) To be sure, those who claim that new souls are made individually completely miss the point, since one may begin to oppose them by asking by what justice of God could a soul that is given anew to a body derive original sin, since it does not come from the propagation of human seed. Those who assert this are evidently constrained by a dilemma that compels them either to call God unjust or to deny original sin. For a soul that is not propagated the way flesh is must not be considered as a partner with the flesh in original sin, and therefore, such a soul is not found to need the sacrament of baptism. And if, in the case of a child who dies without baptism, the flesh alone is polluted with the contagion of original sin and the soul of the unbaptized child is thought to depart this age without iniquity, where then will the child be in the resurrection? In the kingdom of God because of the purity of his soul, or in the eternal fire because of the impurity of his flesh? But wherever one might say the child will be, [in this scenario] one must say that God is either a liar or unjust. He is a liar if he brings an unbaptized person into the kingdom after the Savior himself previously established a very strong condition: "If anyone is not born again of water and the Spirit, he cannot enter the kingdom of God."[417] And God is unjust if he sends a soul into eternal fire along with the flesh, when the soul shares no common sin with the flesh. But it is obvious that everyone is to be condemned to the conflagration of eternal fire if he has not been baptized either by water that has been sanctified in Christ's name, or in

417. Jn 3.5.

his own blood[418] for the name of Christ and for the Church. Therefore, by what justice of divine judgment will the soul be sent into the eternal fire along with the flesh, if it is not held guilty of original sin?

30. Or will someone by chance try to lay hold of this dilemma in order to say that the soul will exist forever separate from the body because of its purity, and to assert that the flesh will deservedly burn in eternal fire because of original wickedness? But the truth of the Catholic faith, which believes in and preaches with great certainty the future resurrection of all men's flesh, destroys the very stupid error of this idea. For if the flesh does not receive a soul, it will not rise, and if it does not rise, it surely will not live either. Therefore, if the flesh cannot live without a soul, how will it be able to feel the torments of that fire without a soul? Consequently, those who want to place the soul of the unbaptized child in the kingdom because of its purity must then deny that the flesh will rise. Even they themselves see that what they say is as absurd as it is impious. Indeed, it is the height of impiety to deny that the dead flesh of a man is going to rise or to say that the soul is going to share in affliction or felicity after the judgment apart from the flesh in which it lived. When our Savior showed that the resurrection of the flesh was going to take place, he said, "For the hour will come when the ones who are in their graves will hear his voice, and those who have done good will enter the resurrection of life, but those who have done evil will enter the resurrection of judgment."[419] Likewise, once the body has arisen, the retribution due to the soul and the flesh on account of the works must be common, for when the flesh has arisen, the body will not continue without the soul, nor the soul without the body. Therefore, the soul and the flesh will share either eternal joy or eternal affliction in common, since the eternal connection of flesh and soul will remain intact. Soul and flesh should not share a common punishment if they do not share a common sin, for it would not be consistent with God's justice if a soul that is given anew to the body and is

418. As when a catechumen was martyred before baptism.
419. Jn 5.28–29.

not propagated with that body (with which it has no common origin) were forced to share the common guilt of propagation.

31. (XX.) Indeed, on this point those who assert that souls are propagated with bodies can demonstrate that God's judgment toward children is just by establishing that original sin is present not just in the flesh or just in the soul, but is common to both. As a result, those who say this may rightly regard the guilt as being shared because of a common source of sin, but on the issue of sperm that dies without leading to conception, let them be completely silent. It is certain that the human soul has attained eternality by the very gift of its creation, and the body, in which the soul lived for however short a time in this world, must receive eternality in the resurrection. Therefore, who would say that sperm that has issued forth (either sperm that has not led to conception [in the womb] or sperm that has flowed as the result of a nocturnal emission) has been ensouled? Every sane person sees how preposterous and completely irrational it is to say that.

32. Therefore, while these factions are taking turns prevailing over each other through propositions of this kind, neither side can win because each of them is defeating the other in such a way that it also defeats itself. And when one side has destroyed the other's proposition, it cannot support what it proposes. Therefore, it will be much better if we refrain from disputing over this issue, which we know we belabor in vain, especially since we have to inquire all the more cautiously and moderately about matters that our holy predecessors left only minimally defined, because we understand that those illustrious men only minimally achieved any resolution of the issues. Therefore, let us ascertain beyond a shadow of a doubt what the Catholic faith believes and preaches, which is that the human soul is certainly a rational spirit, not a body; that it is not a part of God, but a creation of God; that it has not been sent into the body as if into a prison because of certain sins committed before the body existed, but that it has been introduced into the body by the work and decree of God as a result of which the body both lives and

feels. Let us not doubt that original sin envelops the soul along with the flesh in which it is born, and that for this reason, the soul also needs the benefit of holy baptism.

33. (XXI.) By renouncing the true and clear decrees of the Catholic faith stated above, many have fallen miserably into various errors. Tertullian certainly erred grievously when he said that the soul is not a spirit, but a body.[420] He even went so far as to say irrationally that the highest and true God is a body, although we read about God the Creator of all things both that "God is spirit"[421] and that "he makes his angels spirits,"[422] as the Psalm says about the angels whom God created. Similarly, no sensible person would doubt that the human soul is a rational spirit. About that spirit the Apostle says, "For who among men knows [the thoughts] of a man except the human spirit that is in him?"[423] Similarly, the holy evangelist also taught that the rational soul that Christ assumed with the flesh was not a body, but a spirit. Our Savior himself had said, "I have the power to lay down my soul, and I have the power to take it up again."[424] There is no doubt that he then laid it down, as the evangelist says, for on the cross "he bowed his head and gave up his spirit." In truth, the human soul in him is shown to be rational because it is said to have been made in the image and likeness of God. For this reason, men are divinely admonished not to be "like the horse and the mule, which have no understanding."[425]

34. Indeed, the Manichaeans' blind ungodliness leads them to think that the soul is a part of God, that is, it is of one nature with God.[426] They think that God's substance is bound together

---

420. Tertullian, who lived in Carthage in the late second and early third centuries, was the first major Christian theologian to write in Latin. Around the year 206, he joined a rigorist group known today as the Montanists. The passage Fulgentius refers to here, in which Tertullian argues for the corporeal constitution of the soul, is in *On the Soul* 6 (Latin text in CCL 2, 787–90; English translation in FOTC 10, 189–93).

421. Jn 4.24.   422. Ps 103.4 (104.4 modern).
423. 1 Cor 2.11.   424. Jn 10.18.
425. Ps 31.9, following LXX (Ps 32.9 modern).
426. Manichaeism was a dualistic sect that originated in Persia in the third

not only in the bodies of men, cattle, birds, and fish, but also in wood and grass, in trees and vegetables. They are ignorant wretches, and they have not learned that the creature is not the same as the Creator. Although God is immutable, the soul is in fact mutable. Now it knows, now it does not; now it progresses, now it fails; now it has rational intelligence, now it does not; now it remembers, now it forgets; now it hates what it loved, now it loves what it hated; now it falls into the trap of being deceived, now without even having been deceived, it still consents to error. This is certainly what the blessed Apostle points out in Adam and his wife, when he says, "Adam was not deceived, but the woman was deceived and fell into transgression."[427] Therefore, the woman who had been deceived sinned, and the man who had not been deceived consented voluntarily to wickedness. Thus it is ungodly to believe that the soul is a part of God. The soul is sometimes changed for the better, sometimes for the worse, but it is found to be not a part of the divine nature, but a certain part of the divine works. To be sure, it is one of those works that God made, each one definitely good, and all taken together, very good.

35. (XXII.) It is also completely contrary to the faith to believe that before the soul inhabited a body, it fell in any place in heaven or on earth and that it deserved to be placed into the body because of this [prior] sin, which is what Origen is said to have thought.[428] The Apostle Paul opposes him emphatical-

---

century. It was based on the idea of a struggle between light and darkness, and the purpose of religion was to enable a person to release the particles of light within him. Augustine was a Manichaean in the 370s, prior to his conversion to Neoplatonism and then to Christianity. The idea Fulgentius discusses here was common in many forms of Eastern religion, not merely in Manichaeism.

427. 1 Tm 2.14.

428. Origen was the leader of the Alexandrian catechetical school in the early third century. At the time Fulgentius was writing in the early sixth century, Origen's cosmology was considered very problematic, and he would be condemned at the Fifth Ecumenical Council in 553. Notice that Fulgentius's statement "as Origen is said to have thought" suggests doubt about whether Origen actually taught the ideas for which he was being criticized at the time. In fact the textual history of Origen's *On First Principles* is extremely complicated, and it is very difficult to ascertain what Origen himself originally wrote. For the

ly, saying that children who have not yet been born have done nothing good or evil.[429] Indeed, the deeds of those being born are not their own, although they are born bound by the ancient sin of the first man: "For through one man sin entered into this world, and death through sin, and so death passed to all men, because in him all have sinned."[430] Hence, they became sons of wrath and slaves of sin by nature, and by serving sin they became void of righteousness, since they were conceived in iniquity and were also nourished in sin in the womb by their mothers.[431]

36. Because of this entangling bond of original sin, man lost his good freedom of choice when he began to serve sin willingly through his blemish, the freedom to do evil. As a result, all men of any age, from the moment of birth out of the mother's womb to the end of decrepit old age, need the blood of Christ, which has been poured out for the remission of sins and can alone eradicate every sin. "For there is one mediator between God and men, the man Christ Jesus."[432] Whoever has not been buried with him in his death through baptism will not be able to gain the kingdom or to avoid the punishment of eternal fire. Indeed, the Truth says that "if anyone is not born again of water and the Spirit, he cannot enter the kingdom of God."[433] For that reason, all people, small and great, infants, children, adolescents, young and old, must accept what the teacher of the Gentiles faithfully, truly, and rightly says: "For there is no distinction. For all have sinned and come short of God's glory, being justified freely by his grace through the redemption that is in Christ Jesus, whom God put forth as a propitiation through faith in his blood, to show his righteousness for the sake of the remission of previous sins."[434] But when one considers sin in infants, one doubtless finds the preceding sin to be the first sin of the first man, the sin that entered this world through one man.

---

idea Fulgentius mentions here, see Origen, *On First Principles*, Bk. 1, Chap. 8 (ancient Latin version in SC 252, 220–32; English translation in *Origen: On First Principles,* trans. G. W. Butterworth [New York: Harper & Row, 1966], 66–75).

429. Cf. Rom 9.11.   430. Rom 5.12.

431. Cf. Ps 50.7 (51.5 modern).   432. 1 Tm 2.5.

433. Jn 3.5.   434. Rom 3.22–25.

In the originator himself, this sin originally claimed for itself all his progeny. To be redeemed, this race needs the blood of that mediator, who was true God, and while remaining "in the form of God," nevertheless "emptied himself by taking the form of a slave,"[435] so that he might not possess the blot of either original or actual sin.

37. (XXIII.) Therefore, in him and from him true freedom has been restored to us, for no iniquity, original or actual, could exist in him. Hence, what he said is true: "Behold, the prince of the world is coming, and he has no claim against me."[436] He is just and the one who justifies, free and the one who sets people free. He frees by justifying, and he justifies by freeing. He frees men from the power of the devil and frees man's choice from servitude to sin, so that man's choice may be truly free. For after his choice has been salvifically freed, true freedom is present in his free choice so that no iniquity may dominate him. Our Liberator testifies through the following words that he intends to give this freedom through grace: "Everyone who commits sin is a slave of sin."[437] And a bit later he adds, "Therefore, if the Son frees you, you will be truly free."[438] So the Son frees a person from the servitude to sin so that after his free choice has been liberated by Christ's grace, this choice, which formerly served sin in an evil manner, may serve righteousness in a praiseworthy manner. As a result, the fact that sin does not reign in a mortal body[439] is not the result of a man's choice, but is the result of the Liberator's grace, since we are made righteous by faith. And with the help of grace, "God is the one working in us both to will and to accomplish according to his good will."[440] He gives us a good will and provides our ability to do good works. He gives us "every excellent gift and every perfect gift."[441] Without him we can do nothing,[442] in him we can do all things, and from him we receive the grace of power to the greatest extent. The blessed Apostle indeed assumes this with steadfast confidence when he

435. Phil 2.7.
437. Jn 8.34.
439. Cf. Rom 6.12.
441. Jas 1.17.
436. Jn 14.30.
438. Jn 8.36.
440. Phil 2.13.
442. Cf. Jn 15.5.

says, "I can do all things in him who strengthens me."[443] And again he says, "In the work I need to accomplish, I labor according to his work that he accomplishes powerfully in me."[444]

38. (XXIV.) If we hold all these things faithfully and without doubt, we are in no danger even though we do not know how souls are given to bodies. It is enough to know that we have been defiled by our first birth and cleansed by our second birth; that we have been enslaved by our first birth and set free by our second birth; that we are earthly by our first birth and heavenly by our second birth; that we are carnal because of the sin of our first birth and spiritual because of the blessing of the second birth; that we are children of wrath because of our first birth and children of grace because of our second birth; that we are children of this age because of our first birth and children of God because of our second birth. Accordingly, although we cannot know how the soul is given to the body, let us insistently busy ourselves with the tasks of believing rightly and living good lives, so that both our soul and body may be joyful in the kingdom of God. Therefore, if we cannot know how souls are given to bodies, let us be patient in our ignorance. But let us seek the kingdom of God ardently and with perseverance, for there God will doubtless reveal even this to us, for he does not hide this from us here below without a reason, unless perhaps it is because it is not relevant that we know it in this life.

39. Since this is the case, if anyone divinely enlightened by signs of most certain rationality or testimonies of holy authority can either understand or teach that human souls are given anew to individual bodies or are propagated with the bodies themselves, let such a person at the same time defend what the Church's faith holds to be manifestly clear. This is the fact that everyone, from the moment of maternal conception, bears original sin, which must be forgiven in each person who is born by the blood of the one Mediator. This must take place so that the connection with wickedness that comes with the first birth will be resolved by the second, so that through God's Son ("made

443. Phil 4.13.   444. Col 1.29.

from a woman, made under the law"),[445] we may receive adoption as sons. Everyone lost this grace of adoption because of the wickedness of man's sin, so that one may receive that grace back because of the Redeemer's blessing. When someone asserts this without doubt, he will then be able to explain the truth about the origin of souls and will do well to speak and not remain silent. Thus, the question of the soul is rightly dealt with only when there is no doubt about the original sin of the human race or about the benefit of holy baptism, which has been granted to the captives through the grace of the Savior, who has condescended both to take to himself the whole nature of our race (but without sin) and to abolish every offense of our sin.

445. Gal 4.4–5.

APPENDICES & INDICES

APPENDIX I

THE CHAPTERS OF JOHN MAXENTIUS COMPILED AGAINST THE NESTORIANS AND THE PELAGIANS FOR THE SATISFACTION OF THE BROTHERS[1]

1. If anyone does not confess that in our Lord Jesus Christ there are two natures (that is, divinity and humanity) united, or if he confesses one incarnate nature of God the Word but does not mean this in the sense of two united in one subsistence or person (according to what the venerable synod at Chalcedon has handed down to us), let him be anathema.

2. If anyone does not confess that the holy Mary is properly and truly the Bearer of God, but if he instead attributes this title to her only according to a great honor and in name because he believes she bore a man who is said to be God only according to grace, rather than believing that she bore God incarnate and made man, let him be anathema.

3. If anyone does not confess that there has been a union of substances and natures according to which the Word was united to a human nature while remaining God by nature, but if he instead confesses that the union was one of subsistence or person or as a kind of illustration or according to favor or good will, let him be anathema.

4. If anyone does not consent to confess that Christ who suffered for us in the flesh is "one of the Trinity" even with his own flesh (although according to that flesh itself he is not of the substance of the Trinity but is the same as us), let him be anathema.

5. If anyone does not confess that that child whom the holy Virgin Mary bore is by nature God, and that through him all things were

1. As explained in the introduction, this is perhaps the earliest writing by the Scythian monks, written in 519 during the monks' stay in Constantinople, if not earlier. The standard title is *Capitula Maxentii Ioannis edita contra Nestorianos et Pelagianos ad satisfactionem fratrum*. The Latin critical text may be found in CCL 85A, 29–30.

235

made—visible and invisible things, heavenly and earthly things[2]—and that he is the Maker of all, "Mighty God, Prince of peace, Father of the coming age,"[3] let him be anathema.

6. If anyone says that Christ has suffered in the flesh but does not consent to say that God has truly suffered in the flesh (which is precisely what it means to say that Christ has suffered in the flesh), let him be anathema.

7. If anyone says, "God was not made the Christ, but the Christ was made God," let him be anathema.

8. If anyone does not confess that there have been two births of the one Son of God (since God the Word was indeed born from the Father before the ages, and the same one was born from his mother in the last times), let him be anathema.

9. If anyone does not confess that after the Incarnation Christ is a compound,[4] let him be anathema.

10. If anyone says that sin is natural, and in a mindless way ascribes the source of sin to the Creator of natures, let him be anathema.

11. If anyone does not confess that original sin has entered the world through the transgression of Adam (according to the voice of the Apostle when he says: "Through one man sin entered into the world, and death through sin, and so it passed to all men, because in him all have sinned"),[5] let him be anathema.

12. Similarly, we anathematize every opinion of Pelagius and Celestius and of all who think like them. We accept all the actions that have been taken against them in various places and all the writings against them by the prelates of the apostolic see (namely, Innocent, Boniface, Zosimus, Celestine, and Leo),[6] as well as the writings against them by Atticus, bishop of Constantinople,[7] and Augustine [and the] bishops of an African province.

---

2. Cf. Jn 1.3, Col 1.16.

3. Is 9.6.

4. That is, a compound composed of the deity he had always possessed because he had always been God, and the humanity that he added to himself to make himself compound. See note 13 to par. 6 of the monks' letter to the bishops, p. 29 of this volume.

5. Rom 5.12.

6. Innocent, Zosimus, and Boniface were the Roman popes during the Pelagian controversy in the 410s and 420s. Celestine and Leo were the Roman popes during the Nestorian controversy and the early phases of the Semi-Pelagian controversy in the 420s and 430s.

7. Atticus was bishop of Constantinople from 406 to 425.

APPENDIX II

A VERY BRIEF CONFESSION OF THE
CATHOLIC FAITH BY THE SAME AUTHOR[1]

1. "The Father is God, the Son is God, and the Holy Spirit is also God; but there is one God, not three."[2] There is one substance or nature, one wisdom, one power, one dominion, one reign, one omnipotence, one glory. Nevertheless, there are three subsistences or persons, and each person always unchangeably retains what is proper to himself, in such a way that the Father is neither the Son nor the Holy Spirit, and the Son is neither the Father nor the Holy Spirit, and the Holy Spirit is neither the Father nor the Son.

2. And the Son, that is, the Word of God, the Only-begotten God, of the same substance as the Father, remains God in his own subsistence. In the last days this Son assumed human nature from the womb of the blessed Virgin Mary, and as he united flesh to himself, was made man, possessing a rational soul or a mind.

3. Therefore, we must confess that God was born of a woman—not according to his divinity, but according to his humanity. We must confess that God lay in a cradle wrapped in dirty cloths, grew and increased in stature and wisdom[3]—according to his humanity, not according to his divinity. We must confess that God became hungry, thirsty, and tired, and that he rested after a journey—not according to his divinity, but according to his humanity. We must confess that God was grasped by the hands of impious men and that he was judged, condemned, and crucified, and that his side was pierced by a spear—not according to his divinity, but according to his humanity. We must confess that God died, was buried, and rose—not according to his divinity, but accord-

---

1. That is, John Maxentius. The standard title of this work is *Item eiusdem professio brevissima catholicae fidei,* and the Latin critical text may be found in CCL 85A, 33–36.

2. This is a quotation from the Athanasian Creed, art. 15–16. The Latin text and English translation may be found in (*inter alia*) *Creeds of the Churches,* vol. 2, ed. Philip Schaff (Grand Rapids, MI: Baker, reprint 1998), 67. This creed arose in the West sometime in the late fourth or (more likely) early or mid-fifth century.

3. Cf. Lk 2.52.

ing to his humanity. We must confess that God ascended into heaven with his own flesh, that he sat down at the right hand of the Father, and that from there he is about to come again in glory with his own flesh to judge the living ones and the dead ones.

4. We must declare in turn that Jesus Christ, the Son of man, or a man, was born of the Father before the ages, that he is one of the Trinity, and that "through him all things were made, visible and invisible things, and without him nothing was made"[4]—not, however, according to his humanity, but according to his divinity. We must declare that this same man is eternal life, the wisdom and power of the Father—not, however, according to his humanity, but according to his divinity. We must declare that this same man is the figure or image of the Father's substance,[5] and the emanation of the brightness of God—not, however, according to his humanity, but according to his divinity.

5. We must say in turn that the one who is eternal life, the wisdom and power of the Father, was born of a woman according to the flesh. We must say that the one who is eternal life, the wisdom and power of the Father, lay in a cradle wrapped in cloths. We must say in turn that the one who is eternal life, the wisdom and power of the Father, suffered, was crucified, and died according to the flesh.

6. Since these things are so, no one can be a Catholic unless he confesses that in the Word, the Only-begotten Son of God, two natures always remain inseparably united after the union. These two are the natures of the Word and flesh, of God and man, of divinity and humanity. For just as he is one of the Trinity and has been God the Word from the beginning, so also the same one is himself perfect and true man from us.

7. For he is "from the loins of Abraham,"[6] and a child has been given to us from the seed of David;[7] he is "the God of heaven"[8] and "the Prince of peace."[9] And indeed, there are not two persons, but one person of Christ, because "no one ascends into heaven except the one who descended from heaven, the Son of man who is in heaven,"[10] and "Jesus Christ is the same yesterday, today, and into the ages."[11]

---

4. Jn 1.1–3; Col 1.16.
5. Cf. Heb 1.3.
6. Heb 7.5.
7. Cf. Is 9.6.
8. Gn 24.7.
9. Is 9.6.
10. Jn 3.13.
11. Heb 13.8.

GENERAL INDEX

The words "Lord," God," "Christ," and "Jesus" occur on virtually every page and are not included in this index.

grace, ix–x, xiv–xv, 6n6, 11–16,
18–22, 27, 34, 36–45, 47, 53–57,
65–68, 73, 75–79, 81–89, 91, 93,
95–100, 102–3, 106–26, 129–32,
135–44, 146–47, 149–70, 172–76,
178–86, 188, 194, 198–99, 201–6,
214, 217–19, 221, 228–31, 235; assisting, 173, 185; continuing, 148;
cooperative, 100; operative, 100,
181, 185; prevenient, 53, 66, 76,
78, 148, 164, 168, 172–74, 176,
184, 218; subsequent, 88, 174,
176, 185. *See also* mercy
Gregory of Nazianzus, 27–28, 30–31,
39n61, 195
guarantee, 74, 186–87
guilt/guilty, 73, 87, 99–100, 104,
113, 122, 124–26, 128, 131–32,
141, 144, 154, 159, 175, 187, 205,
224–25

Hadrumetum, monks of, 12–13
healing, 9n11, 17, 20, 74, 86–87,
135, 161–63, 168
heart, 40–41, 44, 61, 65, 67, 72, 75–
78, 80–82, 84–85, 89–91, 93–96,
106, 108–9, 111, 113, 116, 129,
137, 141, 144, 146–49, 151, 153,
155, 157–60, 163, 166, 171–73,
175–77, 179, 182–83, 188–90,
192–93, 212–13, 217–18
heaven/heavenly, 31, 36, 41, 49,
53, 60–61, 69, 77, 86, 93, 96–97,
102–5, 118, 121, 125, 156–58,
163–64, 173, 176, 179, 185–86,
191, 196, 198, 203, 210–13, 227,
230, 236, 238
Hebrews, 81, 150, 165
help, 6, 13–14, 20, 26, 33n37, 36,
41, 58, 66, 72, 74, 76, 78–79, 83,
88, 97, 106, 109, 115–16, 120–21,
126, 128, 131–32, 142, 149, 151,
154, 159, 162–65, 167–68, 170,
172–74, 176–85, 187, 189, 206,
218–19, 221, 229
Henotikon, 8–9, 11
heretic/heretical, 18, 25, 29–30, 33,
37, 41, 72, 195
Holy Spirit, 15, 25, 29n14, 32–33, 36,
38, 40, 44–45, 48–49, 53, 55–58,
60, 63–65, 75, 78, 81, 83, 86, 93,

95, 101–2, 108, 110, 114–16, 118,
124, 136–37, 139, 150–51, 156–
57, 165–69, 171, 176, 178–79,
185–86, 195–96, 206–7, 211, 223,
228, 237
hope, x, 9n12, 77, 84, 93, 109, 120,
179, 182, 190–92, 204
Hormisdas, 10–11, 17–19, 119
horoscope, 208
human choice. *See* choice
humanity, ix, 6, 19–21, 26–27, 29–30,
45, 48, 52–53, 58, 61–62, 124,
235–38
human nature. *See* nature
humility/humble, 42, 48, 72, 76–77,
82, 85, 94, 96, 141, 144, 159, 163,
172, 176, 179, 181–82, 189, 192
Huns, 3

immortality/immortal, 9–10, 35, 51,
60–62, 65–66, 69, 87, 190
immutability/immutable/immutably,
29, 46–47, 182, 184, 199–200,
204, 207–9, 227
incarnation/incarnate, xiii, 6–7, 9,
15n27, 20, 25–27, 30–31, 44–45,
47–48, 52, 54, 106, 235–36
infant, 11n15, 72–73, 99–100, 133,
138, 228. *See also* child
Innocent, 39–41, 195, 236
intercourse. *See* sexual intercourse

Jacob, 58, 61, 111–13, 122, 126–27,
129–30, 159, 187
James, 82, 157, 169, 182
Jerome, 222
Job, 72
John (the evangelist/apostle), 31, 47,
55–56, 58, 60, 169, 171, 215–16,
221
John Cassian. *See* Cassian, John
John Maxentius, xiii, 16–20, 25, 28n9,
43, 108, 119n47, 235, 237n1
John of Antioch, 37n33
John of Constantinople, 11, 17
John Thebaeus, 195–96
John the Baptist, 32
justice, 32, 37, 66, 70, 84, 96–97,
123, 130, 137–38, 142–44, 162,
168, 173, 184, 187, 189, 199, 205,
223–24

INDEX OF HOLY SCRIPTURE

In most passages from the Psalms, and occasionally in passages from other parts of Scripture, the ancient and modern numberings of the verses differ. In all such cases, the ancient numbering is listed first, followed by the modern numbering. An example is as follows: Ps 18.10/19.9.

Old Testament